Hadrian's Wall

Archaeological Histories

Series editor: Thomas Harrison

An important series charting the history of sites, buildings and towns from their construction to the present day. Each title examines not only the physical history and uses of the site but also its broader context: its role in political history, in the history of scholarship and in the popular imagination.

Avebury, Joshua Pollard and Mark Gillings

Dura-Europos, Jennifer Baird

Pompeii, Alison E. Cooley

Tarquinia, Robert Leighton

Troy: Myth, City, Icon, Naoíse Mac Sweeney

Ur, Harriet Crawford

Hadrian's Wall

Creating Division

Matthew Symonds

BLOOMSBURY ACADEMIC
LONDON • NEW YORK • OXFORD • NEW DELHI • SYDNEY

BLOOMSBURY ACADEMIC
Bloomsbury Publishing Plc
50 Bedford Square, London, WC1B 3DP, UK
1385 Broadway, New York, NY 10018, USA
29 Earlsfort Terrace, Dublin 2, Ireland

BLOOMSBURY, BLOOMSBURY ACADEMIC and the Diana logo are trademarks
of Bloomsbury Publishing Plc

First published in Great Britain 2021
Reprinted 2021

For legal purposes the Acknowledgements on p. xi constitute an extension of
this copyright page.

Cover design: Terry Woodley
Cover image © Matthew Symonds

A catalogue record for this book is available from the British Library.

Library of Congress Cataloging-in-Publication Data
Names: Symonds, Matthew F. A., author.
Title: Hadrian's Wall : creating division / Matthew Symonds.
Description: London ; New York : Bloomsbury Academic, 2021. | Series: Archaeological histories |
Includes bibliographical references and index. | Summary: "Over its venerable history, Hadrian's Wall
has had an undeniable influence in shaping the British landscape, both literally and figuratively. Once
thought to be a soft border, recent research has implicated it in the collapse of a farming civilisation
centuries in the making, and in fuelling an insurgency characterised by violent upheaval. Examining
the everyday impact of the Wall over the three centuries it was in operation, Matthew Symonds sheds
new light on its underexplored human story by discussing how the evidence speaks of a hard border
scything through a previously open landscape and bringing dramatic change in its wake. The Roman
soldiers posted to Hadrian's Wall were overwhelmingly recruits from the empire's occupied territories,
and for them the frontier could be a place of fear and magic where supernatural protection was
invoked during spells of guard duty. Since antiquity, the Wall has been exploited by powers craving
the legitimacy that came with being accepted as the heirs of Rome: it helped forge notions of English
and Scottish nationhood, and even provided a model of selfless cultural collaboration when the
British Empire needed reassurance. It has also inspired creatives for centuries, appearing in a more
or less recognisable guise in works ranging from Rudyard Kipling's Puck of Pook's Hill to George R. R.
Martin's A Game of Thrones. Combining an archaeological analysis of the monument itself and an
examination of its rich legacy and contemporary relevance, this volume presents a reliable, modern
perspective on the Wall"—Provided by publisher.
Identifiers: LCCN 2020034877 (print) | LCCN 2020034878 (ebook) | ISBN 9781350105348 (paperback) |
ISBN 9781350105355 (hardcover) | ISBN 9781350105362 (ebook) | ISBN 9781350105379 (epub)
Subjects: LCSH: Hadrian's Wall (England)–History. | Walls, Roman–England, Northern. | Fortification,
Roman—England. | Great Britain—History, Military—55 B.C.-449 A.D. | England–Antiquities, Roman. |
Romans—England.
Classification: LCC DA146 .S96 2021 (print) | LCC DA146 (ebook) | DDC 936.2/7—dc23
LC record available at https://lccn.loc.gov/2020034877
LC ebook record available at https://lccn.loc.gov/2020034878

ISBN: HB: 978-1-3501-0535-5
       PB: 978-1-3501-0534-8
       ePDF: 978-1-3501-0536-2
       eBook: 978-1-3501-0537-9

Series: Archaeological Histories

Typeset by RefineCatch Limited, Bungay, Suffolk
Printed and bound in Great Britain

To find out more about our authors and books visit www.bloomsbury.com
and sign up for our newsletters.

For Erin
My Wonderwall

CONTENTS

ILLUSTRATIONS

Maps

Table

Figures

ACKNOWLEDGEMENTS

It is not unusual to hear someone remark at gatherings dedicated to Roman frontiers that these former instruments of division are now bringing people together. This is true. I am grateful for the friendships that have grown out of an interest in mural matters, and this book owes a great debt to the community of Roman frontier scholars. Although it is impossible to name everyone, I am especially grateful to David J. Breeze for his continued help and encouragement over many years, and for commenting on the draft text, as did Richard Hingley. My anonymous peer reviewers also provided valuable feedback. Lindsay Allason-Jones, Paul Bidwell, Anthony Birley, Mike Bishop, Rob Collins, Alex Croom, Heather Davis, Stephen Greep, Ian Haynes, Peter Hill, Nick Hodgson, John Humphrey, Jacqui Huntley, Tatiana Ivleva, Beccy Jones, Mike Luke, David Mason, Al McCluskey, Jan Parker, Andrew Parkin, Andrew Poulter, John Reid, John Scott, Margaret Snape, Sue Stallibrass, David Taylor, Tony Wilmott, and Roger J.A. Wilson have generously offered information and/or assistance that has materially enriched this volume. Naturally, all of them will have their own views about the ideas presented here.

My family and friends have stoically humoured a frontier fixation that has endured – as much to my surprise as theirs – for over two decades. In that time, I have repeatedly trespassed on the good natures of Paul Austin, Mark Repath, D. Partlett, and P. Smith, as well as my parents Malcolm and Linda, my brother Andrew, and of course Erin and Tommy. I couldn't have done this without them.

Thanks are also due to Current Publishing, Andrew and Wendy Selkirk, Rob and Libby Selkirk, and Lucia Marchini. At Bloomsbury, I am indebted to Alice Wright, Lily Mac Mahon, and Georgina Leighton for guiding the manuscript through the editorial process. Merv Honeywood oversaw pre-press. The author and publisher gratefully acknowledge the permission granted to reproduce the copyright material in this book. Every effort has been made to trace copyright holders and to obtain their permission for the use of copyright material. The publisher apologises for any errors or omissions and would be grateful if notified of any corrections that should be incorporated in future reprints or editions of this book.

Dating

All dates are AD, unless otherwise stated.

Frontiers of the Roman Empire

Roman provinces and frontiers in the Hadrianic period

MAP 1 *The Roman Empire during Hadrian's reign (117–138). Courtesy of David J. Breeze.*

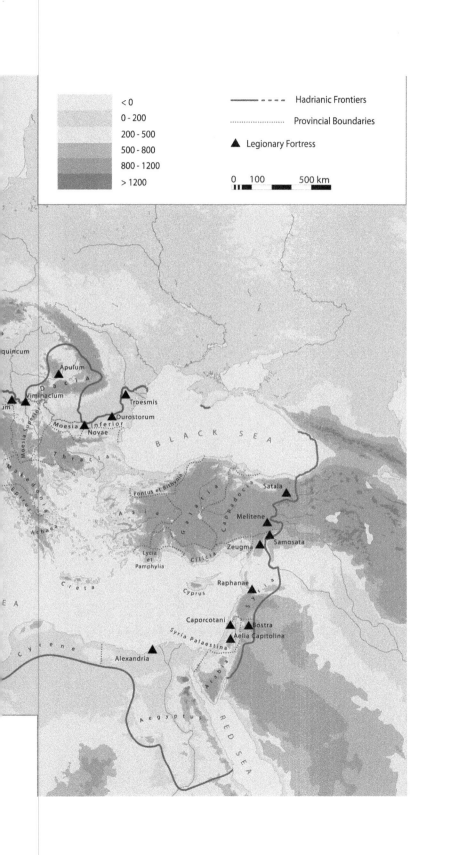

< 0
0 - 200
200 - 500
500 - 800
800 - 1200
> 1200

Hadrianic Frontiers
Provincial Boundaries
▲ Legionary Fortress

0   100   500 km

quincum

Apulum ▲

D a c i a

▲ Viminacium

im ▲

Moesia Superior

Moesia Inferior

Troesmis ▲

Durostorum ▲

Novae ▲

T h r a c i a

Macedonia

Epirus

Achaea

B L A C K   S E A

Pontus et Bithynia

A s i a

G a l a t i a

C a p p a d o c i a

Satala ▲

Melitene ▲

Zeugma ▲ Samosata

Lycia
et
Pamphylia

C i l i c i a

C r e t a

Cyprus

Raphanae ▲

S y r i a

Caporcotani ▲ ▲ Bostra

▲ Aelia Capitolina

E A

Cyrene

▲ Alexandria

Syria Palaestina

A r a b i a

A e g y p t u s

R E D   S E A

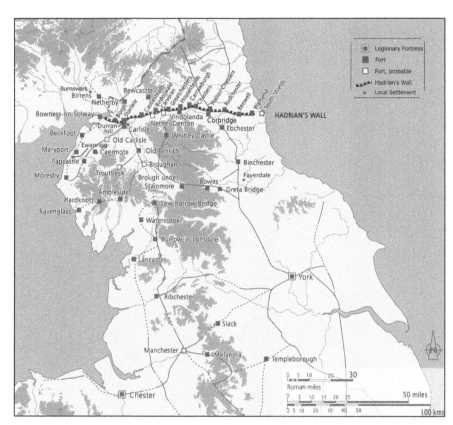

MAP 2 *Hadrian's Wall in its military landscape and select local settlements in the 130s. Courtesy of David J. Breeze.*

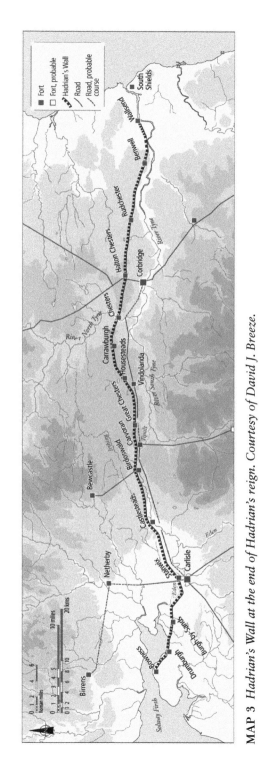

MAP 3 *Hadrian's Wall at the end of Hadrian's reign. Courtesy of David J. Breeze.*

1

Introduction

Into Darkness

[Hadrian] was the first to build a wall, 80 miles in length, to
separate the barbarians from the Romans.
– *HISTORIA AUGUSTA, HADRIAN* 11, 2

Hadrian's Wall hardly fits the profile of a classic archaeological mystery. Even its current name offers answers rather than questions: Hadrian really was the emperor who ordered its construction, while a wall is something we can all relate to. The simplicity of this description is so timeless that its original Roman name seems to have been effectively the same: the *vallum Aelium*, or Aelian Wall,[1] Aelius being Hadrian's family name. As for why his Wall was needed, it is hard to visit the solemn chain of crags crowned by the curtain without sensing you are standing on an edge. This sentiment is borne out by the barrier belonging to a network of frontiers that girded the Roman Empire and, in Hadrian's reign (117–138), stretched for over 10,000km through twenty modern countries on three continents (Map 1).[2] Hadrian's Wall accounts for a modest 117km, or 80 Roman miles, of that total (Map 3), but distinguishes itself by presenting a more formidable barrier than its peers. When it comes to the Wall's purpose, our sole surviving Roman statement on the matter is a throwaway comment in the *Historia Augusta*. This scurrilous ancient document presents a racy and often unreliable exposé of various emperors' lives, which was probably compiled over two centuries after Hadrian's death. Despite this dubious pedigree, the text emphasises that the Wall served as a means to create division by distilling its essence into just four Latin words: *qui barbaros Romanosque divideret*, or 'to separate the barbarians from the Romans'. So, even a rapid sketch of our knowledge seemingly rules out any real scope for mystery. We know what Hadrian's Wall was, who built it, and why. Case closed.

But what did imposing this division on previously open country mean for its inhabitants? Modern visitors can be forgiven for imagining amid the serenity of the crags that Roman military planners indulged their frontier fantasies in an empty wilderness. But if you look closely, traces of more ancient activity can sometimes be made out in the vicinity of the Roman works. Faint blemishes, often no more than smudges on the landscape, mark the enclosures and roundhouses of scattered farmsteads, mouldering beside long untended fields. Follow the course of the Wall away from the picturesque uplands, through what is now gently undulating farmland or settlement, and the evidence for earlier activity rises sharply, even though the visible remnants diminish: levelled by agriculture or urban sprawl. These prehistoric sites testify to landscapes that were inhabited and worked for millennia before the Roman conquest. Our understanding of chronology is rarely all we would wish for, but it is clear enough that long stretches of the Wall split settled, sophisticated, and stable agricultural communities that were centuries in the making. It was once believed that such local groups prospered on the back of a durable peace dividend – the vaunted *pax Romana* – but new dating evidence is challenging this scenario by implicating the Wall in the collapse of some communities. Understanding how Hadrian's Wall upset the rhythm of rural life, though, is hamstrung by our uncertainty concerning who was permitted to pass through it, and under what circumstances. To put it another way, we do not know what the Wall did. Here is our mystery. It hinges on the relationship between the Roman military and local population for almost 300 years while the Wall was operational, and its continuing impact down to today. To set the scene for this enquiry, we will begin by exploring some previous interpretations of the monument.

The writing on the Wall

The question of what Hadrian's Wall did is far from being a new one. Many answers have been offered over the years, multiplying to keep pace with shifts in knowledge, or the foibles of scholarly fashion. These solutions shape our views of the world in which the Wall operated, and indeed the world it helped to create. After all, taking the statement in the *Historia Augusta* at face value presents the Wall as a social fault-line, screening unruly – and un-rulable – savages from cultured Romans; essentially, a bulwark between chaos and civilisation. This broad viewpoint continued to influence scholarship until well into the 19th century, but while the popular appeal of this image remains strong – as we will see when we examine some of the Wall's fictional offshoots – more recent study of the monument has encouraged a nuanced take on its role. Back in 1732, the antiquarian John Horsley envisaged 'defences against the enemy' when he surveyed a barrier seemingly short on crossing points.[3] A surprise followed in the 19th century, though, when a series of gateways through the frontier was discovered, built

FIGURE 1 *John Storey's engraving of milecastle 42, after digging in 1848 revealed a pair of gateways. Courtesy of David J. Breeze.*

into small posts placed at sufficiently rigid intervals to coin the name 'milecastles' (Fig. 1). This demonstration that the Wall curtain was regularly pierced by access passages forced a reappraisal of just how formidable Rome's foes really were.[4] John Collingwood Bruce, then doyen of Wall studies, felt moved to remark that 'the territory north of the Wall was not given up to the enemy'.[5] As well as providing an early example of how knowledge won from digging could recast debate, it also created a headache for Wall scholars that remains acute: who were these gateways for? Were they intended to aid military manoeuvring, or a sop to inconvenienced local groups freshly divided from friends and relatives?

Establishing whether the milecastle gateways eased passage for all is central to gauging the Wall's purpose, but perceptions of this have differed markedly. In 1899, Robert Forster declared the Wall 'a great stone portcullis, which cut off the southern tribes from their northern kinfolk, and so weakened both, depriving the north of the richer resources of the south, shielding the south from the fiery inspiration of northern freedom'.[6] Twenty-two years later, R.G. Collingwood asserted a predominantly passive role for Hadrian's Wall and concluded that it was primarily 'designed to serve simply as a mark to show where Roman territory ended'.[7] In 1976, David J. Breeze and Brian Dobson proposed that 'the purpose of the barrier was to control movement, not to prevent it, as the liberal provision of gateways demonstrates. Civilians, whether merchants, local farmers moving their cattle and sheep or simply local people visiting relatives on the other side of the Wall, would be allowed through the gateways, though only presumably when they had satisfied the guards of their peaceable intentions and on payment of customs dues'.[8] By 1990, John Mann could claim that the Wall was no more than 'a rhetorical statement of Roman power', and 'in no way did the military defence of the occupied part of Britain' depend upon it.[9] These interpretations illustrate the intellectual journey initiated by the discovery of milecastle gateways, as a barrier once seen as effectively a *cordon sanitaire* morphed into one allowing life on both sides to continue with minimum hassle.

Despite the popularity of this model, not everyone has been persuaded. In 1999, Paul Bidwell reiterated the importance of deducing how the access arrangements worked: 'if civilians could not use the milecastle gates, Hadrian's Wall would be virtually a closed frontier'.[10] More recently, the wheel has turned full circle with Nick Hodgson presenting a spirited case for the Wall making a more muscular contribution to provincial security. By this reading, the presence of regular gateways does not disqualify the barrier from being 'designed along conventional lines as a defensible structure',[11] allowing an interpretation reminiscent of the 'defences against the enemy' hypothesised by Horsley. Today, opinion remains split. The two dominant scholarly views of the Wall's purpose can be crudely characterised as either a military barrier capable of repulsing full-blown invasions, or a means to regulate the peaceful movement of people and goods. Although both camps accept the barrier could neutralise nuisances such as raiding, the former position envisions a largely closed frontier, and the latter a highly porous one, amounting to a radical difference in intent.

Scholarly debate about an 'open' or 'closed' barrier sounds eerily prescient in an age when the relative merits of 'hard' and 'soft' borders are once again high on the international political agenda. Such echoes of wider contemporary concerns crop up time and again in Wall studies, emphasising the monument's currency during moments of national debate. Assessing this aspect aids appreciation of why successive generations saw the Wall as they did, and how interpretations of it continue to feed into, and be shaped by, current affairs. Breeze and Dobson's case for it channelling rather than curtailing movement, for instance, was published just three years after Britain joined the European Community, with concomitant shifts to trading patterns and cross-border cooperation. In the 19th century, the Wall offered a model of cross-cultural cooperation when the British Empire needed reassurance, while the medieval period saw it helping to forge a sense of English nationhood. As early as the 6th century AD, Gildas, a preacher, was able to make a point by claiming Christian and British origins for the Wall (with a little help from the Romans). Together, these examples reflect the role of the zeitgeist when formulating archaeological theories and humanity's genius for repackaging the past to suit present needs. That the Wall has been capable of sustaining so many conflicting readings speaks volumes about what the evidence for investigating it can and cannot tell us, making it essential to introduce the principal categories of information available.

A fragmented picture

Titbits from surviving copies of Roman-era literature typically underpin attempts to devise a crude chronology for activity in the frontier zone. While these ancient histories are invaluable for noting epochal events that befell Britain, they are typically short on detail. Few references are longer than a sentence, and even fewer mention the Wall directly. The *Historia Augusta* discloses, for instance, that upon Hadrian's accession in 117 'the Britons could not be kept under control',[12] but nothing about the cause, duration, or geographical focus of this insurrection. Marcus Aurelius' reign (161–180) furnishes another good example, when we learn simply that 'war was threatening'. The emperor responded by appointing Calpurnius Agricola governor of Britain, and sending him 'against the Britons'.[13] Once again, though, the nature of the threat and whether it was focused within or without Roman territory is left ambiguous. A few extra words can make a massive difference, with Dio specifying that the 'greatest struggle' during Commodus' reign (176–192) flared in the early 180s, when 'the tribes . . . crossing the wall that separated them from the Roman legions proceeded to do much mischief and cut down a general together with his troops'. Dio mentions the Wall again when discussing the inhabitants of the 'hostile' portion of Britain during the run-up to a campaign by the emperor Septimius Severus (reigned 193–211): 'the Maeatae live next to the cross-wall which cuts the island in half, and the Caledonians are beyond them'.[14] Despite our gratitude for these gobbets, we must be mindful that this information is not always reliable. After all, numerous ancient sources credit Septimius Severus with constructing the Wall, while only the *Historia Augusta* correctly assigns it to Hadrian.

Despite its shortcomings, the ancient literature carries implications for understanding the role and impact of Hadrian's Wall. Dio's allusions to a barrier that 'separated' hostile peoples from 'Roman legions' and 'cuts the island in half', for instance, echo the desire to 'separate the barbarians from the Romans' expressed in the *Historia Augusta*. This apparent literary tradition of presenting the Wall as a true line of division was gilded in breath-taking style with a tale set down by the 6th-century Byzantine historian Procopius, long after Roman Britain had ceased to exist. He held that 'in this island of Brittia the men of ancient times built a long wall . . . and the climate, and the soil and everything else is different on the two sides of it . . . the inhabitants say that if a man crosses this wall and goes to the other side, he dies straightaway, being unable to bear the pestilential air'.[15] Although Procopius distinguishes Brittia from nearby Britain, it seems certain his barrier is a mythologised Hadrian's Wall.[16] Whether the underlying implication common to all these accounts – that the Wall truly acted as a mechanism for creating division – had any grounding in reality is central to understanding its Roman-era remit.

It is traditional for studies of Hadrian's Wall to collate the crises chronicled in the ancient literature to establish when the frontier was restless or calm. The ancient histories certainly imply that Britain's fortunes waxed and waned. Tellingly, perhaps, the period of most persistent problems seems to fall in the decades immediately after the Wall was raised. From Hadrian onwards, incidents – whether instigated by Britons or Romans, and whether featuring fighting, bribery, mutiny, or punitive measures – are reported during the reign of every 2nd-century emperor who lasted for longer than a year. Although not all of these episodes certainly involved the Wall zone, many probably did. After Severus' early 3rd-century campaign the pattern changes, with the remainder of the century free from turmoil that can be directly tied to the northern frontier. While the early 4th century heralded one or more Roman campaigns, serious challenges only otherwise seem to mount as events spiralled out of control in the twilight of Roman Britain. It was once believed that a formal end to the Roman occupation came when the emperor Honorius (reigned 393–423) wrote to the 'cities of Britain' in 410, telling them to protect themselves, but this missive is now believed to have been directed at the Bruttium region of Italy. Instead, the curtain seemingly fell on Roman Britain in around 409, when its inhabitants were either obliged to repel attackers striking from beyond the Rhine or eject unwelcome units of 'barbarian' troops serving in the Roman army. One or other scenario led the Britons to 'live on their own, no longer obedient to Roman laws'.[17]

A danger with privileging a chronology generated from the ancient histories is that we do not know how many reports of equally relevant events have been lost, and whether they could cancel out the apparent 3rd- and 4th-century lulls. Equally, it was exceptional episodes that caught the eye of distant authors, rather than lesser incidents that probably played a greater role in colouring everyday life. A further handicap concerns the attitude of the Mediterranean elite who wrote these works. Like many groups before and since, the Romans were suckers for a stereotype. People from the east, for example, are frequently shown wearing a type of hat known as a Phrygian cap, a visual shorthand that has all the subtlety of using a kilt, beret, or Stetson today. Other examples include classing Batavians, from the modern Netherlands, as skilled riders, Syrians as natural archers, and so on.[18] Rather than boasting a comparable national talent – however exaggerated – the Britons are typically portrayed in the ancient texts as simple, savage, or strange. Choice descriptions brand them 'inhuman', 'lawless', 'raving', 'tent-dwelling', 'naked', and 'uncivilised'.[19] Dio claims that those living north of the Wall in the early 3rd century 'plunge into the swamps and exist there for many days with only their heads above water'.[20] This has the air of a traveller's tall tale and is a reminder that few of these writers had visited

Britain. Instead, they relied on accounts that were second-hand at best. While there is little reason to doubt the major events recorded in the ancient histories transpired in some form, we can suspect these sources present a generally distorted and unsympathetic view of the Britons. Shades of this can be found in some modern literature describing the Britons as 'natives', a term that can have unhelpful pejorative undertones. Here, the word 'local' will be used instead to denote groups already living in a region when the Roman army arrived.

Centuries of curiosity concerning the frontier, and over 100 years of scientific excavations, have yielded further written sources, which were composed by people with personal knowledge of Roman Britain. Paradoxically, perhaps, the earliest source of major new information about the Wall was often a by-product of its destruction. Stone robbers stripping the monument of masonry for reuse could chance upon inscriptions, which were sometimes deemed worthy of retention, or at least record, creating an invaluable corpus of texts. Roman epigraphy comes in many guises, including monumental proclamations celebrating construction work, dedications on altars, funerary monuments, and even graffiti. As formal texts were often commissioned to convey a particular public message and sometimes contain errors, they must be treated with caution. Even so, they preserve vital details. One example, discovered at Vindolanda fort, is the tombstone of a centurion probably named Titus Annius. The text tells us that he died *in bello* – in war – while the overall style would fit a Hadrianic date.[21] As such, it furnishes a clue that the fighting in Hadrian's reign recorded in the *Historia Augusta* involved the north. Another crossover concerns Calpurnius Agricola, whom Marcus Aurelius sent 'against the Britons'. Calpurnius Agricola features on inscriptions from at least four forts in the northern military zone, suggesting that his energies, too, were focused in that region.[22] Epigraphy can also begin to plug gaps in the ancient histories. One inscription dating to 284 – that is during the apparent 3rd-century lull – from Ostia, in Italy, describes the emperors Carinus and Numerian as *maximi Britanni* or 'most great conquerors of Britain', hinting at an otherwise unknown campaign.[23]

While inscriptions have illuminated a remarkable breadth of subjects, arguably their greatest legacy lies in the frontier's modern name. For many years the builder's identity was fiercely contested, not least because of the ancient histories crediting Septimius Severus with raising a wall in Britain.[24] Building inscriptions from the milecastles were instrumental to settling the matter in Hadrian's favour.[25] This emphasises the tight dating that epigraphy can provide, with some texts assignable to a few years or even just one. Such precision allows important insights to be gleaned from the Wall's convoluted building programme. The curt formal lettering can also preserve touching human details about journeys taken, lovers met – explicitly or implicitly – flourishing careers, gods worshipped, and lives cut short. Such vignettes are an important reminder that the story of life in the frontier zone is not one of generic Romans and Britons, but a mass of individuals trying to make their

FIGURE 2 *Victor's tombstone. By permission of Arbeia South Shields Roman Fort.*

way in life, even if we cannot usually see them as clearly as we would like. One celebrated example is the tombstone of Victor, who was born in Morocco, and served as a freedman to the cavalry soldier Numerianus, before dying at the age of 20 in South Shields (Fig. 2). The quality of Victor's tombstone has prompted speculation that his relationship with Numerianus transcended that of merely master and servant.[26]

Personal details are also a hallmark of the celebrated tablets discovered at Vindolanda fort. In 1973, two slivers of wood were found pressed together during the digging of a drainage ditch. Parting the leaves revealed ink writing that rapidly faded, but became vivid once more under infra-red photography.

That first writing tablet recorded the delivery of socks, two pairs of sandals, and two pairs of underpants,[27] immediately providing a refreshingly informal glimpse of the occupation. Since then, hundreds more examples of casual correspondence and official documents have been discovered, creating an unrivalled collection of textual evidence for Roman Britain. Although Vindolanda fort was initially founded in the mid AD 80s (over 30 years before work on Hadrian's Wall commenced) and tablets dating to the period after the 110s are rarely discovered there, they breathe life into the military north. Highlights include a birthday invitation from one fort commander's wife to another; a unit strength report dating to 18 May – sadly the year is not specified – revealing that of the 752 men in the First Cohort of Tungrians, only 265 were at Vindolanda and fit for service; correspondence between slaves; and an insight into military logistics that exposes infrastructure deficiencies with the line 'I did not care to injure the animals while the roads are bad'.[28] The local Britons are poorly served by the texts, although one tablet does disclose a new insult for them: *Brittunculi*, meaning wretched or little Britons.[29] This crops up in a document critiquing their fighting style, on which score it is notable that the 18 May strength report specifies that six members of the Vindolanda garrison were 'wounded', a subject we will return to (see p. 44).

Despite the details preserved in the assorted written sources, they suffer from the significant downside of providing less than half the story: that of the Mediterranean elite and others of more modest origins whose presence in Britain was almost certainly a product of the Roman occupation. They also offer a predominantly male perspective. We have no written sources that were certainly created by local communities already inhabiting the Tyne-Solway isthmus, leaving its occupants mute. In this regard, the old adage about victors writing the history is wholly apposite. The scale of the challenge thrown up by the disparity in our written sources is perhaps best illustrated by a more modern analogy: would anyone take seriously a history of Soviet Eastern Europe that drew purely on accounts produced for public consumption by the Russian elite, and documents drafted by serving Soviet soldiers and hangers-on from elsewhere in the Soviet Union? We face a similar danger when we over-rely on the written sources available for Roman Britain. After all, the difference between history and archaeology can be crudely boiled down to that between what people say and what people do. As we all know, there can sometimes be quite a gulf between the two.

Giving a voice to those who left no written records is arguably archaeology's greatest gift. The soil of the Tyne-Solway isthmus still holds traces of local and Roman communities alike, presenting a repository from which their rise and fall can be charted. In practice, though, it would be fair to say that archaeological investigation of local settlements has lagged behind that of military sites.[30] In part this is because the Roman remains are more spectacular, and reliably produce far greater quantities of finds. Equally, archaeologists drawn to Hadrian's Wall tend to be motivated by a fascination with the Roman period, and so target sites – such as forts –

emblematic of that era. Although Bruce advocated further investigation of
local sites in the 19th century, and a farmstead at Milking gap was excavated
in 1937, it was the pioneering scholar George Jobey who revolutionised
knowledge of such sites between the 1960s and 1980s.[31] His energetic
endeavours saw him affectionately likened to a one-man Royal Commission,
and over time Jobey developed a model that proposed local-style rural
settlement flourished during the Roman floruit. Since then, several scholars
have called for further study,[32] but it was new planning policy guidance
embedding archaeology in the development process in 1990 that saw a
surge in work on local settlements. This, coupled with technical advances –
especially improved scientific dating methods – is fuelling a reappraisal of
Jobey's thesis (see p. 86).[33] Although there is a long way to go before our
archaeological datasets for local groups rival those available for the military,
this rich seam of comparatively new information is integral to the picture of
Hadrian's Wall presented here.

Archaeology has also laid bare the Wall's basic anatomy. Various types of
structures cumulatively make up Hadrian's Wall, and although in many
cases their broad characteristics are now well documented, this clarity has
often only been achieved over the last 150 years. This is largely a tribute to
researchers active since the dawn of scientific excavations on the Wall in the
late 19th century. Adopting a methodical question-and-answer approach
enabled them to target sites best able to resolve the uncertainties of the day,
which primarily concerned the construction order of the various Wall
components. As well as amassing data that still underpin research, these
early endeavours pinpointed numerous individual Wall installations. It has
been observed that our knowledge of site positions along one stretch of
frontier has barely advanced since archaeologists F.G. Simpson and Ian
Richmond concluded their enquiries in 1936.[34] As time went by, so too
techniques improved. Discrete occupation layers were first recorded at turret
44b on Mucklebank in 1892 (Fig. 3), while a breakthrough followed at
milecastle 48 in 1909–1910 when artefacts were used to date different
phases of activity.[35] The results were refined at Birdoswald fort in 1929 to
create an influential chronology known as the 'Wall-periods framework'.[36]
This dating scheme was subsequently – and with a certainty we criticise
today – applied Wall-wide in the belief that all its installations developed in
parallel, until such time as they were abandoned.

The case of the Wall-periods framework is a salutary one. It envisioned
four phases of activity, interspersed by episodes of destruction, which
prompted comprehensive refurbishment work. The first period commenced
under Hadrian, and closed when barbarians ransacked the frontier after the
usurper Clodius Albinus stripped it of troops in a bid to become emperor in
196–197; the second ended in 286 when another usurper, Allectus, withdrew
soldiers to fight Constantius Chlorus, allowing the Wall to be overrun once
more; the third concluded with the so-called 'barbarian conspiracy' of 367,
when an apparent alliance of Rome's enemies plunged Britain into chaos

FIGURE 3 *Turret 44b on Mucklebank.*

(see p. 125); and the fourth finished when the Wall was finally abandoned in the late 4th or early 5th century. One of the more astonishing features of this framework is that the first two invasions are entirely imagined, while it is nowhere stated that the 'barbarian conspiracy' engulfed the Wall itself.[37] Moreover, the one instance where the ancient histories specify a wall was breached – under Commodus in the early 180s – is absent from the schedule. Crucially, it cannot be assumed that a 117km-long barrier incorporating 270 or so individual posts acted like a single site with one uniform and predictable structural sequence. Over time, it became increasingly difficult to shoehorn fresh dating evidence from newly dug installations into the Wall-periods scheme, but it was only in 1976 that Breeze and Dobson rejected it wholesale.[38] They ushered in modern Wall studies, by establishing the convention of judging all individual Wall posts on their own merits. The demise of the Wall-periods framework left scholars understandably cautious about linking archaeological evidence to historical incidents,[39] although there are signs this is beginning to change.

Achieving a holistic view of the Wall is aided by the impetus for archaeological investigations, the rigour of recording methods, and the timespan under consideration, all evolving in recent decades. Involving archaeology in the planning process led to a new element of the Wall system being recognised in 2000: timber obstacles, typically likened to Roman barbed wire, on the berm between the curtain and ditch (Fig. 4).[40] It is entirely possible that comparable surprises remain in store for the future. Another shift concerns the treatment of late and post-Roman features. A medieval

FIGURE 4 *A reconstruction of the berm obstacles. Credit: Nick Hodgson/Tyne and Wear Archives and Museums.*

peel tower discovered and excavated during the search for a Hadrian's Wall turret in 1911 merited only ten sentences in the subsequent report,[41] emphasising the excavators' preoccupation with Roman material. Over the course of the 20th century attitudes changed, and by 1984 half of the milecastle 35 structural report could be dedicated to post-Roman features. This growing appreciation that the Wall influenced future development of the region paid off handsomely with Tony Wilmott's 1987–1992 campaign at Birdoswald fort.[42] There, he charted the evolution of the fort granaries, which culminated in a post-Roman timber structure reminiscent of a chieftain's hall. Wilmott's sequence indicated that rather than the fort garrison marching away when Roman control ended *c.* 409, it stayed put and gradually mutated into an early medieval warband (see p. 128). This demonstration that the close of the Roman period simply changed rather than ended the Wall's relevance has directly inspired the chronological span embraced by this book.

The questions we ask of excavated materials are also increasingly sophisticated. For many years pottery and coins were primarily seen as a handy dating tool. Because pottery styles change over time, it is often possible to narrow the date range for a collection of Roman sherds from a site to within a few decades. The minting dates for coins can usually be fixed even more precisely, although estimating how long they remained in circulation before entering the archaeological record remains an imprecise science. More recently, artefacts have been prized for the light they shed on people. This helps us tease out the changes that followed in the wake of a Roman occupation force bearing novel modes of dress, cuisine, and various forms of advanced technology. The Roman author Tacitus bragged that the Britons developed a taste for the toga, baths, and fine dining, adding 'the simple natives gave the name of "culture" to this factor of their slavery'.[43] For many years it was assumed that the Britons did indeed gratefully and indiscriminately accept the trappings of their conquerors, but the finds from Roman Britain tell a different story. These reveal discerning consumers of new commodities, and a willingness to use them in unintended ways. At one site, fine wine cups may have been charged with ale,[44] for instance, which is a bit like swigging beer from a champagne flute today. This local insistence on accepting opportunities on their own terms is a recurrent theme, and it is clear that cultural change was not just a one-way street. Sometimes the results are beautiful, such as the sinuous Dragonesque brooches, which were only manufactured in Roman Britain and fuse local and Roman traditions.[45] Such artefacts, and countless more, make the cultural upheaval unleashed by the Roman conquest tangible.

Bones, seeds, and pollen may not always win the same plaudits as spectacular artefacts, but the insights they offer are equally powerful. Human skeletons are rarely available for study in the northern military zone, partially because cremation remained a popular funerary rite, and partially because the abundant acidic soils eat away faunal material. One exception to the cremation rule is the disquieting number of bodies stashed near or within military installations, rather than in formal cemeteries. At Vindolanda, for example, a 9- to 11-year-old child's corpse was found concealed within a fort barrack block. Isotope analysis – made possible because our teeth preserve the geological signature of the region we grew up in – revealed that the child had spent his or her earliest years in the Mediterranean area, perhaps Libya, before dying in a distant land.[46] Such unorthodox disposal of the dead hints at murder, perhaps sometimes ritually motivated.

Where livestock bones are preserved, they reveal that cattle, sheep, and pigs all featured on the military menu. Cattle sometimes endured hard working lives before being butchered, while their skulls could be reused as targets for artillery or sword practice. Spelt wheat and barley were the most commonly cultivated cereals, while an apparent latrine pit at Carlisle preserved the digested remnants of imported and local produce, such as figs, olives, grapes, apple or pear, damson, rowan, blackberry, dill, radish, and hazelnuts. Pollen from flora on the Tyne-Solway isthmus can also track shifts in the wider environment. Although deforestation accelerated in the pre-Roman Iron Age, for example, greater tree cover survived into the Roman period in the western part of the isthmus than the east. In both cases the levels were probably only slightly greater than those prevailing today. The region's inhabitants would have enjoyed a balmier climate than that greeting modern visitors, though, with conditions broadly comparable to modern Kent.[47]

Considering the ancient environment brings us to another critical factor: the landscape. If you picture this in your mind's eye, you will probably imagine dramatic crags, but these only account for about 14 Roman miles of the curtain's 80 Roman mile length. Gently undulating farmland is more characteristic of the Wall's course across the Tyne-Solway isthmus, and it has been suggested that this location was picked because it overlaps with a regional transition from fertile land favouring cereal cultivation to more marginal ground suited to livestock grazing.[48] This oversimplifies the situation, though, as vast tracts of moor and bog exist both north and south of the Wall. Indeed, the Pennine hills forming the spine of Britain leave zones of transition between upland and lowland farming regimes running straight up northern England (Map 2). Selecting the Tyne-Solway isthmus as the location for Hadrian's Wall surely owes more to it being one of two places where Britain narrows abruptly, making a shorter barrier viable. It can be no coincidence that the second such chokepoint, on the Forth-Clyde isthmus, was exploited by another Roman frontier: the Antonine Wall.[49]

Understanding the nature of the Tyne-Solway isthmus hinges on appreciating two river systems, as well as the intervening watershed, which falls in a 2.55km-wide bottleneck of land known as the Tipalt-Irthing gap. The eastern river system includes the South Tyne and North Tyne, which entwine to form the Tyne, while the western one features the Irthing and Eden (Map 3). The Tipalt-Irthing gap connects the valleys of these two systems, creating the finest natural east–west cross-country corridor south of Tweeddale, about 60km distant, and north of Stainmore, 50km away. The terrain also dictates the easiest northern entrances to this passage, which are via the east and west coastal plains, the Tipalt-Irthing gap, and the North Tyne valley. Movement by members of the prehistoric communities living and working within the region must have been influenced by these natural routeways, as well as fording points on the rivers. Such concerns wove a strategic dimension into the landscape, which surely attracted Roman military attention. This is also true of the Tipalt-Irthing gap itself, which is the only place on the isthmus where north–south movement is possible without having to cross a major watercourse.[50] These natural thoroughfares were certainly significant in later centuries, when the region lay in the debatable lands between England and Scotland.

Mentioning the role of the isthmus in medieval border warfare raises the question of comparative studies. Many other cultures have sought to impede or regulate the flow of human movement, with potentially instructive consequences. Examining the former Berlin Wall and current Israeli West Bank barrier can, for instance, help us to frame the ambiguity at the heart of Hadrian's Wall. When complete, the Berlin and West Bank barriers display numerous common features, including controlled crossing points and two or more lines of running barrier, separated by a cleared strip containing a patrol track and augmented with observation points and artificial lighting. Despite this similarity, The Berlin Wall was effectively a 'closed' border where crossings were the exception, while the Israeli West Bank barrier channels and regulates daily movement by thousands of people. Because a general ability to control movement is integral to both systems, this difference is difficult to demonstrate using structural elements alone: it is only the volume of traffic using the crossings that varies.[51] So it is with Hadrian's Wall, where the frontier gateways in the milecastles could have been used by the many or the few, a subject we will return to. Another, perhaps surprising, case study provides a valuable example of the varied responses borders can elicit: the British Isles.

A green and partitioned land?

It is centuries since the island of Britain has hosted an international land border with any bite. Today, the Anglo-Scottish border is free of the violent lawlessness and warfare that blighted it for centuries. At the time of writing, the border is barely visible in the landscape, with the exception of a length of 16th-century earthwork known as the Scots' Dike, running between the rivers Esk and Sark.[52] In the Cheviots, there is a waist-high fence that can be easily stepped over. The border's modern profile is just as low, and Hadrian's Wall is still commonly used as a convenient shorthand, even though the ancient and modern lines do not touch at any point. Indeed, the eastern end of Hadrian's Wall lies almost 100km south of Scotland. The Anglo-Welsh border can be even easier to miss. Although it intermittently crosses the great early medieval earthwork known as Offa's dyke, in places the modern line runs down streets, invisibly assigning the houses on either side to Wales or England. As Britain is an island, the entire coastline also represents a maritime border. Recent migrant sea crossings have raised its profile, but shady shoreline activity is still generally seen through the prism of dark deeds from the past, perpetrated by wreckers or smugglers. The latter have become so ingrained in folklore that the enterprise can seem almost romantic. Today, whether by sea or land, their modern successors engage in people and weapon trafficking, presenting lucrative possibilities for organised crime, although naturally its practitioners prefer to operate discretely.

The land border on the island of Ireland is also inconspicuous for much of its course, but has a public profile that continues to oscillate. The border's route was established in 1921 on the basis of existing 16th- and 17th-century parish boundaries, which sometimes followed rivers, but often meandered through the landscape in a manner best described as 'arbitrary'.[53] Today, the border is chiefly known for the violence perpetrated during the Troubles, which might seem a surprising subject to broach in a study of Hadrian's Wall, but both the conflict and the consequences of demarcation appear instructive. Employing longstanding parish boundaries to create a border, for instance, bisected individual farms and left towns severed from their hinterlands, while no allowance was made for key religious administrative units. Smuggling became rife – in 1938, there were 180 cross-border roads – while the region could attract violence. This reached new levels when the Troubles erupted in the late 1960s, after public disorder developed into a struggle between paramilitaries and a state security apparatus including soldiers, police, and intelligence operatives. Early steps to tighten control of movement saw most cross-border roads blocked, with military checkpoints on the twenty official crossings, while watchtowers sprouted in the border region.[54] These were particularly prevalent in South Armagh, which was strategically significant to the IRA. The presence of such surveillance measures coloured everyday life, with one resident likening the experience to being in an 'open prison'.[55] Unsurprisingly, this fostered the development of a distinct border identity among some residents.

Fighting in Northern Ireland featured a strong component of what is now variously termed an insurgency, guerrilla warfare, small war, or low-intensity conflict. Such operations are common in modern warfare, as the overwhelming superiority technologically advanced armies enjoy in conventional battles forces less-well-resourced opponents to fight by other means. Farther back in time, small wars were so prevalent in the European colonial era that a British officer, Colonel C.E. Callwell, published an influential treatise on the subject in 1896. His language concerning local groups would not be out of place in Roman texts, and as we will see, there is overlap between Callwell's recommendations and Roman responses to comparable conflict. Reference to guerrilla warfare is generally absent from discussion of Hadrian's Wall,[56] but such combat may well be fundamental to the monument's genesis. Guerrilla tactics typically involve springing surprise attacks to inflict losses and then – crucially – making a clean escape before the enemy can respond in strength. Such fighting feeds off and is nourished by a wider sense of discontent, meaning that countering it requires different techniques to winning conventional wars. Unless states waging counterinsurgency are willing to exterminate an entire population, success depends upon driving a wedge between the guerrillas and the community supporting or harbouring them. This is typically achieved by addressing the grievances that originally sparked the conflict, making the local population the most important element in any counterinsurgency strategy. Another key factor is mobility, with conventional forces often developing tactics to diminish the advantage of surprise by mounting a rapid response. Helicopters were widely used in Northern Ireland, and are also emblematic of the most famous 20th-century counterinsurgency: the Vietnam War. Low-intensity conflicts are often dismissed as not proper soldiering by the regular forces involved, while the very nomenclature implies they are trivial affairs of little significance. The truth can be very different.

The Troubles represent the longest war in the history of the British Army and featured its largest infantry deployment since the Second World War.

More than 3,600 people died, over 40,000 were wounded, and thousands of properties were destroyed during the struggle. Despite the conflict being concentrated in urban hotspots, 50% of the available troops were spread across border areas in the countryside, where there were an estimated 137 unauthorised crossing points – often opened by inconvenienced farmers – that security forces struggled to close.[57] Controlling the border was complicated by its cumbersome course, and the United Kingdom Prime Minister Margaret Thatcher reportedly wished it was 'a straight line', which 'would be easier to defend'.[58] Firefights in the border area between soldiers and insurgents, often ranging from roughly seven to thirty strong, could last for over an hour.[59] Some rural areas became more dangerous than others, with insurgents successfully preventing vehicle patrols on roads in Crossmaglen, Armagh, which became known as the 'graveyard of the British Army'.

The conflict is often framed in terms of sectarian violence between Catholics and Protestants, but it was rooted in local economic and political grievances. High unemployment rates and a political system that restricted Catholic representation in areas where they formed the majority fostered a sense of deprivation, discrimination, and disenfranchisement. The resulting civil rights movement, though, sparked a hostile backlash. Although degrees of involvement by Northern Irish society varied, one effect of the violence was to isolate figures calling for moderation or compromise.[60] In broad terms, the protagonists aimed to achieve two opposing end states, with Northern Ireland either joining the Republic of Ireland, or remaining within the United Kingdom, making the existence of a border a central issue. This had a practical as well as a symbolic value, because securing it was necessary to cut off the IRA from weapons dumps and safe havens in the Republic of Ireland.[61] Naturally, there are fundamental differences with the situation on Hadrian's Wall – not least the absence of a continuous artificial border barrier in Ireland – and these events prove nothing about Roman Britain. But they do provide a sense of the complexities that can follow creating a border on previously open land, as well as the nature of resistance that regular forces may encounter in such regions. Indeed, considering the British Isles in general emphasises the spectrum of responses borders can illicit, from near-ignorance of their presence through organised crime to armed opposition.

Murus mystery

This brings us to the intended scope of this book. As this summary of categories of evidence illustrates, seeking to understand Hadrian's Wall is akin to using assorted jigsaw pieces from numerous different puzzles to try and assemble a single coherent image. Nevertheless, this book aims to unravel the mystery of Hadrian's Wall by examining why it was built, what it was intended to do, and what it really did, both in the Roman period and beyond. Any serious attempt to achieve this must draw heavily on archaeological material. Given its ambiguities, interpretation can sometimes be more honestly described as speculation. Indeed, readers will soon realise from the profusion of cautious qualifiers like 'seemingly' and 'perhaps' that almost every reading of every aspect of Hadrian's Wall is contested by someone. There is no scope to rehearse all of these arguments, or even exhaustively examine every detail of the barrier within this slender volume, but those wishing to venture into the vast labyrinth of Wall literature will be guided by the references.

We begin over the next two chapters by considering who the Romans and Britons were, and why the conquest of Britain ran out of steam. The Wall during the Roman period forms the focus of chapters 4–6, but concluding our survey when imperial control collapsed would sell the monument's true impact short. After all, its influence remains keen today, not just in terms of grounding national discourse, but also the economic boost to the region delivered by around three million tourist visits a year.[62] Fans of *The Eagle of the Ninth* and *Game of Thrones* will know that the Wall has also expanded in a more or less recognisable guise into the realm of pop culture. To cover this, chapters 7–9 will address the Wall's physical, political, and cultural legacy. On one level, this is the story of an extraordinary monument that shaped Roman Britain and continues to influence our world. On another, it is about winners and losers, as individuals grappled with the opportunities and adversity bestowed by the Wall. At its heart, though, it is about change, and how a decision taken almost exactly 1,900 years ago continues to shape lives in unpredictable ways.

2

Rome and Britain

When Worlds Collide

We still have a strange relationship with the Roman Empire. Until 2013, the history taught to English school children began with the Roman invasions. As early human activity in Britain stretches back at least 950,000 years, restricting pupils to the last 2,000 or so missed a good chunk of the story. This span does loosely coincide with the introduction of writing, though, so it can be claimed as the entirety of Britain's history in its strict sense. But that did not stop pupils in Wales from delving farther back in time to learn about Iron Age peoples traditionally referred to as Celts. Why this difference? In Wales, it allowed Celtic origins for the modern Welsh to be emphasised, and in England, too, the opportunity was taken to anchor the present in the past. Rather than focusing on the Roman era as a foreign occupation, the curriculum followed the line about them bringing civilisation. As one recent study put it, 'the English educational system emphasises . . . that the Romans were rather like us . . . The Iron Age peoples seem, by contrast, somewhat "other"'.[1] The gulf between England's focus on the benefits flowing from Classical culture and Wales' perception of free Celts enslaved by despotic Romans plays out in varying guises among many other European countries, reflecting the Empire's status as a keystone for national mythologies.[2] Naturally, rooting modern European identities – with all the sense of ownership that creates – in the Celtic or Roman past is profoundly unhelpful when seeking to understand what these groups were really like.

Sympathy for the Romans is not just encouraged by the English national curriculum. Francis Haverfield, the father of Romano-British studies, Camden Professor at the University of Oxford, and Hadrian's Wall excavator, argued in 1905 that Rome's legions selflessly shielded the occupied provinces, allowing civilisation to take root.[3] Surprisingly, perhaps, it is only really in the last four decades that more critical appraisals of Rome's motives in Britain have been advanced. David Mattingly's 2006 treatment, for instance, skewered an earlier tendency to cast Roman Britain 'as a prequel to the heyday of the British empire', by portraying an occupation that one reviewer epitomised as 'nasty, brutish and long'.[4] But this shift mirrors growing unease about aspects of the British Empire, so it too may be bound up in perceived parallels between us and the Romans. In some ways this sense of kinship is understandable: Classical-style architecture still conveys power in many modern cities; the English alphabet and copious words betray Latin roots; plenty of towns and routes reflect Roman precursors. This list could go on and on in the noblest tradition of 'what have the Romans ever done for us?' But the differences are also stark. The Roman Empire was effectively a military dictatorship, it was sustained by slavery, portents of the future were sought in the flights of birds and entrails of animals, human blood sports flourished, public executions could be staged as twisted theatre, and so on. The Romans were not just like us, and neither were the Iron Age inhabitants of Britain. Nor should we seek to pigeonhole either as simply 'good' or 'bad'. A prerequisite for successfully assessing Hadrian's Wall is to see these groups as they really were, not as we wish them to be today. In that spirit, the remainder of this chapter will be devoted to introducing our protagonists.

Attraction of opposites

When considering Iron Age Britons and Roman invaders, an incisive recent observation is of a trend to cast them as opposing pairs. Examples include describing Iron Age communities as rooted, spiritual, and rural, while Romans furnished the yang to their yin by being mobile, rational, and urban.[5] Testing these qualities exposes the glorious complexity obscured by such labels. Before starting, though, it should be stressed that neither group was static over time. Quite apart from the seismic upheaval in Britain, the all-conquering Roman Empire of the 1st century AD was a different beast from that relinquishing control in the 5th century. Our two groups also varied across space; a factor exacerbated by the Roman failure to complete the conquest of Britain. This left some local communities subject to Roman dominion for the best part of four centuries, others periodically invaded and occupied, while those in north-west Scotland lay beyond the reach of Roman arms. Such differences in circumstance influenced the way these groups developed. Equally, the various emissaries of empire engaged in the colonial project, ranging from slaves to the Roman governor appointed to run Britain, must have experienced the province in very different ways.[6] We can be certain that Hadrian's Wall also provoked conflicting reactions from those living in or travelling through its hinterland. To appreciate them, we must attempt to reconstruct some sense of the worldviews of those involved.

It is useful to begin by clarifying what is meant by 'Roman' and 'Briton'. References to the former could imply people who grew up in the city of Rome, or were at least Roman citizens. Instead, the term can mask an extraordinary diversity of origins. It has been pithily observed that the Roman invaders of

Britain were 'actually not Romans, but Gauls, Germans, Spaniards, Numidians, Thracians, and lots of others with a few Italians pretending to be Romans for appearances sake'.[7] To explain this we need look no farther than Rome's soldiers. While the elite legions did indeed comprise Roman citizens, they were supported by units of *auxilia* (Fig. 5). Literally translatable as 'helpers', these auxiliary soldiers were predominantly recruited or conscripted from among conquered peoples. Many 'Roman' soldiers, then, were born into communities classed as 'barbarian' prior to their submission and incorporation within the Empire. Mastery of this manpower was a matter of Roman pride, with Tacitus bragging that 'of all these [German] races the most manly are the Batavians . . . set apart for fighting purposes only, they are reserved for war'.[8] Auxiliary units included cavalry known as *alae*, and cohorts of infantry or mixed infantry and cavalry. Unit names often referenced the region where they were originally raised, but it is unclear how many soldiers were still sourced from there decades or centuries later. Recruitment practices could certainly be fickle. In AD 117, for instance, the *cohors I Lusitanorum*, which bore a Spanish name and was based in Egypt, received 123 new members from Asia.[9] Equally, such monikers need not be meaningless. An Asturian *ala* that transferred to the Hadrian's Wall fort at Chesters, for instance, may have named it '*Cilurnum*' after the Cilurnigi region of their homeland. If so, presumably Asturians or their descendants could still be found within its ranks. After 25 years of service, retired auxiliary soldiers received Roman citizenship, until the early 3rd century, when the emperor Caracalla (reigned 198–217) granted it to almost all freeborn provincials.

FIGURE 5 *The three reenactors on the left are dressed as legionaries, those on the right as auxiliaries.*

The word 'Briton' also carries deceptive connotations, as it implies a level of unification that simply did not exist prior to the Roman conquest. Rather than being ruled by a single, centralised entity, pre-Roman Britain was home to many rival kingdoms. As such, most people presumably identified with one of them, rather than as Britons. Following the conquest, Rome was keen to promote notions of a unified province and created seventeen new *auxilia* units named *Britannica*, *Brittonum*, or *Brittanorum*.[10] Consequently, referring to Britons runs the risk of reinforcing Roman propaganda, rather than Iron Age realities. Recreating such realities, though, is fraught with difficulty. To take the Tyne-Solway isthmus as an example, this is often viewed as lying on the fringe of territory controlled by the Brigantes, a powerful kingdom in northern England. Yet handmade local pottery is widely distributed in the east of the region, but scarce in the west,[11] indicating a very different uptake of material culture across the isthmus. Equally, Roman inscriptions suggest that groups of *Carvetii*, *Textoverdi*, and *Corionototae* existed on or nearby it,[12] pointing to the local population being far from homogeneous. Suspiciously, the very name Brigantes, which means 'uplander', has the ring of something imposed by outsiders. It has been proposed that the Brigantes were an artificial confederation, assembled from numerous disparate peoples by Roman diplomacy to create a more biddable centralised entity.[13] If so, we are once again seeing the world as Rome ordered it. Either way, the complexity of the situation emphasises the value of a convenient shorthand, so Roman and Briton will be used here, but should be understood in their widest sense.

At a much larger scale, questions also remain about whether the Britons can be classed as part of a wider collection of European peoples traditionally called Celts, a name that has been fiercely critiqued in recent decades.[14] Ancient authors used the term frustratingly inconsistently, but the core Celtic regions seem to have included portions of France, Germany, the Netherlands, and Spain. Tellingly, Britain was not included, with the Roman-era geographer Strabo explicitly distinguishing it from adjacent 'Celtica'.[15] Nevertheless, the Britons spoke what modern linguists call a 'Celtic' language, and they participated in wider European traditions, such as the production and use of 'Celtic art'. Even in the Celtic heartlands there was no single cultural package, implying parallels with modern labels like European, which encompass a wealth of different traditions. Even so, what was and was not Celtic is far from being a moot point on Hadrian's Wall. Because a disproportionately large number of auxiliaries were recruited from north-west Europe, plenty of 'Roman' soldiers had 'Celtic' ancestry.[16] Indeed, because citizenship was extended to some conquered territories, such soldiers could also serve in the legions. These troops – just like those recruited elsewhere – would have carried local beliefs into the Roman army, while descendants may have persisted with certain old-country traditions.[17] As such, some so-called Celtic styles of expression evident on Hadrian's Wall may have been imported by the *auxilia* serving there, and have appeared just as alien to the local Britons as mainstream Classical influences. In other cases, overlap between the traditions of continental Celts and Britons can make establishing a source difficult. To avoid confusing this key issue the terms Briton and Celt are not used interchangeably here. Instead, only people hailing from the continental Celtic heartlands will be referred to as Celts. That said, the convention of referring to Celtic art, languages, and gods will be retained.

Going mobile

Turning to our list of opposing attributes, describing Romans as 'mobile' and Britons as 'rooted' might seem wholly reasonable. The Empire afforded extraordinary opportunities for movement within its bounds. One example is Titus Haterius Nepos, who in the AD 90s conducted a census of the *Brittones Anavion[enses]* – probably the inhabitants of Annandale in south-west Scotland – perhaps as a prelude to conscripting eligible menfolk into the Roman army. Annandale lies just north of the western end of Hadrian's Wall, but by the time work on it commenced in the early 120s, Nepos was already a Roman world away, serving as Prefect of Egypt.[18] Inscriptions indicate that individuals from as far afield as Spain and Syria or Germany and Morocco served on Hadrian's Wall, with 'almost every corner of the empire . . . represented'.[19] A tombstone set up by Barates at South Shields fort captures how different cultures and traditions could mingle. Barates was from Palmyra in what is now Syria, and the tombstone carries a bilingual inscription in Latin and Palmyrene. It was dedicated to his deceased freedwoman wife, Regina (Fig. 6). She was a Briton, but not a local, as the text describes her as a member of the Catuvellauni: an Iron Age kingdom and Roman *civitas* in the Hertfordshire region. Anomalies in the Latin suggest that the text was originally composed in Greek – presumably Barates' second language after Palmyrene – before being translated into military Latin. It is also possible that 'Catuvellauni' constitutes a rendering of spoken British Celtic in Latin script. If so, four different languages combined to create Regina's epitaph.[20] Of course, both Barates and Regina's presence was presumably enabled either directly or indirectly by the military. Most people probably could not roam the Empire at will, and the reality is that opportunities for mobility were unequally distributed.[21]

Whether local farmers in the Wall zone considered a southerner like Regina to be just as much a migrant as Barates is an interesting question, but there can be little doubt that movement on a regional scale was normal. As early as the Mesolithic period (*c.* 9600–4000 BC), there seem to have been sizeable seasonal gatherings of people at the River Eden near what is now Carlisle. By the Neolithic period (*c.* 4000–2500 BC), there are signs of a long-distance routeway running through north-east England towards the Tyne, broad stretches of which were later adopted by the major Roman highway now known as Dere Street.[22] The arrival of metal technology in the

FIGURE 6 *A laser scan of Regina's tombstone, on display at Arbeia South Shields Roman Fort. The Palmyrene text is at the bottom. Credit: Newcastle University.*

Bronze Age (*c.* 2500–800 BC) depended on securing and processing raw materials, as well as exchanging finished goods, meaning it was underpinned by movement. Indeed, most of the copper used in early British metalwork arrived from Ireland.[23] Maritime links with the Continent also grew, not just across the Channel, but also via the Atlantic from Spain, Portugal, or France to Cornwall, Wales, and Ireland,[24] with tin from Cornwall apparently reaching Israel.[25] While this probably arrived via cabotage rather than direct voyages to the eastern Mediterranean, it is entirely possible that some Britons travelled as far as their tin.

International links seemingly fragmented in the Iron Age,[26] but the growth of larger settlements and seemingly more centralised political units in southern Britain can only have increased demand for effective communications and regional movement. The largest pre-Roman Iron Age centres in Britain, which presumably acted as royal seats, can contain ritual centres, funerary complexes, metalworking sites, and imposing halls, as well as sizeable spaces that were seemingly unoccupied. A fine outlying northern example of such a centre is the Brigantes' probable capital at Stanwick, in north-east England, which girded *c.* 270ha within stone-faced perimeter ramparts. Much of the interior was apparently empty, perhaps because it was dedicated to hosting seasonal gatherings of people and, if there was a link to the annual cycle of transhumance, also livestock.[27] Such scenarios mean that rather than farmers on the Tyne-Solway isthmus being rooted to their land, yearly travel allowing some to participate in major congregations at Stanwick is a real possibility. By the Roman conquest, then, modes of movement by land and sea around Britain had been finessed over thousands of years, and were presumably a fact of life for traders, pilgrims, druids, envoys, farmers attending markets, shepherds droving livestock, travellers bound for gatherings, and seasonal labour, while one-off journeys for marriage surely also occurred. As we have seen (p. 14), the landscape would have funnelled terrestrial traffic towards natural nodes, such as fords, thereby shaping regional development.[28] This must, in turn, have influenced Roman military activity, making mobility crucial to understanding pre-Roman and indeed Roman Britain.

Magic and miracles

When it comes to understanding life, belief was as important as movement, which brings us to the notion of spiritual Britons and rational Romans. The most famous manifestation of Iron Age spirituality must be the druids, about whom little is known and much is written. Yet again we draw on Classical sources, which mostly concern Gallic druids, although Caesar notes the sect purportedly arose in Britain.[29] The druids were powerful figures who acted as priests – Pliny the Elder calls them 'magicians' – teachers, and justices.[30] Despite this wide-ranging brief, we tend to fixate on the druids' role in human sacrifice. Sufficient potential sacrificial victims – including individual bodies placed in pits – have been unearthed to suggest that the practice was widespread, though perhaps not frequent, in Iron Age Britain.[31] When it comes to worship more generally, purpose-built shrines were becoming more common in southern Britain towards the end of the Iron Age. Even so, most sacred places were probably simply significant places in the landscape, where individual gods were believed to dwell, such as groves, springs, bogs, and rivers. In this regard it may be significant that Stanwick has something of a watery focus.[32] The quantity of high-status material fished from the Thames has seen it branded a sacred river, and on this score the Tyne is pre-eminent in the north.[33] While Bronze Age and early Iron Age artefacts are most common from the Tyne, later material suggests it remained ritually potent.[34]

Major manmade structures could also receive special deposits. Hillfort defences sometimes seem to be associated with human sacrifices,[35] while limited investigation of the ditch at Stanwick produced portions of five skulls, and it has been calculated that a similar distribution along its entire

course would require over 500 crania.[36] Everyday houses and settlement or
field limits could receive more innocuous special deposits, with quernstones
seemingly used in various ways, including to mark the creation or
abandonment of boundaries.[37] Pits dug into the earth and containing burnt,
broken, mundane, and unusual material are also widespread.[38] Such deposits
were often branded refuse when excavated, but the presence of suggestive
artefacts and the repetitive nature of this behaviour must make a ritual
dimension likely in some – though not all – cases. A site at Doubstead, on
the Northumberland coastal plain about 80km north of the Tyne, provides
an excellent example. This modest enclosed farmstead contained at least
two roundhouses. Excavating the north ditch terminal of the enclosure
revealed animal bone, broken pottery, a broken quern, a late-1st- or 2nd-
century hinged bracelet, and spiral finger-ring. The interest in round objects
implied by the last three artefacts was continued by a shale disc within a
nearby pit sunk into the entrance passage.[39] Such discs are viewed as 'not
uncommon' in the Iron Age and Roman north, and a ritual purpose has

FIGURE 7 *The Battersea Shield, dating to c. 350–50 BC and now in the British
Museum.*

been tentatively proposed for some.[40] Representations of solar discs are a feature of later European prehistory,[41] although in this case the colour of shale seems a poor fit. What such apparent offerings signified can only be guessed at, but they may well reflect key moments in the settlement lifecycle.

An illustration of how far ancient beliefs could differ from modern western worldviews comes from considering Celtic art. On one level, the quality of Iron Age pieces such as the Battersea Shield – which is believed to have been manufactured in Britain – gives the lie to Roman slurs about the island being populated by ignorant savages (Fig. 7). The imagery on Celtic art can be highly sophisticated, with vegetation, humans, animals, or fantastical beasts often lying concealed within graceful, sinuous decoration. Such figures remain defiantly intangible, merely hinted at before dissolving once more into ambiguous swirls. Despite its splendour, this artistry was probably primarily prized for its perceived power, and may have been judged magical.[42] What such sorcery accomplished is a matter for speculation, but it hints at a world where the boundaries between natural and supernatural states were blurred. Martial kit emblazoned with Celtic art appears popular, so perhaps the creatures conjured by the imagery lent their powers to the owner. Alternatively, the technological proficiency enabling such sumptuous artefacts may have been popularly perceived as a product of occult skills.[43] Some decorative details are so subtle that they conceivably acted as protective devices aimed at divine powers rather than a human audience.[44] Here, we are moving into a realm where things we consider mere objects were seen to possess elements of personhood, including a power to influence behaviour.[45] To cynical 21st-century minds this may sound like a plot device from *The Lord of the Rings*, but the potency of these objects is reflected in the careful manner of their disposal. Rather than entering the archaeological record by chance, many examples of Celtic art were deliberately deposited, be it in lakes, rivers, bogs, pits, burials, or elsewhere. Iron Age Britons, then, were undoubtedly spiritual. But so were the Romans.

On one level we all know this. The names of their chief gods remain familiar, not least because some still hang in the heavens as planets, while Roman temples enliven many an archaeological itinerary. At the head of state, the emperor served as *pontifex maximus*, or high priest. But perhaps we sometimes overlook the degree to which superstition pervaded Roman society. Because Roman temples had boundaries demarcating the extent of the sacred compound, it is easy to imagine that the space beyond was secular, but this was not the case. Rather like Iron Age Britons, Romans believed that a *genius loci* or protective spirit of the place dwelt within landscape features. Intriguingly, dedications to *genii loci* in Roman Britain most commonly occur in military zones, perhaps in an attempt to placate spirits whose tranquillity had been violated by army activity.[46] Human males also had their own genius, which was formed at birth, while military units and institutions gained one at the moment of their inception.[47] Parallels between the practices of Britons and Romans include buildings or boundaries sometimes receiving foundation or abandonment offerings, while apparent ritual pits are plentiful. One Pompeian fresco illustrates how far belief was bound up in the mundane. It occupied a corridor leading to a tavern toilet and features a squatting man protected by serpents and Fortuna, while the text cautions readers to beware the evil eye – what we might think of as bad luck – when defecating.[48] Averting its malign influence could be aided by various amulets or symbols, with phallic imagery proving a particularly popular safeguard.[49] Such magical protection was sometimes concealed from view, offering a parallel to the devices on some Celtic art.

The Empire's size ensured that many gods were worshipped within its bounds, but while some pre-Roman practices prospered, others did not. Human sacrifice was famously prohibited by Rome, but it is less clear how stringently this was enforced. As the modern world reminds us, making something illegal does not mean it immediately stops happening. There are hints that Roman-era human sacrifice occasionally occurred in Britain, including at least eight bodies found in bogs in the northern military zone.[50] In Kent, during the 2nd century two sets of paired babies – one decapitated – were placed at temple corners and have been interpreted as harrowing evidence for human foundation sacrifices at a religious complex focused on the waters at Springhead.[51] Removal of the crania is interesting, as Strabo insists that another practice stamped out by the Romans was ritual headhunting.[52] This grisly practice is closely associated with the Celts, but there is also evidence for it in Britain and Ireland.[53] Ancient literature speaks of enemies' heads being taken by warriors and displayed, preserved, or even fashioned into sacred vessels for pouring libations or drinking from.[54] One Irish literary tradition held that depositing a head in a well gifted it magical properties.[55]

Despite Strabo's testimony, headhunting survived in the Roman world, and could even be found in the army. Trajan's Column, which presents a visual narrative of that emperor's Dacian wars, captures the awkward moment when two auxiliary soldiers presented a nonplussed Trajan (reigned 98–117) with the severed heads of their foes.[56] A potentially broadly contemporary example from Lancaster, in the British military zone, occurs on the tombstone of Insus, an auxiliary soldier from what is now western Germany. He served in the *ala Augusta* and is shown on horseback, gripping the head of a decapitated enemy (Fig. 8).[57] That Insus' heir wished him to be publicly depicted as a headhunter suggests that the practice was not only tolerated, but could deliver a degree of social kudos.

There is also evidence for a head cult or cults on Hadrian's Wall, where skulls are sometimes found associated with defences, paralleling the situation at Stanwick. One example, from a Severan ditch at Vindolanda, came from a young man who grew up in south-west Scotland, which seems to have been a notable trouble spot. Crania found in such contexts are sometimes claimed to be the heads of enemies or criminals that were mounted on poles, before tumbling into a ditch, but at least some seem to have been carefully placed within defences. Skulls also occur in pits and wells, including a

FIGURE 8 *The Insus tombstone, on display in Lancaster City Museum. Credit: Lancashire County Museum Service, Lancashire County Council.*

portion of that of an adult female, which was 'filled with coins' and deposited at a shrine known as Coventina's Well, beside Carrawburgh fort.[58] An ·interest in heads is also apparent from pots with decorative human faces sometimes being seemingly deposited as substitutes for the real thing. Equally, crudely carved stone sculptures known as 'Celtic heads' have been found at numerous places along the Wall. These are often poorly dated and it was once assumed they were crafted by local communities. But such stone heads are a poor fit with pre-Roman artistic traditions in Britain, while the existence of continental parallels makes it probable that the idea arrived with the Roman army.[59]

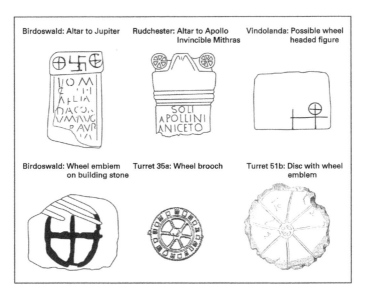

FIGURE 9 *Six objects bearing possible or certain wheel emblems (not to scale). After* RIB *1877, 1397,* RIB III *3448, from Woodfield 1965, courtesy of the Society of Antiquaries of Newcastle upon Tyne.*

Following Roman conquest, acceptable local gods could undergo a process that Tacitus called *interpretatio Romana*.[60] This formally associated such deities with members of the Roman pantheon sharing similar attributes. A classic example from Hadrian's Wall is an apparent local warrior god, who was combined with his Roman counterpart to become Mars Cocidius. Although this technique is often feted as an act of religious tolerance, the local gods were effectively subjugated by Roman ones, and worshipped in Roman style.[61] Not all devotees were so passive, though. One powerful deity with a cult presence on Hadrian's Wall is not named on any known inscription: a Celtic sky god associated with a wheel emblem (Fig. 9). As Miranda Aldhouse-Green has pointed out, the wheel appears to be an ancient solar symbol, which was used at least as early as the Bronze Age. The hub was presumably the sun itself, while the spokes represent rays, and the rim its nimbus,[62] with some artistry suggesting that the wheel was towed through the heavens by a solar horse. This sky god was often associated with Jupiter, a celestial deity who acted as father of the Roman pantheon and the focus of displays of fealty to the Roman state. Sometimes Jupiter was depicted holding the wheel, but on other occasions this emblem was inserted onto his altars, as occurs at Birdoswald, Castlesteads, and Maryport forts (Fig. 9). The Celtic sky god's apparent association with the sun is alien to classical representations of Jupiter, so when he is forced to adopt this attribute, he rather resembles a victim of *interpretatio Celtica*.[63]

With the exception of coins and some rock carvings, the wheel emblem is relatively rare in pre-Roman Britain, suggesting this god was not widely revered on the island. This makes it all but certain that the deity's presence on Hadrian's Wall was a consequence of soldiers or incomers with Celtic heritage. A stone mould for making wheel emblems or brooches found at Gateshead, just south of the Tyne at Newcastle, is paralleled by one found at Bibracte in France.[64] Petroglyphs in the Camonica Valley of the Italian Alps feature wheel representations,[65] and also an ithyphallic horse image tentatively dated to the 4th century BC, which bears some similarities to the striking example incised on a building stone at Birdoswald fort on Hadrian's Wall (Fig. 10).[66] As wheel symbolism is also known from this fort (Fig. 9),[67] a connection with the solar horse might be suspected. While there is more evidence for mainstream Roman deities, such as Jupiter, Minerva, Mars, Mercury, Juno Regina, and Fortuna, being worshipped on Hadrian's Wall, the army clearly introduced provincial cults from elsewhere in the Empire, emphasising the importance of seeking out worship conducted in a less than Classical manner.

Roman military bases are often seen by archaeologists and the public as profane places, but the classic 2nd-century fort ground plan had the *aedes* or shrine of the unit standards at its heart. This sacred space lay within the *principia* (headquarters building) and was usually aligned on the principal fort gateway, which in turn was positioned to face either the enemy, or east towards the path of the rising sun. As such, a mainstream military design presents a carefully choreographed display of supernatural power. There are grounds to suspect that the *aedes* could be ritually decommissioned when a fort was abandoned, thereby ensuring the appropriate disposal of sanctified material.[68] While this is usually the only formal religious space within a fort, magical protection could also be present. Excavations at South Shields fort revealed stones bearing phallic imagery built into the front walls of two barrack blocks, in a fashion that rendered the carvings invisible.[69] An alternative means to ward off evil may be illustrated by a building stone depicting a human head from milecastle 35 (Fig. 10).[70] Such imagery is comparatively rare in Iron Age Britain,[71] but once again comparable carvings do occur in areas of Iron Age Europe, so the milecastle head presumably reflects the Celtic mania for crania.[72] Elsewhere along the Wall, there are sundry examples of what appear to be offerings made at pivotal moments in the lifecycle of a military post, testifying to small acts of faith.[73] Indeed, by building the Wall, the soldiers seemingly sired their own supernatural entity. One altar to Mars Cocidius also invokes the *Genio Vali*, presumably to be translated as 'Genius of the Wall',[74] meaning it was believed to have a protective spirit. If so, the Wall was deemed capable of extending both physical and supernatural protection.[75] Belief that gods could dwell in special places, such as rivers, springs, bogs, and manmade edifices like the Wall, emphasises that the army 'operated within a ritual landscape, as well as a military one'.[76]

FIGURE 10 *The milecastle 35 head (above) and Birdoswald horse (below). For the head, credit: Great North Museum: Hancock. From the collection of the Society of Antiquaries of Newcastle upon Tyne.*

Town and country

The final calling point on our whistle-stop tour is the question of urban Romans and rural Britons. Roman civilisation depended on a sophisticated urban system, and towns were also an essential tool for creating governable provinces. Most Roman towns in Britain can be classed as *civitas* capitals, which administered the inhabitants of former Iron Age kingdoms, or agglomerations thereof. Because civic authorities enjoyed some independence, towns created an arena where compliant former ruling classes could compete for positions on the council and retain some say in the running of their former territory. This was traditionally achieved by bankrolling new amenities and thereby currying favour with the electorate, although it would be fair to say that local elite civic munificence appears less extravagant in Roman Britain than in towns on the Continent. Even so, many Romano-British towns were founded near or within former Iron Age centres, emphasising the importance of pre-Roman proto-urban powerbases in 'rural' Britain. Stanwick provides an intriguing exception to this, as the Roman *civitas* capital for the Brigantes was built much farther south at Aldborough, placing it quite close to the legionary fortress at York.

Given the pre-eminence of towns, discovering the true extent of rural settlement proved eye-opening for archaeologists in both Britain and Italy. In the 1950s–1970s, the South Etruria Survey revealed an unexpected density of rural sites in Italy, after the introduction of deep-ploughing methods exposed long-buried artefacts.[77] In Britain, aerial photography first began to reveal the density of rural settlement, but the true revolution followed archaeology becoming part of the development process in 1990. The importance of this for understanding the Wall zone can hardly be overstated. Developer-funded excavations on the Northumberland coastal plain – in the vicinity of the eventual course of Hadrian's Wall – have revealed a settled Iron Age community inhabiting sites that surprised by virtue of their scale, quantity, and longevity.[78] One enclosed farmstead had a comparable footprint to the Roman fort at Wallsend, which was designed to garrison over 500 men (Fig. 11). It has been estimated that enclosed settlements occurred approximately every kilometre on the coastal plain, with more modest habitation in between, potentially housing a pre-Roman population of 10,000–15,000 over an area of approximately 675km^2. This population developed over several centuries, and as well as speaking of a stable community, it hints that families occupying the high-status enclosed settlements drew some prestige from ancestral claims to the land.[79] These farmers – like many others in the region – practised mixed agricultural regimes combining crops and livestock, with the gentler climate permitting cultivation of land no longer productive today. Mobile groups are harder to detect archaeologically, but raiders were probably a hazard, while the Tyne-Solway isthmus is admirably suited to transhumance,[80] making it likely that Iron Age cattle drovers were also active. Although they worked distant uplands in the spring and summer, their seasonal – and doubtless sometimes fractious – interactions with the settled lowland farmers would have contributed much to the region's character.

Frontier cultures

We may seem to have strayed some distance from Hadrian's Wall in this chapter. But it is crucial to appreciate that the differences between Britons and Romans was often one of degrees, rather than absolutes. While some Romans enjoyed greater opportunities for long-distance mobility, for instance, movement was also crucial to life in Iron Age Britain. Concerning spirituality, both parties accepted that the world was rife with gods and magic. While practices could vary, and the Roman elite disapproved of

FIGURE 11 *Local farmsteads (including West Brunton, Blagdon Park 2, and Pegswood, which lay north of the Wall and were abandoned in the early 2nd century) compared to Wallsend fort. Credit: Nick Hodgson/Tyne and Wear Archives and Museums.*

human sacrifice, they were content that animals delivered a comparable result. It is also essential to be mindful of the impact of beliefs borne by members of the *auxilia*. Such soldiers ensured that the Roman army acted as a vector to spread non-Roman beliefs alongside the official ones, but it is the latter category that often receives most attention on Hadrian's Wall. While Stanwick indicates that local Britons believed skulls had an apotropaic power, some of the more baroque evidence for head cults along Hadrian's Wall is most closely paralleled on the Continent, suggesting the arrival of influences from Celtic Europe. Accepting that belief motivated behaviour also means that we must move beyond seeing the Wall as simply a structure running through a picturesque landscape. It belonged to a world where artefacts and natural features could be supernaturally charged with aspects of personhood, and where the Wall itself could seemingly acquire a spiritual identity. Yet this barrier did not just cleave apart a landscape populated with myriad local gods, it also threatened local Iron Age power structures. If elite status was conferred by ancestral claims to land, its unilateral division must have jeopardised existing hierarchies. The stakes, then, could not have been higher. In the next chapter we will examine how the conquest period laid the foundations for Hadrian's Wall.

3

Battling for Britain

Conflict and Collaboration

In 55 BC, the safe return of the first Roman army to land in Britain occasioned an unprecedented 20 days of thanksgiving in Rome. The army was Julius Caesar's,[1] and the roots of this rapturous reception lay in a Classical belief that the inhabited world – comprising Europe, Africa, and Asia – was surrounded by an all-encompassing ocean. This was a place of mystery and danger, populated by gods, monsters, and mythical lands.[2] As Britain lay within this realm, Caesar had effectively carried Roman arms beyond the edge of the world. Other than his success in impressing his target audience in Rome, though, the operation appears to have been disappointing. Loot was thin on the ground, and Caesar's political opponents in Rome did not appear overly dismayed by his escapade. While Caesar was preparing for a second British foray, Cicero waspishly wrote to a friend that 'It is also now ascertained that there isn't a grain of silver on the island nor any prospect of booty apart from captives, and I fancy you won't expect any of *them* to be highly qualified in literature or music!'[3] After Caesar departed from Britain a second time in 54 BC, having secured further hostages and the promise of an annual tribute from the 'conquered' island, troubles in Gaul arose once more. It would be 97 years before another Roman army made landfall.

In the interim, Britain remained an agenda item. Augustus, the first emperor, seemingly mulled invasion in the last few decades BC.[4] Intensified contact with the Roman world also heralded change in Britain,[5] with Roman imports even reaching Stanwick, the Brigantes' powerbase in northern England. If this was a product of conscious Augustan diplomatic activity,[6] courting such a distant polity would illustrate the sophistication of Rome's groundwork. A dribble of refugee British royals headed in the other direction, finding sanctuary at successive emperors' courts, doubtless in case they proved useful. Gaius (reigned AD 37–41) – the famously unhinged emperor we know by his nickname of Caligula or 'little boot' – was the next to assemble an invasion force. The ancient sources gleefully describe this degenerating into farce, with Gaius ordering his army to collect seashells on the Gallic shore.[7] An explanation for this odd episode may lie in his men's reluctance to cross the ocean.[8] Gaius' excesses ultimately ended in assassination, and during the ensuing chaos his uncle Claudius was proclaimed emperor. Claudius (reigned 41–54) had something of a chequered reputation for competence and coveted a military victory to shore-up his position in Rome. An exiled British prince in Claudius' court presented an excuse for military action, although his soldiers initially, once again, proved reluctant to cross the ocean.

Claudius struck in 43. His invasion force comprised four legions – the *IX Hispana* redeployed from Pannonia, and the *II Augusta*, *XIV Gemina*, and *XX Valeria* from the Rhine – representing a paper strength of over 20,000 men. They were supported by *auxilia*, who probably increased the invasion force to about 40,000. After landing, the army advanced rapidly, seemingly in part because the Britons shunned set-piece battles. Instead, they 'took refuge in the swamps and the forests hoping to wear out the invaders in fruitless effort',[9] which suggests a reliance on small-scale surprise attacks. This tactic fits with Iron Age martial kit from Britain, which has been judged best suited to 'highly mobile and loosely formed' warfare.[10] The Britons did hold major rivers in force, though, and the invaders twice forced passage when a unit of auxiliaries – perhaps Tacitus' dread Batavians – swam the river in full armour. On the second occasion, Roman forces were also able to cross via a bridge upstream, illustrating the army's knack for turning existing infrastructure against its creators. By late summer, Claudius was present in person, to administer the *coup de grâce* at Camulodunum: modern Colchester. Before Claudius left Britain to celebrate his Roman triumph, he instructed Britain's first Roman governor to conquer the rest.[11] It proved an unattainable goal.

UnRoman warfare

There is no call to rehearse the conquest period exhaustively here, but considering a handful of aspects helps illuminate subsequent events on Hadrian's Wall. One is to salute Rome's diplomatic nous. Cultivating friendly kingdoms paid off handsomely, ensuring the Empire literally divided and conquered, rather than facing a force fielded by an alliance of all British kingdoms. As Roman battlegroups set about completing the conquest, their flanks were secured by allied kings presiding over a substantial chunk of the south and east, while the equally compliant Queen Cartimandua's Brigantes held the north. But the speed with which Roman forces advanced must not blind us to the disruption following in their wake. Occupation often ignites a period of what is essentially civil war among the conquered, after existing power structures are fatally weakened by military defeat. It is easy to imagine vying factions within Iron Age kingdoms settling scores and struggling for influence during a post-conquest power vacuum. That an increase in Briton-on-Briton violence dogged the legions is implied by Tacitus' observation that 'originally the people were subject to kings, now the quarrels and ambitions of petty chieftains divide them'. This is later followed by a cryptic reference to his father-in-law, and governor of Britain, Gnaeus Julius Agricola protecting states that sued for peace: 'no newly acquired district of Britain submitted with so little interference from neighbours'.[12] The modern world furnishes ample examples of nations intervening in the affairs of destabilised neighbours to foment a favourable outcome,[13] and it was surely the same among the British kingdoms. Upheaval is seemingly also apparent in the deposition of Celtic art, as a notable spike in 40–65 is suggestive of societies in crisis.[14]

Violence certainly characterised Rome's early dealings with the Silures. This group occupied south-eastern Wales, and successfully resisted domination for a quarter of a century, from 49–73/4. Roman military efforts were hamstrung by a confluence of calamities, including the expiration in office of two governors, the succession of Nero (reigned 54–68) – who reputedly harboured reservations about retaining Britain[15] – and the Boudican revolt. Even so, credit must also go to the Silures, who proved adept at targeting vulnerable Roman soldiers. Legionary cohorts detailed to construct installations, a foraging party, and two auxiliary units bent on plunder all paid a price for inadequate vigilance. In the case of the mauled legionary cohorts, it was only a Silurian failure to cut the lines of communication that allowed word to reach nearby forts and a rescue to be mounted. But when the army brought its superior strength to bear, 'the enemy escaped with trivial losses'. Tacitus' description of smaller ambushes sprung on Roman forces is often rendered in translations as 'irregular' or 'guerrilla' fighting.[16] His original phrase is *in modum latrocinii*, or 'in the manner of banditry', conveying palpable disdain for such desultory combat. Once again, these episodes played out in 'forests and marshes'; precisely the environments where soldiers trained for fighting in formation would be most disadvantaged. Unlike the brief encounters in 43, though, this time resistance appeared resilient. The calculated manner in which the Silures exploited Roman weaknesses to strike and escape suggests astute planning. At the end of the 19th century, Callwell observed that irregular forces often exercise superior intelligence gathering. He despaired that regular soldiers' 'camp gossip ... flies from mouth to mouth until it reaches the ears of the enemy', while the languid, predictable movements of regular forces simplified observing and ambushing them. Callwell added that such campaigns 'are always most trying to the [regular] troops'.[17]

The Romans were certainly riled. One commander threatened the Silures with genocide, which unsurprisingly did nothing to quell resistance. So how were they bent to the imperial yoke? Tacitus is vague, saying simply that the end came in the 70s, when the governor Julius Frontinus 'reduced the Silures ... he surmounted not only the valour of the enemy, but also the physical difficulties of the land'.[18] Archaeology can help here, because it was around this time that a network of forts interspersed with smaller fortlets along key communication routes was established in Wales (Fig. 12). This web of posts appears unprecedented in Britain, but parallels what Callwell advocates as the best bet for victory against guerrillas: 'the sub-division of the theatre of war into sections, each with its commander, its chain of posts, and its mobile columns'. He explains that a combination of larger and smaller posts is essential to safeguard supplies and communications.[19] Luck

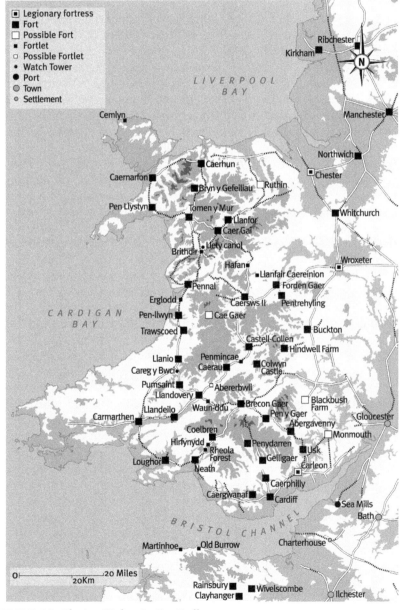

FIGURE 12 *Flavian Wales. By Ian Bull.*

or canny judgement may also have brought an even more modern technique into play. The Silures eventually received their own semi-autonomous *civitas* capital, *Venta Silurum*, where obliging elites could have retained a measure of authority. Finding a political solution that addresses the initial complaint, in this case presumably loss of autonomy and land, is a hallmark of modern counterinsurgency strategies. Although the foundation of *Venta Silurum* is dated to the early 2nd century, finds indicate activity by the 70s, which has been linked to the potential development of a local, civilian market.[20] If so, we could be seeing a sophisticated military and political strategy operating in tandem. While the forts and fortlets tightened the screw on insurgents, fostering a civilian centre presented the promise of a pathway to a meaningful future for those willing to play ball. Such subtle blends of coercion and consent are judged essential to modern pacification operations.[21]

As the network of forts and fortlets extended throughout Wales, sustained guerrilla warfare was probably fiercest in, rather than restricted to, Silurian territory; an inference supported by the ancient literature.[22] In this regard it is valuable to consider the case of Anglesey, which was a major druidic religious centre. Tacitus paints a vivid picture of the initial assault on this island in 60, with Roman soldiers massacring 'all who met them' and destroying 'the groves consecrated to [the druid's] savage cults'.[23] Mattingly notes that these priests 'could expect no quarter now they had nowhere left to run', but their backs were not quite against the wall.[24] We have already seen how the Atlantic seaways had bound Wales and Ireland together for millennia, while Holyhead on Anglesey remains an important ferry port. As boats must have been present – it is an island after all – an exit was available to those who did not wish to fall with their groves. Given that we know imperilled British royals sometimes fled to emperors' courts, there seems no reason why elite refugees could not try seeking sanctuary with Irish leaders.[25] Some may even have fled and then returned, as the island was repopulated before the Roman army took it a second time in 77 or 78. Tacitus also mentions that Agricola later sheltered an expelled Irish ruler, with an eye to invading the island. If word of this ambition reached Irish leaders, it would provide a motive to keep Rome busy elsewhere by discretely aiding resistance in Wales. It may well be no coincidence that Roman fortlets, which were arguably the fortification type best suited to countering low-level resistance, are concentrated in western Britain, facing Ireland.[26]

There and back again

Tacitus traced the turmoil that forced Rome's advance northwards in 69 to a sex scandal involving Queen Cartimandua of the Brigantes. Given, though, that similar slurs have been used to undermine powerful women through the ages, it might be wondered if anti-Roman factions concocted this tale to turn public opinion and perhaps even Cartimandua's own husband against her. Either way, Roman *auxilia* managed to rescue Cartimandua, and the army then set about subduing the Brigantes.[27] By the winter of 72–73, a fort was being constructed at Carlisle: the earliest Roman installation known on the Tyne-Solway isthmus (Fig. 13). The choice of site is an interesting one.

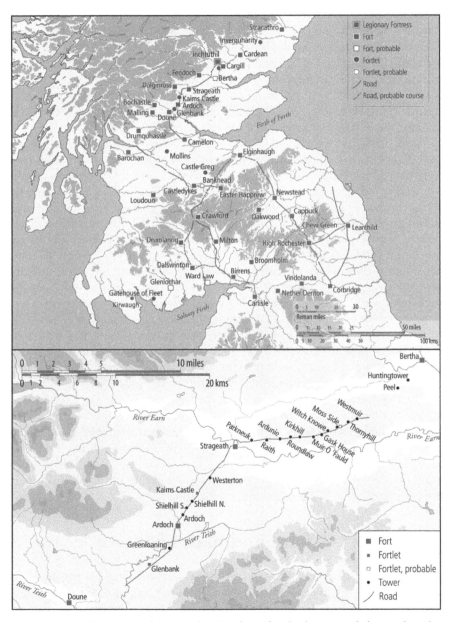

FIGURE 13 *Flavian northern England and Scotland (above), and the Gask Ridge (below). Courtesy of David J. Breeze.*

The fort occupied a commanding position later exploited by a medieval castle, while an important seasonal meeting place appears to have existed nearby as early as the Mesolithic period. Neolithic axes from Carlisle could imply subsequent ritual activity,[28] and it has been suggested that the area acted as a local centre in later prehistory.[29] Although traces of Iron Age settlement remain scarce, archaeologists find this period hard to date in Cumbria. An important pre-Roman river crossing probably existed nearby, and it is intriguing that the Roman name for Carlisle is *Luguvalium*, meaning something like 'strong through Lugus': a Celtic deity. Whether this references its existing name, or was coined by Celtic-speaking members of the *auxilia* is a different matter. It is conceivable, though, that Carlisle fort lay near or upon some kind of local gathering place, perhaps with a religious dimension. Farther south, Brougham fort was certainly founded in a ritually sensitive region.[30] An interest in demonstrating military control of such places might also explain why the primary Roman fort ditches at Ambleside, in the Lake District, clasp a prominent rocky knoll, which was explained as 'an improvised corner tower' (Map 2).[31] Yet this outcrop lies near the head of Lake Windermere, while the fort was surrounded by marsh, and given the importance of watery places to Iron Age belief it conceivably held spiritual significance. Naturally this is speculative, but founding forts at such sites would have conveyed a message about Rome's power over local gods.

Initially, the Tyne-Solway isthmus was just another region to be conquered. The earliest fort in the east was probably founded in the mid 70s at Red House. This was abandoned in the mid 80s, in favour of nearby Corbridge, while forts were also established at Vindolanda and Nether Denton (Fig. 13). By then, the army was campaigning far to the north in Scotland, where Tacitus again chronicles adversaries adept at slipping away into marshes and forests. These foes seem to have been especially bold, directly attacking forts and even mounting a nocturnal assault on a legion within its temporary camp. Eventually, in 83 or 84 a set-piece battle took place at Mons Graupius, somewhere on the Highland fringe. There, the Roman army once again demonstrated the futility of fighting them in this fashion. Agricola used his *auxilia*, especially Batavian and Tungrian units, to inflict a crushing defeat, claiming 10,000 enemies slain for the loss of just 360.[32] In the aftermath, forts were positioned in the mouths of Highland glens, presumably poised for a fresh offensive.

To the rear of the glens a highway was established, which received special protective measures along a stretch crossing the Gask Ridge (Fig. 13). There, the fort-fortlet-fort model seen in Wales was employed again, this time alongside a chain of towers, some under 900m apart. This configuration would help ensure that communications could not be cut to isolate units, although the Gask Ridge has also been viewed as a component of a prototype land frontier.[33] The closest Roman word to frontier – *limes* – originally meant a road, and the great 2nd-century systems certainly built on the basic Gask Ridge premise of arranging forts, fortlets, and towers along a linear feature. Despite the army's apparent preparations for further advance, it did not have long to savour victory at Mons Graupius. Trouble on the Danube saw *Legio II Adiutrix* and presumably its supporting *auxilia* rushed to the Continent *c.* 87, never to return. For everyone else, a gradual retreat ensued. In Tacitus' judgement, Britain was 'subdued and immediately let go'.[34] It took the Roman army about two decades to return the northern frontier to the Tyne-Solway isthmus, a reverse that the surviving ancient histories remain resolutely silent about. Archaeology, though, shows that surrendering so much territory was not the original intention. Instead, an attempt was made to retain the region south of the River Tweed, anchored on a key fort at Newstead (Fig. 13).[35] Perhaps the authorities assumed that the army only needed to hold on until the *II Adiutrix* returned and the advance could continue, but if so they waited in vain.

The Vindolanda writing tablets provide a key source for this period. Although they shed little light on the momentous events unfolding in the north, these documents convey the nitty-gritty of military life on the Tyne-Solway isthmus. The tablets span the late 1st to the early 2nd century, covering the period when a unit of Tungrians, then Batavians, then Tungrians again were in residence, with many of these soldiers probably veterans of Mons Graupius. Topics range from work details, requests for leave, and sourcing supplies, to absentee soldiers and even a man being deported from the province in chains.[36] One letter from a decurion named Masclus seeks both orders and beer for his men, while referring to the Batavian commander as 'his king'. This could be sycophancy or even playful cheek, but it is possible that a Batavian royal had found that military service was a way to retain status.[37] If so, at least some of the unit's soldiers were still being sourced from among the people commemorated by the unit name. Masclus' letter is far from being the only reference to Celtic beer or brewers among the tablets.[38] Hilary Cool has noted the health risks posed by unpurified water meant that 'prior to the advent of tea and coffee, much of what was drunk in Britain was alcoholic'.[39] Presumably, then, plenty of booze was being quaffed, but we can only speculate about how diligently – and even-handedly – half-cut or hungover soldiers fulfilled their duties.

Some local unrest is implied by a unit strength report noting six wounded soldiers.[40] Another tablet might be a critique of local conscripts, but appears a natural companion piece to accounts of guerrilla warfare elsewhere in Britain: 'the Britons are without body armour. There are very many cavalry. The cavalry do not use swords nor do the wretched Britons mount in order to throw javelins'.[41] Both documents point to low-level violence well within occupied territory. That discontent may have been aggravated by legal discrimination is implied by another letter, in which a petitioner complains about being beaten with rods until he bled. The appellant argues this was unjust because he was 'a man from overseas' and, what is more, 'innocent'.[42] The subtext is that locals had less rights and could expect more brutal treatment than immigrants.

When it came to dispensing justice, another tablet reveals that a *centurio regionaris* (regional centurion) presided at Carlisle,[43] a location that fits with the site having an established prominence among local communities. Documents from Egypt demonstrate how much power such centurions wielded, by acting as a link between the provincial governor and local settlements.[44] Far from restricting themselves to military matters, these soldiers received petitions from ordinary Egyptians on many subjects. One example is a woman seeking to reclaim her dowry, while another claims 'I was talking to . . . shepherds, concerning what they owe me as damages for grazing by their flocks, they belaboured me with blows, shamelessly refusing to pay'.[45] Friction between pastoral and arable farmers was far from unique to Egypt, and such problems would probably have resonated with the regional centurion at Carlisle, given the area's suitability for both crops and transhumance. The existence of this post emphasises the depth of the military administration's reach into local affairs, and also its ability to keep tabs on their activities.

Stanegate system

Knowledge of local sentiment would have become critical during the reign of Trajan (98–117), because the Roman army had completed its withdrawal to the Tyne-Solway isthmus by 105.[46] There is no doubt that military control of the isthmus was subsequently tightened, but precisely when and to what end remain contested. Discussion focuses on the founding of additional forts, fortlets, and towers alongside the pre-existing bases at Carlisle on the Eden, Corbridge on the Tyne, and intervening Vindolanda and Nether Denton. The resulting cordon is traditionally called the Stanegate system after the medieval name for the metalled Roman highway connecting Carlisle and Corbridge (Fig. 14). A scholarly schism concerns whether these measures simply protected traffic on a key outlying highway or served as a full-blown frontier prior to Hadrian's Wall. This debate typically focuses on the role of the Stanegate fortlets and towers.[47] The two certain fortlets, at Haltwhistle Burn and Throp, together with a probable third at Boothby, once again create a fort-fortlet-fort configuration. Associated towers seem to be sited for surveillance, allowing them to act as the eyes for larger installations. Haltwhistle Burn and Throp both feature a design quirk that placed the main gateways on adjacent stretches of rampart, an arrangement that appears geared towards easing traffic circulation through them (Fig. 15).[48] As Haltwhistle Burn also contained probable storage facilities, a logistical role is likely. Callwell's treatise on small wars furnishes one possible explanation for this, as he advocates using comparable posts to resupply mobile columns hunting guerrillas.[49] Naturally, though, such depots would be equally appropriate to either frontier defence or highway security.

A significant complication for perceptions of the Stanegate system has emerged over recent decades. Evidence is increasingly pointing towards the

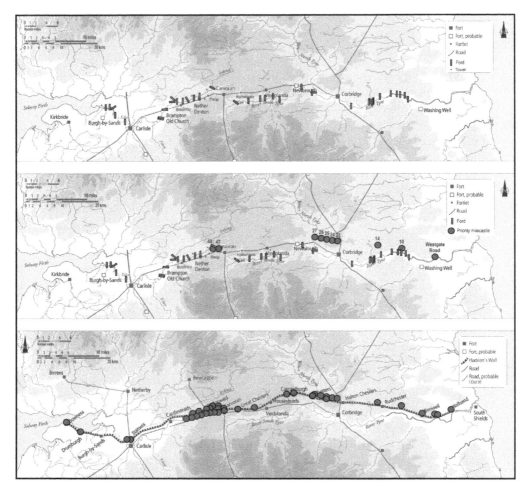

FIGURE 14 *The Stanegate system (top) and apparent Broad Wall 'priority' Hadrian's Wall milecastles (middle) alongside ford locations marked on 19th-century Ordnance Survey maps. The distribution of unusual Wall features more generally shows a concentration around the Tipalt-Irthing gap (bottom). Courtesy of David J. Breeze.*

military cordon being established before the engineered Stanegate road, which was perhaps installed during Hadrian's reign (117–138).[50] Given the system's modern name, this situation is somewhat ironic. Despite this development, the traditional term will be retained here for convenience. Eliminating the metalled road from the equation does not mean there was no linking track, because a reasonably robust route must have existed since at least the mid 80s to service Vindolanda. Indeed, as the Stanegate road passes a pair of probable Bronze Age standing stones, this could easily be another 'Roman' route with prehistoric origins (Fig. 16). Given that the earliest datable milestones in Britain name Hadrian, he may have overseen the first concerted attempt to engineer an integrated network of metalled

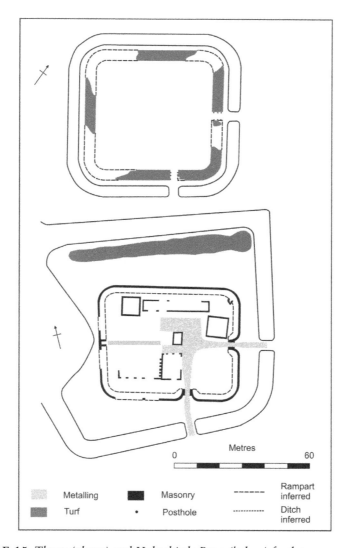

Metres
0 — 60

Metalling Masonry Rampart inferred

Turf • Posthole Ditch inferred

FIGURE 15 *Throp (above) and Haltwhistle Burn (below) fortlets.*

highways. If so, in large parts of the country the existing prehistoric infrastructure presumably fulfilled army needs for around 80 years.

Assessing the relationship between the wider landscape and the Trajanic cordon may help determine its purpose. Specialists distinguish between eastern, central, and western sectors of Hadrian's Wall, with the eastern sector lying east of the River North Tyne, the central sector falling between it and the River Irthing, and the western sector running west of the Irthing (see Map 3). Applying a similar approach to the Stanegate system is revealing. In the west, all of the military posts apart from two towers lie south of the

FIGURE 16 *The Mare and Foal, standing stones close to the course of the Roman Stanegate road.*

River Irthing or Eden, with a notable concentration of installations occurring directly west of the Tipalt-Irthing gap. Stanegate posts in the central sector, though, controlled approaches to the River South Tyne from the north, rather than the south. In the east, Corbridge held a key Tyne crossing, but beyond that no certain 'Stanegate' posts are known in the Tyne valley, although a fort at Gateshead is certainly possible (Fig. 14).[51] This scarcity of 'Stanegate' posts in the east seems symptomatic of a wider imbalance between the north-east and north-west of England, with appreciably more Roman military garrisons established in the latter region (Map 2). It has long been suspected that this points to local communities in the east being friendly, or even allied, while those in the west were more hostile.[52]

That the military did discriminate between different threat levels across the isthmus is supported by factoring in ford locations. Although we have no direct knowledge of their Roman-era positions, fords marked on 19th-century Ordnance Survey maps – some of which demonstrably existed in the same general area for the best part of a millennium – can be compared with the distribution of 'Stanegate' posts (Fig. 14). In the west, forts and fortlets are well placed to control these fords. If – as is likely – a fort existed at Burgh-by-Sands, then all of the 19th-century Irthing and Eden fords in this sector lay within 4.5km of a 'Stanegate' site, and most were considerably closer. Indeed, the concentration of posts directly west of the Tipalt-Irthing gap becomes explicable as a response to a localised abundance of Irthing fords. Garrisoning river crossings in this fashion would fit with an attempt to use the Irthing and Eden as the backbone of a control system. The end result resembles a modest example of the river frontiers developed elsewhere by the Roman military.

In the central sector, military installations are also explicable in terms of 19th-century ford locations. This time, though, access to the South Tyne crossings was controlled from the north, and the measures appear lighter touch. The region east of Corbridge is different once again, as this is the only place on the isthmus – so far as we know – where concentrations of 19th-century fords occur without a Roman military post standing sentinel nearby. This resonates with a near-contemporary arrangement that Tacitus describes on the Danube: 'with [the Hermunduri] alone of Germans, business is transacted not only on the riverbank . . . They cross the river everywhere without supervision . . . we let other people see only our fortified camps'.[53] Conceivably, then, the Stanegate system was calibrated to the temperaments of the local communities inhabiting the isthmus. These bespoke measures potentially ranged from a preclusive river frontier in the west, to free movement remaining permissible in the east.[54] But they failed.

Fighting elusive enemies?

It could be argued that this chapter has distorted the military situation in Britain by devoting scant attention to the battles of the Boudican revolt and Mons Graupius, or the many operations mounted to capture local population centres. Yet the ancient histories suggest that the Roman army in Britain was most often confronted – and confounded – by guerrilla warfare.[55] This fits the archaeological evidence for sophisticated Roman counter-strategies being employed in Wales, Scotland, and on the Tyne-Solway isthmus. Although the early 2nd-century Stanegate system appears explicable as a move towards an orderly border, it arguably grew organically out of preceding counterinsurgency strategies. As well as replicating the fort-fortlet-fort principle potentially employed to counter insurgents in Wales and perhaps also on the Gask Ridge, it is intriguing that the apparent storage facilities at Haltwhistle Burn match a provision recommended by Callwell.

More recent counterinsurgency literature emphasises the corrosive effect such fighting can have on the morale and discipline of regular soldiers. While there can be a belief that only small groups of regular soldiers would be targeted by guerrillas, the reality in Roman Britain was that anything from foraging parties to a substantial portion of a legion could be attacked while unprepared. But when the army attempted to retaliate by bringing its superior strength, training, and equipment to bear, the perpetrators simply melted away into the landscape. Such hit-and-run attacks are a classic feature of insurgencies. In Britain, the army apparently responded by discriminating between local groups, with the Stanegate system arguably applying very different levels of control over north-south movement to communities living in the east and west of the isthmus. One shortcoming with this approach was that it incentivised anyone causing disruption in the west to detour east and bypass the security measures, thereby diffusing the problem. As we will see in the next chapter, the military solution took the form of a monumental barrier, easily surpassing anything previously seen in Europe.

4

Drawing a Line

Hadrian and His Wall

Hadrian's Wall was engineered on such a scale that in places the scars scored into the landscape still seem fresh almost 2,000 years later. But the impression this permanence conjures of a confidently executed masterplan is an illusion. The Wall's design was experimental and featured numerous elements that were refined while work was underway. As we will see, some of these revisions were subtle, but others cumulatively suggest that there was a significant change of plan during construction. Such shifting end goals complicate analysing the monument, because upon completion at least two different operational concepts were fossilised in its fabric. A further difficulty is that the precise timescale for construction operations remains hotly debated. Current estimates range from work starting *c.* AD 120–122 and being brought to fruition in 126, to the project languishing unfinished when Hadrian died in 138.[1] Despite this uncertainty, teasing out how the military implemented and adapted the initial plan for the Wall offers our strongest opportunity to understand its purpose. The longstanding archaeological attention lavished on disentangling the construction schedule has bequeathed a wealth of evidence to draw upon. This chapter will capitalise on that, by delving into the detail of how the Wall was delivered, and what its repercussions were.

Hadrian's Wall is here taken to mean the entire barrier system at any given time, and the overriding impression gained from assessing a schematic plan of it is one of order (Fig. 17). When complete, the Wall generally consisted of three separate linear barriers, with a ditch to the north, the curtain behind it, and a massive earthwork known as the Vallum running to the south. Small military installations called milecastles and turrets were carefully spaced along the curtain, resulting in a manned post approximately every 495m, or ⅓ Roman mile.[2] Larger forts, usually capable of accommodating an entire auxiliary unit, lay at lengthier intervals, generally given as between 7⅓–7⅔ Roman miles.[3] There was also a purpose-built gateway known as the Portgate, where Dere Street crossed the Wall in the east, with a presumed counterpart

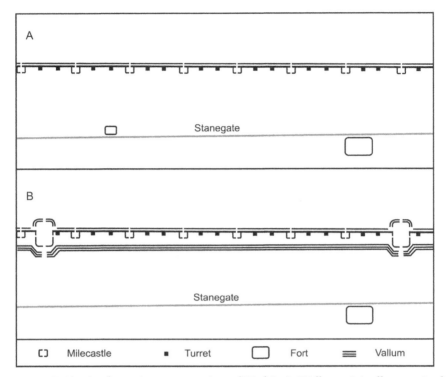

FIGURE 17 *A schematic representation of Hadrian's Wall as originally conceived (A), and after the fort decision (B). After Breeze and Dobson 2000.*

north of Carlisle to serve the main western highway. Establishing what order these components were built in and how – if at all – they interacted has been a source of scholarly curiosity since at least Bede's day in the 8th century AD. We now know that all these elements belong to Hadrian's reign, when two broad frontier concepts can be distinguished. The first comprised a comparatively lightly manned barrier featuring the ditch, curtain, milecastles, turrets, and – presumably – road gateways. It was seemingly only after construction was underway that the auxiliary forts and Vallum were added to the system, a revision known to specialists as 'the fort decision'. Until recently, it was generally accepted that work on the first concept began in 122, with the fort decision following sometime between 123 and 126. As we will see, it is perhaps possible that both dates can be nudged a little earlier.

Despite the standardised approach evident from the overall Wall concepts, the closer you look at the detail of its execution, the more obvious it becomes that this uniformity is a veneer. One eye-catching difference is that only the eastern two-thirds of the Wall were originally built of masonry, which is referred to as the Stone Wall. By contrast, the western third initially comprised earth, turf, and timber milecastles and curtain, alongside masonry turrets, forming the Turf Wall. Further variation is apparent from the Stone Wall curtain. This was originally built to a width of about 3m or 10 Roman feet, a gauge known to specialists as 'Broad Wall', before being decreased to a 'Narrow Wall' of *c*. 2.3m, which is approximately 8 Roman feet, at around the time of the fort decision. Thanks to this reduction we can see where early work was underway, revealing clues about overall military priorities. The same is true of those instances where the army elected – for want of a better phrase – to break their own rules and depart from the generic Wall template. Establishing the motivation for these deviations presents a way to understand the purpose of the Wall system.

A key player in the Wall's gestation was Publius Aelius Hadrianus: the emperor we know as Hadrian (reigned 117–138; Fig. 18). In modern parlance he was a maverick, and displayed an appetite for flouting convention that contemporaries found 'strange and baffling'.[4] Hadrian not only spurned the traditional path to imperial martial glory via territorial expansion, but also relinquished some of Trajan's conquests. As emperor, Hadrian proved an avid traveller with an eye for bolstering frontier security. His

FIGURE 18 *The emperor Hadrian, as rendered on a statue fragment found in the Thames, and now in the British Museum.*

FIGURE 19 *The Ilam Pan. Credit: Peter Savin.*

measures to safeguard the Empire's edges took many forms, including furnishing Upper Germany with a stout timber palisade. In 122, Hadrian visited Britain, where modern accounts often state he ordered the Wall's construction, although he may instead have inspected a work in progress (see p. 67). This monument proved to be the greatest legacy of Hadrian's frontier fixation, and the emperor seemingly took steps to ensure he received due credit. One indication of this is a small skillet or patera known as the Ilam Pan, which carries text naming four forts and seemingly also the *Vali Aeli* or Aelian Wall, suggesting the barrier originally bore Hadrian's family name (Fig. 19).[5] Indeed, it has been conjectured that some of the Wall's more outlandish conceits were personally masterminded by Hadrian.[6] We know he dabbled in architecture from an anecdote dating to Trajan's reign, when Hadrian's opinion was rubbished by the architect Apollodorus of Damascus. Clearly Apollodorus' keen eye for design was balanced by a tin ear for politics, and following Hadrian's accession the architect found himself exiled and then executed.[7] Conceivably, Hadrian's twin passion for architecture and frontiers found expression on the Tyne-Solway isthmus.

The division bell

Hadrian's reign did not start auspiciously. Following his accession in 117, Hadrian faced turmoil that included Britons who 'could not be kept under

Roman sway'.[8] As resistance was seemingly simmering in the decades leading up to the building of Hadrian's Wall, what brought it to boiling point? As we have seen, much remains uncertain about the cause, location, and duration of this insurrection, but local communities' loss of resources and prestige following the Trajanic build-up on the Tyne-Solway isthmus presented potential flash points. The Roman army was a voracious consumer of victuals, timber, leather, textiles, ceramics, metal, and masonry, among other commodities. It has been calculated that a unit with 500 horses needed around 650ha just to feed their steeds,[9] so military requisitioning of land must have come at a cost to local farming communities. If the Stanegate system restricted north–south movement in the west and centre of the isthmus, it would also have threatened pre-existing lifestyles dependent on such mobility. Presumably the greatest disruption occurred where control seems tightest: in the west. If a preclusive river frontier was attempted there, then groups practising transhumance would find routes to the lowlands impeded, while local elites were eclipsed by the Roman military monopoly on regional power, and the ritual landscape was fractured. It is easy to see how this could create fertile ground for resistance.

The potential impact of obstructing access to religious sites can be illustrated by considering springs. These have long been associated with healing in Britain, and if such beliefs were shared by local communities on the Tyne-Solway isthmus, then preventing or hindering visits could have been construed as an attack on communal welfare. Some springs certainly attracted Roman ritual activity, which might have developed from an existing reverence for these places. An inscription dedicated to the goddess Ahvarda was set up at springs near Vindolanda fort, for instance, probably in the years before work on the Wall commenced. Ahvarda can be translated as 'water, the sublime', making her a Celtic deity who sits comfortably alongside others worshipped in Britain, but whose name was Germanicized by the Tungrian auxiliary unit that erected the inscription. Sulphur springs also lay near Vindolanda, and these may have received a shrine as well.[10]

Events would have given succour to any belief that the occupiers could be driven out. Relinquishing Scotland demonstrated that the military did surrender territory, violating Callwell's 'one great fundamental rule' when facing guerrillas: 'to seize and to keep the upper hand, to advance constantly'.[11] One of Hadrian's first acts as emperor was to abandon three recently captured provinces in the east;[12] if word of this reached local communities on the Tyne-Solway isthmus, the fledgling emperor would have appeared susceptible to pressure. Equally, the army's recent track record hardly encouraged locals weighing up their options to jeopardise existing social ties by throwing in their lot with occupiers whose presence – and therefore protection – proved fleeting in southern Scotland.[13] As such, some disgruntled local communities had both a motive and grounds to believe they would prevail. We can only guess at the nature of the ensuing combat, but a dramatic intensification of the guerrilla warfare seemingly favoured in the north must be a possibility.

Several sources allude to conflict in Britain at around this time. Inscriptions include Annius' tombstone at Vindolanda, which fits with fighting in the north (see p. 7). Others refer to a prefect of the *cohors II Asturum* participating in a British war sometime between 89 and 128, while Maenius Agrippa and Pontius Sabinus served on an *expeditio Britannica* – that is, a military expedition or taskforce dispatched to Britain – under Hadrian.[14] A sense of magnitude comes from a letter written by Fronto. He recalled heavy losses when consoling the emperor Marcus Aurelius (reigned 161–180) about military casualties: 'under the rule of your grandfather Hadrian what a number of soldiers were killed by the Jews, what a number by the Britons'.[15] That Britain came second only to Judea, which revolted in 132 under the leadership of Bar-Kokhba, speaks volumes about the violence. Dio claims that 585,000 Jews were killed in action, alongside countless others who perished in 'famine, disease, and fire', the last alluding to ferocious Roman reprisals.[16] We hear that 'many Romans' died in the carnage in Judea, and a case can be made for one or perhaps two legions being annihilated. An *expeditio Iudaica* was dispatched, while mounting losses led to emergency measures, including members of the fleet being transferred to a legion, and recruits levied far from the conflict zone.[17] Hadrian's ablest general, Julius Severus – then governor of Britain – was sent to suppress the rebellion. Dio notes Severus' unconventional tactic of 'intercepting small groups' of enemies,[18] rather than fighting them *en masse*, a doctrine suited to tackling insurgents that he could easily have developed in Britain.

There is cause, then, to suspect significant Roman casualties in Britain during Hadrian's reign. But if local groups had gambled on breaking Roman resolve, Hadrian's post-conflict response unmistakably signalled a long-term commitment to the region. Seeking to understand the Wall's immediate origins is complicated by hints that there was not just a single outbreak of fighting in Britain. Specifying that the Britons 'could not be kept' under control certainly implies more than one episode of violence, a scenario supported by other sources.[19] The close of one phase of hostilities is potentially commemorated on Roman coin issues bearing Victory, Britannia, or Securitas (security), which are dateable to 119 or soon afterwards.[20] Fighting confined to 117–119 is difficult to square with the epigraphy, though, as Sabinus' career suggests a later date for the *expeditio Britannica*. Many years have been proposed, but Anthony Birley has stressed that the emperor should be present during an *expeditio*, which would place it in 122, when Hadrian was in Britain. This seemingly fits with coin issues of around 122–123 alluding to an *expeditio Augusti*.[21] Birley prefers to see 122 as the true end of the one and only Hadrianic war, dismissing the coin evidence for a 119 cessation as 'unfounded'.[22] One complication with this reading is that the earliest datable milestones from Britain reveal that engineered highways were being built under Hadrian in 119–120 and 120–121.[23] Resourcing such an initiative seems a distraction during the throes of a desperate struggle, but would fit with post-conflict infrastructure improvements to enable faster troop movements in future.

Work on Hadrian's Wall commenced either before or just after the apparent 122 *expeditio*. If before, this would again support an earlier cessation in open warfare, as large numbers of soldiers were assembled for the Wall labour force. Indeed, an inscription fragment found reused at Jarrow explicitly assigns the Wall's genesis to the aftermath of fighting. The reconstructed text, which presumably refers to Hadrian's endeavours, states that 'after the barbarians had been dispersed and the province of Britain recovered, he added a frontier line between either shore of the Ocean for 80 miles'.[24] If building did commence prior to the emperor's presence, the wider preparatory work of planning, clearance, surveying, troop movements, and logistics could easily have taken a year or two. A hypothetical start to actual building in early 121 would, then, also fit with victory in 119. If an *expeditio* followed in 122, it raises the possibility that the very act of commencing building work on Hadrian's Wall brought violence to a head once more. To assess this, we will examine the components of the original Wall system, and establish how closely the start date for construction operations can be fixed.

Wonder Wall

The initial plan for Hadrian's Wall envisioned a formidable obstacle manned by a relatively modest garrison (Fig. 17). Its course closed off access to the lateral valley corridor on the Tyne-Solway isthmus from the north, while its backbone was provided by the milecastle and turret cordon, which employed adapted versions of posts known elsewhere as fortlets and towers. Roman military records from Egypt reveal that fortlets were manned by small, rotating detachments of soldiers, posted away from their home fort or fortress for periods of months or years. These garrisons were overwhelmingly drawn from the *auxilia*, and typically comprised infantry and cavalry, under the command of low-ranking or even ordinary soldiers.[25] Before the decision was taken to add forts to the Wall line, the intention was presumably to source the milecastle and turret garrisons from the web of forts spun through northern England (Map 2).

When compared to most earlier fortlets, the milecastles appear rather novel. Although fortlets come in many shapes and sizes, the milecastles were built to a standardised plan, with variation generally stemming from cosmetic differences in gateways and the orientation of an installation's long axis (Fig. 20). Milecastles were also abnormally small, with known internal areas ranging from just 181m² to 644m². Most milecastles originally enclosed under 300m², but if early excavation results are accurate, even this allocation frequently proved unduly generous. Although two milecastles – numbers 47 and 48 – have produced evidence for built-up interiors dominated by a pair of barrack blocks, others seemingly held a single, small building, set within a quantity of surplus space that is exceptional for fortlets.[26] A garrison size of thirty-two soldiers has been estimated for the

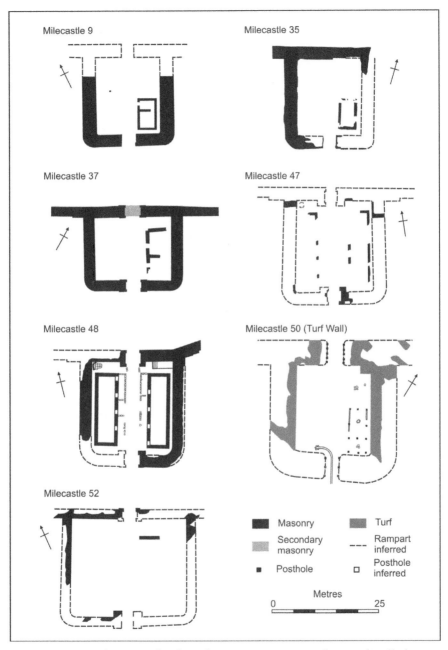

FIGURE 20 *Hadrian's Wall milecastles 9, 35, 37, 47, 48, and 50 Turf Wall, showing what the excavators considered to be the first phase of occupation. The later stone rebuild of milecastle 52 is also included.*

double barracks, plummeting to just eight in the single ones.[27] Documents
from Egypt indicate that fortlet garrisons probably ranging from just under
twenty to around thirty strong were tackling hostile bands of eighteen to
sixty-one 'barbarians'.[28] As the milecastles were originally the largest posts
on Hadrian's Wall, a capability to repulse greater enemy forces directly on
the Wall line does not seem to have initially been judged necessary.

Under the original scheme, the milecastles also contained all of the known
passageways through the frontier, apart from the two crossings serving
the main highways. Determining whether civilian traffic was documented,
searched, and taxed in the milecastles, or if these gateways simply aided
military manoeuvring, is therefore key to understanding the Wall's remit.
That access was not the sole consideration is highlighted by the number of
milecastles poorly placed for north–south transit. Between milecastles 33
and 37 inclusive, for instance, the north gateways uniformly open onto bogs
or steep drops impassable to wheeled vehicles, and in two cases all passage
appears impossible. Milecastle 35 lay directly south of a 30m vertical drop
and was seemingly never equipped with a north gateway, while subsidence
led to that in milecastle 37 being blocked before the post was completed
(Fig. 20).[29] As both posts were still manned in the usual fashion, there was
clearly more to the garrisons' role than operating frontier gateways.

Consigning some milecastles to flawed positions was a side-effect of their
most radical facet. As their name implies, they were placed at intervals of
approximately one Roman mile (1,479m), in stark contrast to the established
principle of siting military posts carefully within the landscape. This orderly
cordon has inspired an east–west numbering scheme, starting with milecastle
0 near Wallsend and running to milecastle 80 under Bowness-on-Solway.[30]

FIGURE 21 *Milecastle 37 opens onto a steep drop impassable to wheeled vehicles,
just east of a pass on level ground. Credit: Newcastle University.*

Although milecastles do deviate from precise mile intervals, the greatest recorded difference between a measured and actual distance is just 213m. While this allowed minor tweaks to be made to individual installation positions, it presented scant scope for meaningful flexibility.[31] The distance between two neighbouring milecastles is known as a Wall mile, which is designated long or short, depending on whether it is greater or less than the theoretical distance of one Roman mile. Inevitably, imposing a regular spacing system on irregular terrain threw up absurdities, especially amid the central-sector crags (Fig. 21). Milecastle 48, for instance, occupies a one-in-five slope. Countenancing such an approach implies that the nuances of the landscape were irrelevant to the smooth running of the Wall. As we will see, this impression is deceptive.

Two turrets subdivided the space between each pair of milecastles, resulting in a manned post roughly every 495m along the curtain (Figs. 17 and 22). Today, turrets are referred to by the same number as the adjacent milecastle to the east, and distinguished with an 'a' or 'b'. Some suspect that the original plan was to rotate turret garrisons – perhaps as small as two soldiers – from neighbouring milecastles for the duration of a single shift.[32] If so, each milecastle was presumably responsible for the flanking turrets immediately to its east and west, rather than the pair to the west implied by the modern

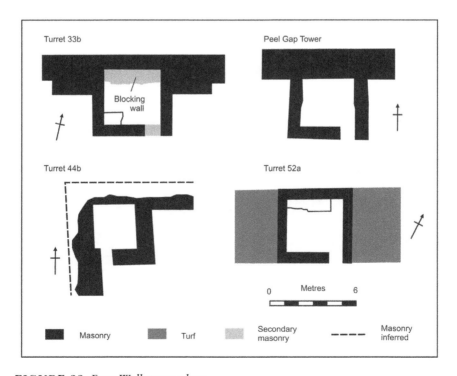

FIGURE 22 *Four Wall turret plans.*

numbering convention.[33] Like milecastles, the turrets were built to a standardised plan, with minor variation in details like doorway position. Little is known about upper elements, including overall height and whether the top floor was open or roofed (Fig. 23). This complicates assessing purpose, although signalling, shooting, and surveillance are popular possibilities.[34] David Woolliscroft has noted that some subtle deviations in milecastle and turret spacing would help establish a visual signalling link with Stanegate posts.[35] As these larger military bases initially represented the only substantial source of reinforcements on the isthmus, it is easy to see how a means of rapid communication would seem attractive. As for shooting, projectiles such as slingshot, arrows, and artillery bolts and balls have been found in or near a handful of milecastles and turrets.[36] At least some posts, then, probably held missile troops for a time, aiding efforts to prevent incursions across the curtain. Overall, though, the closely spaced installations arguably make most sense as a means to minimise opportunities for infiltration. Even though the regular spacing left some installations working against rather than with the landscape, the result was a surveillance system on a scale previously unseen in Britain.

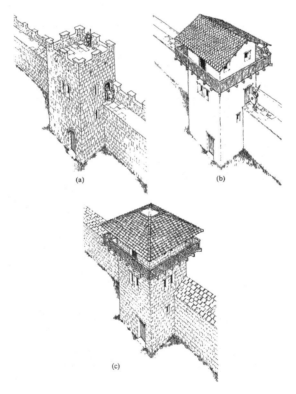

FIGURE 23 *Three possible reconstructions of the Wall turrets. Copyright Michael J. Moore.*

Milecastles and turrets were attached to and connected by the Wall curtain (Fig. 24). It might seem natural to assume that this was capped by a wall-walk and parapet, but the demonstrable absence of an elevated patrol way along the Hadrianic palisade in Upper Germany has invited questions about whether Roman frontiers needed such a facility.[37] Nevertheless, there is persuasive circumstantial evidence for a wall-walk on Hadrian's Wall.[38] Bridges physically carried the curtain over rivers, for instance, which is a curious provision if no one was walking along it. Equally, the scale of the Stone Wall curtain is otherwise hard to explain. Admittedly, the original Broad Wall gauge of *c*. 3m was reduced to the Narrow Wall width of *c*. 2.3m relatively soon during the construction phase. Even so, narrower curtain widths could still accommodate a wall-walk. The 1.8m wide rampart of a late Roman fortlet on Alderney had one, for example. On that basis, it seems most likely that the Wall curtain acted as both a barrier and elevated patrol way. Extrapolating from a flight of stairs in milecastle 48 and the north gateway arch in milecastle 37, places this

FIGURE 24 *A reconstructed stretch of Wall. Copyright Michael J. Moore.*

wall-walk roughly 4.3m above ground level.[39] As for why it was judged superfluous in Germany, but beneficial in Britain, an explanation may lie in local population numbers. Settlement beyond the Upper German barrier seems to have generally been both sparse and distant, while Hadrian's Wall scythed through populous farming communities. The greater risk of a backlash from this disruption to local interests could have made incorporating a wall-walk seem like a sound precaution.[40]

The masonry used in the Wall curtain is sometimes described as ashlar, creating a misleading impression of a prestige building project. In reality, most Wall facing stones can be classed as 'squared rubble', often held fast with light mortar or clay.[41] Steps may have been taken to conceal their true quality to observers, though, as fallen plaster render from the south face of the curtain at Denton was scored with false joints seemingly mimicking the finely dressed appearance of ashlar.[42] A stone from Peel Gap also preserved what appears to be traces of whitewash, assuming this was not lime that had leached from mortar.[43] If this plaster render and whitewash were used together, it could mean that stretches, or perhaps the entirety, of the Stone Wall were originally envisioned as 'a gleaming white line cutting across the landscape'.[44]

Despite such a potentially striking appearance, the internal fabric of the curtain also displays a pragmatic approach to construction. Few stretches of Broad Wall curtain make much use of mortar, and the known exceptions can be attributed to either very early work or later repair.[45] Either way, early procurement problems probably led to mortar use being restricted. Analysis of lime from mortar in the Hadrianic bathhouse associated with Wallsend fort indicates that it was probably transported about 52km from the central sector. Apparently, the army failed to appreciate that a more convenient source was available just 8km distant at South Shields. That lime production was well established in the central sector is confirmed by an earlier reference in a Vindolanda tablet to a work party being detailed to 'burn stone', while one certain and two possible Roman lime kilns are known in the region.[46] In the absence of mortar, the curtain's rubble core was generally packed with earth, clay, or sand.

The decision to build a Turf Wall in the west, commencing at the River Irthing, has also been explained by a shortage, in this case of sufficient easily accessible stone (Fig. 25). As the Turf Wall was ultimately rebuilt in stone, though, we know masonry construction was possible, so why not erect it that way from the start? One suggestion is that as turf and timber were the Roman military's building materials of choice in Britain at this time, it is the Stone Wall that represents the true anomaly, perhaps pointing to a shortage of turf in the central and eastern sectors.[47] Alternatively, the Turf Wall may have been chosen because it enabled much faster construction – conceivably taking a single year or even just a few months to complete – in a region where there were security concerns.[48] This possibility is supported by the Turf Wall coinciding perfectly with the region where the western Stanegate posts exercised tightest control over river crossings, once again suggesting

FIGURE 25 *A section through the Turf Wall. Credit: Stephen Greep.*

special measures in a restless region.[49] If the Turf Wall was seen as a suitable countermeasure, then its design should tell us something about the anticipated nature of the threat. While small, dispersed garrisons in the milecastles and turrets would be powerless against a full-blown army, they appear well suited to frustrate low-level guerrilla warfare.[50]

Variety is also apparent in the range of dimensions and profiles exhibited by the Wall ditch.[51] The wide and deep stretch on the eastern flank of the North Tyne valley, for instance, finds its antithesis in a length still languishing unfinished near milecastle 30 (Fig. 26). There, dolerite bedrock famously defeated digging operations at the misleadingly named Limestone Corner. Elsewhere, decisions to forgo the ditch could be entirely voluntary. It was deemed redundant where the curtain capped high crags, for instance, and only resumed in narrow defiles. Omitting the ditch beneath the crags does, though, raise questions about why the curtain crosses their summits unbroken, given that they naturally prevent movement by wheeled vehicles, horses, and cattle. On the Roman frontier in Tunisia, for instance, lengths of wall called *clausurae* block valleys, but do not crest intervening ridges of high ground.[52] Hadrian's Wall clearly aimed for tighter control. As gullies between the slender dolerite columns forming the crag faces present a means for intrepid humans to scramble up, a desire to prevent such movement offers one explanation for a continuous curtain.

Efforts to minimise infiltration across the Wall are also evident from the obstacles installed on the berm between the Wall ditch and curtain (Fig. 4). Although it is unclear precisely what form they took, suitably spiky branches,

FIGURE 26 *Unfinished Wall ditch at Limestone Corner.*

perhaps something like blackthorn, were probably set in serried ranks to tear at trespassers.[53] These obstacles have only been proven by excavation in the vicinity of Newcastle, but geophysical survey has revealed possible examples in the Tipalt-Irthing gap and near Birdoswald fort,[54] making it increasingly likely that they were present for much of the Wall's course. Taken together, the ditch, obstacles, curtain, milecastles, and turrets presented a formidable barrier to unauthorised north–south movement.

The eastern and western Wall termini may also have been selected with an eye for preventing covert pedestrian access. Although the lowest reliable 19th-century Tyne fords lay at Newburn, south of milecastle 10,[55] there were places below this point where the river could be negotiated on foot at times. Indeed, in the Middle Ages, the Tyne was reputedly sometimes crossable at low tide beside Newcastle.[56] Prior to the fort decision, the Wall may have been intended to end nearby, perhaps placing it just beyond the easternmost point where people could simply walk across the river when conditions permitted. A comparable situation probably prevailed at the Wall's western end, which lay a short distance west of Bowness-on-Solway. This was the lowest fording place on the Solway in the early 20th century,[57] and so here, too, the curtain's course may have been deliberately calibrated to run just beyond the last spot where sporadic north–south pedestrian passage was possible.

Considering the Wall's western coastal flank offers some support for this suggestion (Fig. 27). A cordon of posts extended the milecastle and turret sequence – known along the shore as milefortlets and towers – for at least

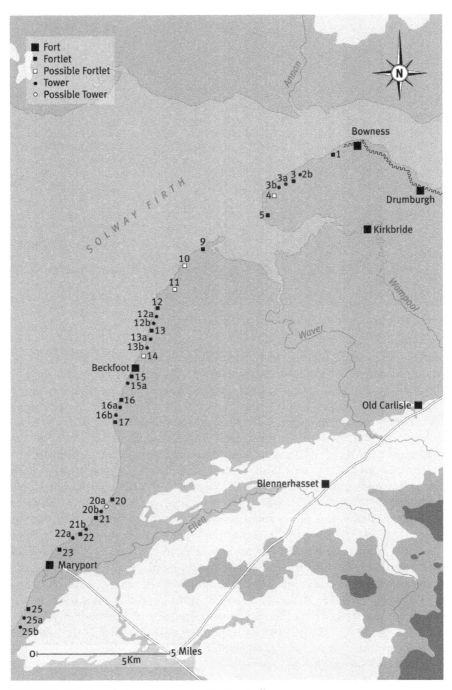

FIGURE 27 *Cumbrian coast posts. By Ian Bull.*

35km beyond the Wall terminus, with apparent gaps in the chain perhaps attributable to erosion or even a failure to complete the system. Although it has been claimed that linear palisades or ditches were also installed along this length of coast,[58] some apparent examples have subsequently proven to be modern field drains and in all cases an association with the frontier works seems doubtful. Continuing the regular installation cordon without any artificial linear barriers would emphasise that in certain circumstances the curtain – like the ditch – could be judged unnecessary.[59] In this case, it was surely because the Solway presented a sufficient barrier to movement below its lowest fording point, once again pointing to pedestrian access being the deciding factor. Presumably the milefortlet and tower garrisons were tasked with forestalling incursions by boat, arriving either from the adjacent Scottish shore, or via the Irish Sea.

Made of stone

Despite a widespread belief that building operations commenced in 122, earlier years have periodically been proposed.[60] Although our evidence remains resolutely ambiguous, Erik Graafstal has identified two pointers to an earlier start date.[61] The first is that dendrochronological dates show some trees used in the Upper German palisade were probably felled in advance of Hadrian's visit, perhaps to give him something to inspect. Graafstal's second observation concerns a set of formal building inscriptions from the milecastles. Six examples are known, in whole or in part, and these probably or certainly come from milecastles 37, 38, 42, 47, and the Turf Wall (TW) version of 50.[62] The surviving slither of a timber dedication from the last is particularly valuable, because it can plausibly be reconstructed to name not only Hadrian, but also Aulus Platorius Nepos. He arrived in 122 – presumably with Hadrian – and replaced Pompeius Falco as governor of Britain. Nepos' name also appears on four of the Stone Wall milecastle inscriptions. Only that found near milecastle 47 fails to mention him, or any other governor. This is usually attributed to the milecastle being built after Nepos' tenure expired in around 126, but such an explanation is an awkward fit with the milecastle fabric. Milecastle 47 has Broad Wall ramparts, and so should have been started early. While milecastles 37, 38, and 42 all display some Broad Wall features, they also incorporate narrower elements, suggesting the reduction in width was already underway before they reached completion. That should make them later than milecastle 47. If its inscription does not post-date Nepos' governorship, then one inference is that it was cut before he arrived in Britain. That would imply milecastle 47 was either complete or substantially complete by the summer of 122. Either way, plenty of preparatory work must have preceded any actual building.

Clearance operations would have been the first step in some areas, as army surveyors required extended sight lines to plot the Wall's course.[63] Much woodland had probably already been felled by local farming communities, although some stands of trees may have survived, while pockets of scrub were presumably grubbed up by local levies or auxiliaries. Land was also requisitioned, and traces of earlier agricultural activity have been detected underneath frontier infrastructure in numerous places.[64] Whether this land was being worked on the eve of construction commencing is usually unknown, but often a reasonable suspicion. The course surveyed for the Wall is characterised by long, straight alignments, some stretching for kilometres. These typically shadow southern, rather than northern, lips of high ground, which sometimes left dead ground to the north, but aided establishing a visual link back to the Stanegate forts.[65] Commencing building operations brought a surge in written sources, including quarry graffiti, which are usually undatable, formal building inscriptions, and texts commemorating specific work parties cut into Wall facing stones. These last are called centurial stones, but sadly only one of over 300 known gives a date. Such sources disclose that construction was initially handled by building gangs drawn from the three legions in Britain. Indeed, the subtle variations in turret and milecastle design can probably be attributed to the foibles of the different legions.[66] Although the Wall ditch has not produced any building inscriptions, it was probably dug with auxiliary involvement. In places, the ditch seems to have been the first element completed and may sometimes have been exploited as a source of building material for the curtain.[67]

The legions identified on building inscriptions are the *II Augusta*, the *XX Valeria Victrix*, and the *VI Victrix*. Of these, the *VI Victrix* is most significant, as it arrived in Britain within a few years of Hadrian and Nepos in 122. Two altars dredged from the Tyne at Newcastle were dedicated by the legion to Oceanus and Neptune, perhaps giving thanks for its successful arrival by sea.[68] The *VI Victrix* presumably replaced the *IX Hispana*, which has achieved infamy as the 'lost legion'. In 107–108, this unit was undertaking building at its home fortress in York,[69] but at some point between then and the 160s, the *IX Hispana* disappeared from the Roman army list. Its fate has excited much speculation. The legion was once assumed to have been annihilated in Britain, but its tile stamps have been found at Nijmegen, and it is now widely accepted that the unit was redeployed and destroyed in either the Bar-Kokhba revolt or in Parthia. Intriguingly, though, no inscriptions from the Turf Wall name the legion responsible for its construction, and it has been wondered if the *IX Hispana* had a hand in this.[70] Given the potential this presents to concoct a speculative scenario linking a doomed legion, a troublesome region, the deaths of many soldiers during Hadrian's reign, and an apparent *expeditio* in 122, it seems prudent to note Nick Hodgson's suspicion that disaster might have befallen much of the *IX Hispana* in Britain.[71] Naturally, this is conjecture, and doubts have been expressed about the legion being destroyed before the mid 120s.[72] Equally, Wall building may not have started until after the *expeditio*. Even so, we have seen how the Silures savaged legionary cohorts engaged on construction duties, emphasising their vulnerability at such times. Given that the milecastle and turret cordon makes most sense if resistance was anticipated to involve low-level guerrilla warfare, any attack on such a scale is likely to have come as a nasty shock.

When work first commenced, small milecastle garrisons certainly seem to have been judged sufficient to tighten control of the Wall line. Peter Hill, a professional stone mason, has estimated that the surviving Broad Wall elements could have been delivered with just three or four months' labour. He also proposed that individual milecastles and turrets would not normally be carried above a height of 1.5m during initial construction work, as that is the maximum attainable without scaffolding.[73] Hill reasoned that this would only be assembled when lengthy stretches were ready for completion. As Broad Wall curtain is concentrated in the eastern sector, blocks of such milecastles should occur there. Instead, they are scattered along the Stone Wall (Fig. 14). In all cases, the ramparts are too poorly preserved to clarify whether they were completed to full height during the Broad Wall phase of construction, but the seemingly early milecastle 47 building inscription would only have been installed when the post was nearing completion. Equally, excavating the neighbouring milecastle 48 exposed some Broad Wall rampart preserved to a height of 2.7m,[74] making it plausible the post was completed to this gauge. As milecastles 47 and 48 are also the two posts containing pairs of large barrack blocks (Fig. 20), these may be a product of early construction and reveal the original garrisoning intentions for the milecastles. But given that completing individual posts was inconvenient, why would the army bother delivering milecastles 47 and 48 early? The answer probably lies in their location: they occupy the critical natural junction created by the Tipalt-Irthing gap, which held the key to controlling regional movement (Fig. 28).[75]

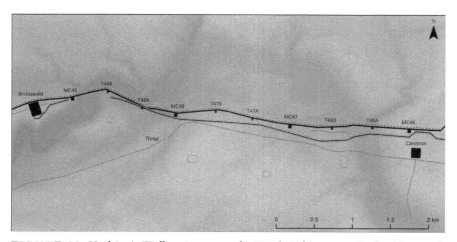

FIGURE 28 *Hadrian's Wall as it crosses the Tipalt-Irthing gap. Credit: Newcastle University.*

Highways to the danger zone

If terrain dictated the early completion of milecastles 47 and 48, can comparable measures be detected elsewhere? Widespread use of turf in the west means early Broad Wall elements only occur in the central and eastern sectors. Stubby wing-walls projecting from Stone Wall turrets to bond them into the curtain reveal that most were started to the Broad gauge. For the milecastles, though, modular construction was seemingly favoured. Although some have entirely Broad Wall or Narrow Wall ramparts, many Stone Wall milecastles have Broad north ramparts, and Narrow side and south ramparts. This bias towards the north ramparts might be because installing the gate towers allowed increased surveillance coverage.[76] If so, building operations appear geared towards incrementally tightening control of the Wall line. This makes the handful of milecastles that were probably or certainly entirely Broad Wall in plan – numbers 10, 14, 23-27, 47, and 48, and one known as the Westgate Road milecastle because its place in the numbering scheme is not clear – particularly interesting. All of them can be associated with potentially important routeways (Fig. 14). Milecastle 27 blocked the natural thoroughfare presented by the North Tyne valley, while milecastle 23 lay adjacent to Dere Street, a Roman highway that in places followed a prehistoric precursor.[77] The intervening milecastles could have redirected traffic from the North Tyne to Dere Street for processing, while also blocking access to Tyne fords at Hexham, assuming these had Roman counterparts. Measures to tighten control of further fords left unsupervised by the Stanegate system could also explain milecastles 10 and 14, which occupied the northern approaches to crossings recorded on 19th-century maps.[78] Those at Newburn, south of milecastle 10, were particularly important.[79] For centuries they represented the lowest reliable Tyne fords, with invading Scottish armies exploiting them in 1346 and 1640. The prehistoric equivalent must have been equally significant.

Farther east, the Westgate Road milecastle oversaw the approaches to a Tyne bridge named *Pons Aelius* in honour of Hadrian. This crossing meant that 'few points on the Wall are of such tactical importance', and it is often assumed the bridge was one of the first elements of the frontier works to be installed.[80] Its significance is emphasised by it being the only such structure known to have taken an emperor's name outside of Rome.[81] Whether or not the Roman army can be credited with creating the first crossing near Newcastle is a different matter. A pre-Roman bridge across the River Tees is suspected farther south at Piercebridge,[82] so perhaps a counterpart existed near the later site of *Pons Aelius*. Alternatively, maybe – as during the medieval period – this part of the Tyne could be crossed on foot at certain times. It certainly had spiritual significance, as the quantity of prehistoric metalwork dredged from this general stretch of the river is without parallel in the north. Ceremonial gatherings stretching back to around 1000 BC have been proposed, with the habit of making votive deposits potentially enduring into the Roman period.[83] If so, Roman military activity once again seems to impinge on an important local ritual site.

On one level, prioritising posts for construction is an admission that the regular spacing system did not produce uniformly useful installations. Instead, some were better placed to advance military agendas than others. On another level, if diminished local prestige, north–south mobility, land access, and the dislocation of ritual landscapes had played any part in sparking a 117–119 war, Hadrian elected to double down by exacerbating all of these tensions. The Wall was clearly capable of implementing tighter control than the Stanegate system, while the course of the curtain suggests a determination to clamp down on access wherever pedestrian passage was possible. The cold logic of such an aim meant that running the Wall through the eastern portion of the isthmus was essential, even though communities possibly once considered allied would be on the receiving end. Fast-tracking a handful of 'priority' milecastles to tighten control also risked a backlash, as occupying key routeways must have signalled Roman intentions to local communities. In those cases where internal buildings were installed – as potentially at milecastles 47 and 48 – there is no real reason to doubt they were manned before the Wall was completed. The impact that these garrisons had on everyday movement was presumably governed by whether the ultimate aim was to regulate or block access. Much, then, depended on whom the milecastle gateways were for.

Our strongest clues come from milecastles 35 and 37 (Fig. 20). These are the posts where north–south transit appears impossible during the Hadrianic period, because the former lay on the brink of a precipitous drop and probably lacked a north gateway, while that at the latter was blocked up before the milecastle was finished. Both installations seemingly originally contained small barrack blocks suitable for garrisons of about eight. Comparable provisions were made in milecastles 9 and 50 TW, even though cross-border passage was possible there. The surprising implication is that the presence or absence of frontier gateways had no impact whatsoever on the number of soldiers required to operate a milecastle. This, in turn, suggests that those using the portals required minimal supervision, pointing to the gateways being primarily a military convenience.[84] That is not to say civilians never used them, though. Surviving documents from elsewhere in the Roman world suggest many soldiers had a weakness for bribery and dubious financial schemes of all shades. One soldier seeking a transfer in Egypt despaired that 'nothing will be accomplished without money, and letters of recommendation will have no value unless a man helps himself'.[85] This notion of soldiers helping themselves would probably have resonated with some low-ranking troops manning the milecastles on Hadrian's Wall, who found themselves in the potentially lucrative role of gatekeepers to Roman Britain. Susceptibility to bribes all but guarantees instances of irregular use. Circumstances must have made some official exceptions expedient, too, perhaps including produce destined for the army and 'contractors' serving them. Even so, the signs are

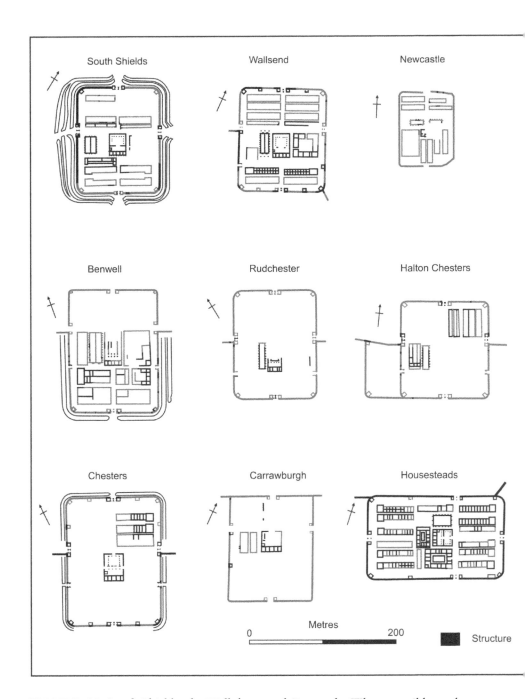

FIGURE 29 *South Shields, the Wall forts, and Bewcastle. Where possible, early internal layouts are shown as excavated, although all forts on the former Turf Wall are shown in their stone phase, except Drumburgh. Equally, the later extension of Halton Chesters and the early 3rd-century granaries at Birdoswald are included.*

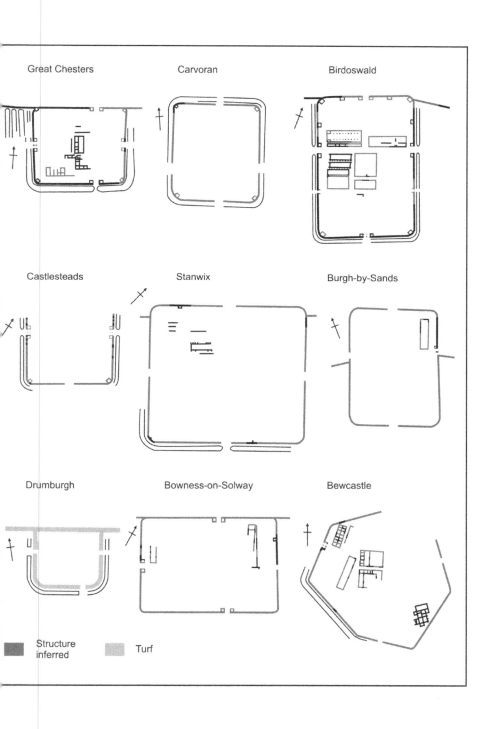

Great Chesters

Carvoran

Birdoswald

Castlesteads

Stanwix

Burgh-by-Sands

Drumburgh

Bowness-on-Solway

Bewcastle

Structure
inferred

Turf

Table 1 *South Shields, the Wall forts, and Carvoran*

Modern name	Ancient name(s)	Construction date	Size (hectares)	Distance from eastern neighbour (in Roman miles)	Unit given in *Notitia Dignitatum* (following Hassall 1976)
South Shields	*Lugudunum*(?), *Arbeia*	*c.* 160s (but Hadrianic fort presumed nearby)	Originally 1.67 Extended to 2.10	–	*numerus barcariorum Tigrisiensium*
Wallsend	*Segedunum*	Hadrianic	1.66	–	*cohors IV Lingonum*
Newcastle	*Pons Aeli(i)* or *Aelius*	Late 2nd or early 3rd century	0.64	3⅔	*cohors I Cornoviorum*
Benwell	*Condercum*	Probably completed by 126	2.06	2⅓	*ala I Asturum*
Rudchester	*Vindobala*	Hadrianic	1.80	7	*cohors I Frixagorum*
Halton Chesters	*Onnum*	Probably completed by 126	1.74	8	*ala Sabiniana*
Chesters	*Cilurnum*	Hadrianic	2.32	6	*ala II Asturum*
Carrawburgh	*Brocolitia*	Probably completed 130–133	1.60	3⅔	*cohors I Batavorum*
Housesteads	*Vercovicium*	Hadrianic	2.02	5⅔	*cohors I Tungrorum*
Great Chesters	*Aesica*	Completed during the period 128–138	1.20	6⅓	*cohors [II] Asturum*
Carvoran	*Magna*	Rebuilt in stone *c.* 136–138	1.65	3	*cohors II Dalmatarum*
Birdoswald	*Banna*	Hadrianic	2.15	3⅓	*cohors I Aelia Dacorum*

Castlesteads	*Camboglanna*	Hadrianic	$7\frac{1}{3}$	c. 1.5	[*cohors II Tungrorum*]
Stanwix	*Uxelodunum, Petriana*(?)	Hadrianic	9	3.96	*ala Petriana*
Burgh-by-Sands	*Aballava*	Hadrianic?	6	2.04	*numerus Maurorum Aurelianorum*
Drumburgh	*Congabata*	Hadrianic	$4\frac{1}{3}$	0.8(?) in turf phase	*cohors II Lingonum*
Bowness-on-Solway	*Maia*	Hadrianic	4	2.31	?

that milecastle gateways were generally reserved for military use. If so, Hadrian's Wall presented a formidable barrier to north–south movement.

The need for more speed

A dawning realisation among local communities of what was afoot could easily have sparked more violence. One stumbling block to the supposition that Wall building work commencing c. 121 provoked conflict and brought an avenging *expeditio* in 122 comes from the Turf Wall. Because the inscription from milecastle 50 TW seemingly names Nepos, it poses an awkward question. If the Turf Wall was so built because it was urgently needed, and if it could be raised in a year or less, why would it still be incomplete when Nepos arrived in 122? While this potentially supports the traditional 122 start date for the Wall, a beginning in 121 still appears compatible with work on the Turf Wall continuing into the summer of 122, especially if progress was disrupted by conflict. One additional possibility is that the decision to build in turf rather than stone was only taken after work on milecastles 47 and 48 was underway, and progress judged too slow for comfort in the restless west. The Antonine Wall may offer a parallel here, as the decision to erect most of it out of turf rather than stone was seemingly taken after building commenced (see p. 90–91).[86]

An outbreak of warfare would also explain the abrupt reconfiguring of Hadrian's Wall known as the fort decision, which by Hill's calculations may have followed just a few months of construction (Figs. 17 and 29; Table 1). That the auxiliary forts representing the most celebrated revision to the format were not part of the original Wall concept is all but proven by semi-built or complete turrets being demolished to make way for Housesteads and Chesters forts, while milecastle 43 was levelled for Great Chesters. These forts are often treated as an obvious necessity that had somehow been overlooked, and therefore undeserving of serious scrutiny. Yet here, as in so many ways, the reality is that Hadrian's Wall was abnormal. The new Wall forts held units with paper strengths running from just under 500 to over 1,000 men, placing approximately 9,090 troops in the immediate vicinity of the Wall curtain.[87] Elsewhere in the Empire, dispersed forces best suited to establishing a line of control rarely overlapped directly with chains of larger units capable of projecting concentrated military power outwards. Even on the Upper German and slightly later Raetian frontiers, the forts were often – though by no means always – set back from the cordon of towers and fortlets arranged along the palisade. What then, did the rethink on Hadrian's Wall achieve?

Assessing the landscape once again presents possibilities. The Wall's eastern terminus may have been extended from Newcastle to Wallsend at around this time, although some believe this endpoint was always intended.[88] Either way, the Wall ultimately ran from adjacent to Wallsend fort, to a little beyond Bowness-on-Solway fort (Map 3). In between, forts were founded at intervals of approximately 7⅓–7⅔ Roman miles,[89] although this spacing was employed less stringently than the original milecastle and turret framework (Table 1). The finest example of flexibility is Chesters fort, which – like Broad Wall milecastle 27 – occupied the North Tyne valley. Chesters' original garrison appears to be a cavalry *ala*, leaving it perfectly placed for rapid deployment north into the uplands beyond, or south into the lateral river valley corridor.[90] Tellingly, this position was only achieved by reducing the interval with its western neighbour at Halton Chesters to 6 Roman miles. Over time, the fort cordon was itself refined, with an extra fort built 2⅔ Roman miles west of Chesters at Carrawburgh, probably in the early 130s (Fig. 30).[91] Farther west, the Stanegate fort at Carvoran was retained on the eastern flank of the Tipalt-Irthing gap, while its western flank received a new fort just 3⅓ Roman miles distant at Birdoswald (Fig. 28). A third fort lay 3 Roman miles east of Carvoran at Great Chesters. This left a conspicuous concentration of force focused on the key north–south ingress points of the Tipalt-Irthing gap and North Tyne valley, corroborating the implication of the priority milecastles.[92] The largest Wall fort lay in the western sector at Stanwix, beside a major highway north. This base ultimately housed the pre-eminent auxiliary unit in Britain: a thousand-strong cavalry force known as the *ala Petriana*, which was well placed to strike into south-west Scotland. Once again, then, major natural and artificial features in the landscape received special treatment.

FIGURE 30 *Looking east over Carrawburgh, where the fort was built over the Vallum. The modern road mostly overlies the course of the Wall curtain. Credit: John Reid.*

Further new forts were probably founded both north and south of the Wall line (Maps 2 and 3). A screen of three outpost forts beyond the Wall in the western sector amounts to additional special measures there. Perhaps these were always intended, but a distinctive style of bathhouse found at several Wall forts also occurs inside the outpost fort at Bewcastle (Fig. 29), suggesting they were part of the same building programme. Bewcastle fort was probably known as *Fanum Cocidii*, which means the shrine of Cocidius, while surviving altars and votive plaques indicate that the low, flat-topped hill occupied by the military base was indeed a place of worship dedicated to this probable local warrior god.[93] Given the Iron Age and Roman belief that springs were special places, it is notable that one issues from the hillside. We have seen that Roman forts have form for occupying religiously sensitive places, but as Al McCluskey observed, this particular case could well have played into the hands of local figures urging resistance.[94] Hints that Bewcastle fort was judged especially at risk include breaking from the generic installation template to allow the rampart to follow a more defensible course, and placing the unit bathhouse inside rather than outside the fort defences.

South of the Wall, the Cumbrian coast also received new foundations, some of which lay well beyond the apparent end of the milefortlet and tower cordon. One fort, at Moresby, produced an inscription suggesting construction sometime between 128 and 138.[95] Other forts, though, may already have been intended or even in existence. Maryport, for instance, occupies a prominent whaleback-ridge at the junction between the Irish Sea and Solway (Fig. 27).[96] Today, the fort is most famous for a remarkable series of altars, which were dedicated to Jupiter Optimus Maximus and document a succession of Hadrianic commanding officers, one of whom was a personal acquaintance of the emperor. In the Roman period, Maryport would have been crucial for controlling the shore. After all, the Irish Sea had acted as a maritime roundabout connecting communities in Ireland, Scotland, Wales, and England for millennia.

Other developments that occurred at around the time of the fort decision include reducing the curtain to the Narrow Wall width and installing an enigmatic earthwork. This latter ran to the south of the curtain, occasionally deviating to skirt fort sites, and was referred to as the Vallum – meaning 'rampart' – by Bede in the 8th century (Fig. 17). His name has stuck, even though the most prominent feature of the Vallum is a massive flat-bottomed ditch or *fossa* roughly 6m wide and 3m deep. Two earth-and-turf mounds usually run parallel to the ditch, creating an obstacle about 36m wide, which – like the Turf Wall – had the merit of being comparatively fast to construct. The Vallum was already in place at Carrawburgh in the 130s, when the additional Wall fort was built over it (Fig. 30).[97] This fort may well have been roughly contemporary with the connecting stretches of Narrow Wall, meaning that there – and presumably elsewhere – the Vallum was completed before the curtain. Causeways across the Vallum were only retained opposite forts, which would have complicated access for construction teams, suggesting

FIGURE 31 *The Vallum at Limestone Corner.*

there was a good reason for countenancing such an impediment. This impression is reinforced by the Vallum being driven straight through the very same dolerite at Limestone Corner that defeated the Wall ditch diggers (Fig. 31). Although the Vallum has no known parallels on Roman frontiers, Poulter has noted similarities between it and a ditch component of Caesar's siege works at Alésia, emphasising that such earthworks could be used to protect extended military fortifications.[98] Equally, its width would deny access to cavalry – an advantage if the mounted Britons documented on the Vindolanda tablet were still a menace.[99] The sudden need for such a feature south of the Wall certainly suggests that threats did emerge from that quarter.

Could these measures be a response to conflict sufficiently severe to justify an *expeditio* in 122? Naturally that depends on Wall construction being underway by then, but aspects of the forts and Vallum do fit with work on the original scheme attracting local opposition in 121. We know from diplomas conferring citizenship on retirees that on 17 July 122, fifty auxiliary units in Britain discharged veterans. The involvement of so many units is without precedent in Britain. Although it has been suggested that discharge was delayed so that these soldiers could be honoured by the emperor's presence at their ceremony,[100] the situation would also fit with lengths of service being temporarily extended to quell a preceding crisis. Both Pompeius Falco and his successor as governor Platorius Nepos are named on the diplomas, suggesting the latter had recently arrived in

Britain.[101] As Nepos also appears on inscriptions from Benwell and Halton Chesters forts,[102] we can be confident they were delivered during his tenure, which probably expired in 126. The Benwell inscription also records building by members of the British fleet (*classis Britannica*), perhaps hinting at a diminished legionary workforce. A centurial stone discovered at Chesters fort, and another found about a kilometre away, also support wider involvement, as they record construction by cavalry rather than infantry. It is plausible that both relate to work on Chesters fort,[103] and their texts are also notable for specifying the length of rampart built. This detail is seemingly first included on stones from a handful of forts, but examples begin to occur along the Wall curtain later in the Hadrianic period. The diplomas and inscriptions could, then, fit with the immediate aftermath of combat, conceivably causing the kind of casualties that Fronto assigns to Britain during Hadrian's reign.

This inference is amplified by epigraphy from the Vallum. As it is an earthwork, inscriptions are rare, but a handful of slabs inserted against the mounds name work teams, and where a unit is specified it is an auxiliary one.[104] While entrusting the less technical task of ditch digging to the *auxilia* seems prudent, one apparent Vallum inscription hints at a more diverse workforce. Although the text is heavily damaged, it may commemorate construction by civilian corvées drawn from the *civitas* of the Durotraces of Ilchester in southern Britain.[105] If correct, the implications are significant. Further *civitas* stones are known from the Wall curtain and have traditionally been associated with 3rd- or 4th-century repairs, although some scholars advocate a 2nd-century date.[106] So far as we know, the Vallum is purely Hadrianic workmanship, apart from a possible re-cutting of its ditch, which must make a Hadrianic date likely for the inscription. Any implication that all the *civitas* stones are therefore Hadrianic creates problems, not least because some come from stretches of Turf Wall supposedly only replaced in stone decades later in the second half of the 2nd century.[107] Although the dating evidence for that rebuilding is far from unimpeachable (see p. 83), civilian corvées could easily have been employed more than once. If sailors and southern levies were present in the 120s, it could reflect the workload created by the fort decision. It does, though, eerily foreshadow measures enacted during the Bar-Kokhba revolt in Judea to remedy severe Roman casualties.

Another reason for suspecting the fort decision followed fighting is the way it enhanced the Wall's capabilities. We have seen that military routine and construction duties can leave regular soldiers vulnerable to guerrillas (p. 39). Little could be more predictable than building gangs setting forth from their construction camps to continue work where it concluded the day before. The Vallum would substantially reduce the risk of such parties being ambushed from the south. Even if insurgents slipped across it under cover of darkness and lay in wait, the rapid escape essential for successful guerrilla warfare was compromised. A quirk in Wall fort placement suggests a complementary motivation was in play there. Several early forts, including Chesters in the

North Tyne Valley, were built astride the curtain, leaving three of the four principal gateways opening to its north (Fig. 29). This is evocative of a counterinsurgency cliché whereby regular armies seek to accelerate their response time in order to engage elusive enemies before they vanish. That cavalry squads were chasing down 'barbarians' is confirmed by an altar that probably came from Chesters and commemorates a prefect of cavalry 'slaughtering a band of *Corionototae*'.[108] A second dedication, seemingly in a similar vein, was found in Carlisle. Both inscriptions are usually dated to later in the 2nd century,[109] but the tactic could easily be Hadrianic.

Making the forts project certainly has the air of a knee-jerk reaction, because this placement interfered with the choreography of a fort layout. The main internal east–west road showed off the fort's architectural power to visitors, and was also beneficial from a logistical point of view, by providing access to the fort granaries. Installing projecting forts placed this key thoroughfare north of the Wall curtain, while traffic was surely concentrated to its south. Although smaller, single-portal east–west gateways existed south of the Wall curtain, they offered a less impressive and less convenient passage through the fort. Equally, the number of gateways opening north of the Wall curtain could rapidly prove excessive. At Halton Chesters fort, for instance, both portals in the main west gateway were apparently blocked before it was even finished.[110] The corresponding gateway at Chesters was probably also closed off early. These factors might explain why later Wall forts, like Carrawburgh, do not project north of the Wall. Although we only have limited evidence for the identity of primary fort garrisons, it has been proposed two upland forts at Great Chesters and Housesteads accommodated infantry, while the remainder housed cavalry or part-mounted units.[111] This arrangement fits Callwell's observation that open lowland and close upland terrain favour different forms of guerrilla warfare, with enemy cavalry rarer in the latter.[112] As such, what little is known about fort garrison distribution would fit with measures to counter distinctive forms of low-intensity conflict in the uplands and lowlands. Both forts and Vallum, then, arguably make sense as a response to a sudden intensification in guerrilla warfare.

These new components seemingly also had an impact on the original milecastle and turret cordon. If the double barracks capable of holding around thirty-two soldiers in milecastles 47 and 48 do represent the original intention, there is a good chance that adding forts to the Wall prompted the reduction to single blocks housing about eight men. This would equate to the projected total milecastle garrison size being slashed from roughly 2,592 soldiers to just 648, although the forts meant there were now also approximately 9,090 soldiers on the Wall line. Yet this apparently sharp reduction in milecastle garrison strength may be deceptive. Presumably, the original milecastle garrisons were intended to be self-sustaining, with perhaps about a third of the soldiers – that is roughly eleven men – on duty at any given time, while the remainder rested. If the milecastle garrison sent two men to each of the neighbouring turrets, that would leave about seven soldiers undertaking tasks in and around the milecastle. After the change in plan, troops could be sent directly from the forts to the milecastles and turrets for the duration of a shift. As such, barracks suitable for about eight soldiers in the milecastle could suggest the number of on-duty soldiers remained broadly constant.[113] Even so, the addition of forts unmistakably added concentrated strike power to what had previously been a dispersed force in the milecastles and turrets.

Most Stone Wall turrets were at least started during the Broad Wall phase of construction, but the few entirely Narrow Wall examples suggest that another change was greater flexibility being permitted to position posts sensibly within the landscape. Turret 44a is probably a Narrow Wall structure, while turret 44b is certainly one; both lie unusually distant from their measured locations, allowing them to dominate fissures leading through the crags (Figs. 3 and 22). This new pragmaticism also saw a third turret added in Wall mile 39, where it was built against standing Narrow Wall superstructure, supervising an otherwise unobserved defile at Peel Gap.[114] Selecting such a small installation suggests the primary concern was small groups attempting covert access, rather than sizeable hostile forces that could overwhelm a turret garrison. At the other end of the scale, experimentation with smaller forts at closer intervals is suggested by the apparently 0.8ha post at Drumburgh, which breaks the 8⅓ Roman mile interval between Burgh-by-Sands and Bowness-on-Solway, and holds a place where the Solway could be intermittently forded.[115] Such heightened sensitivity to the landscape would help tighten control over the Wall line.

Walk the line

There is a general consensus that the Wall could have been constructed in roughly four or five years.[116] Even if work started in 122, it should have reached fruition by about 127. But there are strong signs that construction dragged on beyond that date.[117] Great Chesters fort, for instance, has produced a building inscription that should not be earlier than 128.[118] Although the final form of this installation may only have been fixed after it was decided to retain the neighbouring Stanegate fort at Carvoran, Great Chesters is bonded into the adjoining stretch of Narrow Wall curtain, implying this also remained incomplete in 128. Carrawburgh fort, which was probably constructed in the early 130s,[119] may also be bonded into Narrow Wall curtain. Of course, such hints of a lengthy construction timescale may simply expose some modern scholars' estimates of Roman military productivity as over-optimistic. Yet there are sites along the Wall where work started, before being interrupted long enough for peat or earth to envelop masonry.[120] A delay of some years seems in order, perhaps because sporadic violence continued to flare. It is certainly suggestive that Hadrian's ablest general, Julius Severus, was governor of Britain in the 130s, before arriving in Judea with a fully developed counterinsurgency strategy.

One potential pointer to the rate of progress comes from Carvoran fort. Inscriptions reveal it was rebuilt in stone *c.* 136–138, and also advertise in exuberant style the length of rampart built.[121] Carvoran lies adjacent to Walltown Crags, where the Narrow Wall curtain adopts an unusually sinuous course, allowing it to draw maximum advantage from the terrain. Such a flourish, coupled with the command of the topography exercised by the associated turrets 44a, 44b, and 45b – at the expense of occupying their measured location – could mark this stretch out as the culmination of late Hadrianic attempts to finesse the Wall format. Conceivably, then, the Walltown stretch was completed just before work rebuilding Carvoran commenced, in the final years of Hadrian's life.[122] The broader stretch from Carvoran to Great Chesters fort certainly emphasises the degree to which both the initial and post-fort-decision versions of the concept were refined as construction progressed. As well as more flexible spacing being used to maximise the impact of the small Wall posts, their placement also permitted a visual link to the neighbouring forts, effectively integrating these pre- and post-fort-decision elements.[123] Carvoran and Great Chesters lie only 3 Roman miles distant, presenting a notable divergence from the original concept of approximately $7\frac{1}{3}$–$7\frac{2}{3}$ Roman mile intervals between forts, supporting a move towards smaller, closer installations.

The Turf Wall also received attention at around this time. Its fabric only had a limited lifespan and would probably have needed replacing after 15–20 years, as weathering and slumping impaired its effectiveness as an obstacle. Sure enough, the easternmost portion of the Turf Wall was being rebuilt in stone before the end of Hadrian's reign. Once again, there are signs of the milecastles and turrets being integrated with forts, as the course of the Wall was rerouted for 2 Roman miles at Birdoswald, probably because the original course rendered a visual link westwards from the fort impossible.[124] Other oddities along this stretch include milecastles 49–54 being rebuilt in stone with unprecedentedly large internal dimensions (Fig. 20). It seems unlikely to be a coincidence that they lie directly north of the cluster of Irthing fords that coincided with a concentration of Stanegate posts, suggesting special measures were once again necessary there.[125] If an unusually large proportion of the unit based at Birdoswald was initially dispersed among the milecastles, it might help explain why the standard stone fort granaries were not built until the early 3rd century.[126] Although most of the Turf Wall is traditionally believed to have been rebuilt in stone two decades or so after Hadrian's death, the principal dating evidence for this is a sherd of Samian pottery that could be either Hadrianic or Antonine in date.[127] Despite this ambiguity, it would not be straightforward to slot replacing the entire Turf Wall in stone into our understanding of the building programme during Hadrian's reign, so the traditional model is preferred here.

Impact assessment

Once the Wall was largely in place, what did it do? Regulating trade is often assumed to be a core role, but while merchants surely did peddle their wares via the two north–south highways, evidence for commercial goods crossing the Wall remains sparse. Torbanite, a rock outcropping north of the Wall at Bathgate in West Lothian, and shale-like rocks from Midlothian, seem to have travelled south as raw materials before being carved into bijouterie. Whether this was transported by land via the Wall, or by sea, is a different matter. In any case, the trade only seems to take off in the 3rd and 4th centuries, and so tells us little about the early years of the Wall.[128] Local handmade pottery found either side of the Wall in the east,[129] by contrast, might primarily reflect activity before the frontier was founded. Isotope analysis of cattle teeth from South Shields fort indicates some livestock was raised in either the Lake District or south-west Scotland.[130] This raises the possibility that commodities flowing south were less immediately archaeologically obvious, such as slaves, cereal, livestock, timber, and so forth. Our evidence is such that this cannot yet be clarified one way or the other, but it is worth stressing that military procurement patterns could easily be different to those of merchants targeting primarily civilian markets. There is certainly no sign at present that cross-Wall trade occurred on a sufficient scale to justify – let alone pay for – the military presence in and of itself.

That non-military transit was possible at the major highway crossings is implied by unusual activity nearby. This is best documented north-east of the Portgate, where metalwork ranging from the later prehistoric period through to the early medieval period has been found scattered over a wide area at Great Whittington, 2.2km north of Halton Chesters fort (Fig. 32). Repeated and sizeable gatherings with origins in the pre-Roman period are probably the explanation. A market or regular camping site for caravans are two possibilities, although Richard Hingley has pointed out that ritual activity is another.[131] If so, pilgrims were presumably also able to utilise the highway gateways, perhaps after being taxed. Tolerating traditional gatherings in the shadow of the Wall could be militarily beneficial, as northern participants would present a valuable source of information, and perhaps even a means to spread Roman disinformation. This might sound far-fetched, but an identical technique was used by French forces in Vietnam, who would dig a well or hold markets to attract the local population.[132] Collecting long-range and local strategic intelligence must have been part of the Wall garrisons' role. Surviving references to the gathering and use of information in the ancient literature highlight the breadth of Roman techniques, ranging from formal units of *exploratores* (scouts) to *speculatores* (spies).[133] On Hadrian's Wall, the presence of cavalry units on roads or natural routeways north implies an intention to respond rapidly to problems brewing some distance away. Knowledge of such threats would depend on effective intelligence gathering, and at least some of the outpost forts housed

FIGURE 32 *Finds from Great Whittington. Credit: Newcastle University.*

exploratores at times.[134] Indeed, the Wall's capability to collect long-range intelligence on this scale once again marks it out as exceptional among Rome's frontiers.[135]

As the Wall became operational, so too its impact on local populations must have intensified. While the paucity of Iron Age material culture in the west complicates dating farmsteads, at least some lying south of the Wall seem to survive into the late period. One, at Durranhill, was within 5km of the Wall near Carlisle, and activity probably continued from the prehistoric period into the 4th century AD.[136] In the east, about 47km south of the Wall, an extraordinary farmstead has been excavated at Faverdale. This was probably founded in the late Iron Age, and lies just 10km from Stanwick. Finds from Faverdale testify to an enthusiastic fusion of local and Mediterranean styles, making the site as genuinely Romano-British as Roman Britain ever got. What look to be ritually deposited quern stones fit the established local pattern, while wheel-turned Roman-style pottery was mimicked by local ceramicists making handmade vessels. Analysis of mortaria revealed traces of leafy plants, indicating a taste for Roman cuisine, but local butter was preferred to olive oil. Most extraordinary, is what appears to be a mid-2nd-century local adaptation of a bathhouse. Built using Roman technology, this compact complex may have been devoted to meetings and entertainment at a pleasing temperature, rather than bathing.[137] Here, then, are unmistakable signs of a discerning adoption of new ways, and growing prosperity. Indeed, it has been observed of Roman Britain in general that formalising the frontier was followed by a century of opportunity that saw the number of rural settlements peak.[138] Although the scale of the Wall seems excessive to counter raiding alone, its ability to shield southern farmsteads from this menace quite possibly contributed to their prosperity.

It is a different story north of the Wall. Finds and radiocarbon dates from four farmsteads on the Northumberland coastal plain indicate such settlements developed over centuries (see p. 33; Fig. 11), before being abandoned in the period around 120–140. Artefacts from other sites in the wider region would fit with a longstanding way of life petering out over the course of the 2nd century.[139] New evidence could yet change this picture, but if accurate, these farmers survived the initial Roman conquest in the 70s intact, only to vanish from the archaeological record at around the time the Wall entered service. It seems reasonable to link these two developments. What precisely triggered the collapse is unclear, but severance from southern markets, the creation of a cleared military zone north of the Wall, or a shift to extensive ranching to supply the Roman army have all been mooted.[140] Environmental evidence suggests vegetation did not regenerate after the farmsteads were abandoned, implying continued human activity in the region.[141] Two possible conclusions are that either some permanent settlements did survive, or land once occupied by settled farmers was now roamed by mobile pastoralists. Either way, though, life in the Wall's north-eastern hinterland seemingly changed dramatically.

A former hillfort locked in the embrace of two Roman camps at Burnswark in Scotland also testifies to upheaval at a population centre in the Wall's north-west hinterland. Debate continues about whether the archaeology is more suggestive of a full-blooded assault on a local community, or simply the establishment of a Roman military training facility.[142] The first possibility is gaining momentum, but both scenarios imply disruption, as finds indicate occupation of the former hillfort continued into the 2nd century. Given that the military activity is judged Hadrianic or Antonine, the options seem to be that the local inhabitants were either directly attacked, or forcibly displaced to make way for a training complex. The principal objection to a genuine military siege is that the army could easily have stormed the hilltop, making a blockade unnecessary. Yet Dio specifies that Julius Severus' tactic in Judea involved 'depriving [enemies] of food and shutting them in', enabling him 'rather slowly ... but with comparatively little danger, to crush, exhaust and exterminate them'.[143] This broadly contemporary policy fits the visible remains at Burnswark. Could Severus have developed his doctrine there, or might a successor as governor have adopted this strategy? Either way, at least some local communities seemingly succumbed to unwelcome change north of the Wall in both the east and west. Its legacy had begun.

Like a wheel within a wheel

While life was changing in the Wall's hinterland, the thousands of soldiers in the forts created an unprecedented population density along its line. Feeding and supplying this force relied on supply networks stretching to the south of England and the Continent. Fine pottery, for example, was imported from Gaul and Germany, while a scarcity of wine amphorae has raised suspicions that this essential commodity was arriving via barrels from the Rhineland. Remarkably, relatively non-descript coarse pottery could also be brought in from a considerable distance, with all of the Wall forts seemingly receiving black-burnished ware or BB1 pottery from production sites centred on south-east Dorset.[144] Coinage was sent from the Continent, sometimes after a spell circulating in Gaul,[145] while the evidence for modest metalworking along the Wall implies that much large-scale production was occurring elsewhere. Despite this reach, the forts would also have been endowed with territories where food, fodder, and other commodities could be secured closer to home.

Given the apparent *vallum Aelium* and *Pons Aelius* names for the Wall and bridge, variations on the theme of 'Fort Aelius' might be anticipated for the Hadrianic chain of Wall forts. Instead, all known names are Celtic in whole or part (Table 1).[146] As we saw at Carlisle, there are sometimes grounds to suspect forts might reference existing local place names. In other cases, new ones were seemingly coined by resident garrisons of Celtic-speaking auxiliaries. Wallsend, for instance, was *Segedunum*, meaning 'strong enclosure'. This befits a fort, but hardly suits the farmer's field preceding the military base.[147] Such overt Celtic influence emphasises that Hadrian's Wall was not just a melting pot for Roman and British traditions. Instead, beliefs carried by incomers who grew up across the Empire could make their presence felt. To slip briefly beyond the confines of the Hadrianic period, the tombstone that Barates raised for Regina at South Shields, for instance, displays the artistic influence of his Palmyrene homeland (Fig. 6).[148] A large number of auxiliary units bear names suggesting an origin in north-west Europe, and it has been stressed that northern Gaul and Germany remained an important source of military manpower for Britain well into the 3rd century.[149] As such, strong continental Celtic influences might be expected. Although the overlap between some imported and British practices makes certainty difficult, there are signs that this was the case.

Celtic religious symbols can potentially shed light on how the Wall functioned. Allason-Jones has inferred that soldiers manning milecastle 35 and turret 35a were drawn from nearby Housesteads fort, because all three posts yielded wheel emblems linked to worshipers of the powerful Celtic sky god (see p. 30–31; Fig. 9).[150] This is backed up by a lead sealing from milecastle 35 bearing the abbreviation CIT, which relates to the *cohors I Tungrorum*,[151] a unit that enjoyed a lengthy residence at Housesteads. Wheel motifs dating to various periods have been found along the Wall, with some smuggling the deity's iconography onto altars to Jupiter, and indeed other gods, as well as building inscriptions and architecture (Fig. 9).[152] A proposed Christian symbol from Vindolanda also bears an intriguing resemblance to a rendering of a Celtic-style stick figure or structure incorporating the wheel emblem.[153] At Wallsend, part of a miniature votive wheel was found in a 3rd-century ditch, while a broken full-size wheel crammed into a pit in Carlisle probably also amounts to an act of devotion.[154] A ritual deposit said to have been found near Backworth, Tyne and Wear, included a patera and three gold wheel models – two on necklaces and one on a bracelet – that could be a priest's regalia.[155] All of this emphasises how significant cults not directly attested by epigraphy could be.

Looking at material culture from local farmsteads and broadly contemporary Roman military bases can feel like gazing into two different worlds, but there is some overlap. The presence of two broken querns and a mortar in Wall curtain core near Wallsend,[156] for instance, might be a foundation offering echoing the association between boundaries and querns evident at some local farmsteads. An apparent bias towards circular objects in ritual deposits at Doubstead (see p. 26) also has parallels on military sites. Round artefacts are certainly conspicuous among the 2nd- to 4th-century objects from the spring shrine known as Coventina's Well, outside Carrawburgh fort, as well as a 4th-century deposit in the fort ditches at South Shields, and the Backworth find.[157] Intriguingly, statuary showing Roman-era children from the healing sanctuary at the Seine springhead in France often depicts these young pilgrims wearing round talismans.[158] Such comparatively unambiguous examples of circular symbolism allow isolated examples to be divined with more confidence. Possible parallels for the stone disc from Doubstead include a tombstone cut into a far larger circle found at milecastle 42, and a small sandstone example from turret 51b (Figs. 33 and 9).[159] This last is particularly intriguing as it apparently also bears the spokes and hub of a wheel. If some discs did hold a celestial significance, adding wheel elements is suggestive of a melding of local and Celtic sky symbolism. Circular objects from Coventina's Well and South Shields were also found with representations of human heads or genuine pieces of crania, hinting at a possible connection with ritual headhunting – whether traceable to local or Celtic origins – by some Wall soldiers.

Turret 39a furnished another grisly find, in the form of apparent human body parts lying directly north of the military post, while a nearby coin may continue the circular object theme.[160] This macabre deposit brings to mind the skulls, limbs, and so forth periodically encountered at Iron Age and Roman sites, sometimes associated with defences and boundaries. Explanations range from the propitiating power of ancestors' remnants to severed foes being

FIGURE 33 *A tombstone cut into a disc found in milecastle 42.*

ritually displayed as the 'ghastly decoration' of revenge warfare.[161] Body parts found in a military ditch at Vindolanda have been tentatively linked to aberrant burial rites, with the possibility of a ritual dimension left open.[162] Maybe these grim measures were believed to have an apotropaic effect on defences and so amount to an additional protective element. While such finds are unusual, these are far from being the only body parts used in surprising ways on the frontier. Indeed, two additional – more complete – skeletons were found buried inside turret 39a, lying parallel to its west wall. Parts of the skulls were absent, and the deceased were possibly associated with a round object in the form of a ring. A headless corpse was also buried parallel to and just outside the south rampart of milecastle 9,[163] recalling the decapitated infants potentially acting as human foundation offerings at Springhead. At the south-east corner of the milecastle rampart, 'some bones' were found, including portions of a male and a female skull.

To return to the Hadrianic period, rather tamer rituals probably played a role when the course of the curtain was rerouted at Birdoswald. This entailed abandoning milecastle 50 TW for a stone successor on a new site. Closure operations at the milecastle included opening two pits, one of which produced the surviving slither of a building inscription. This echoes the fragmentary epigraphy that can occur in deposits seemingly laid down during abandonment ceremonies in fort *principia*.[164] The milecastle 50 TW pits also included a wooden writing tablet, broken pottery, a coin, leather, bracken and heather, and a sole shoe. This might seem a miserly offering, but many of these items find parallels in the rather more impressive deposits found in some forts. The new length of curtain was also endowed with stone phalli, to combat the evil eye.[165] By the end of Hadrian's reign, then, the Wall was protected by both fort garrisons and magical devices, and was perhaps believed to have its own guardian spirit or genius.

Wall to Wall

There is only scope for a cursory introduction to the Antonine Wall here, but it provides a fitting coda to this chapter, as finessing the Hadrian's Wall format arguably informed its successor's design. Roman forces marched north to reconquer southern Scotland within a year or two of Hadrian's death in 138. Not only did the new emperor, Antoninus Pius (reigned 138–161), desire a military triumph, but relinquishing Hadrian's frontier system in favour of advance must have delivered a powerful symbolic break with an unpopular policy of retrenchment, which some considered militarily self-defeating.[166] Along Hadrian's Wall, milecastle gates seem to have been removed, while stretches of the Vallum mounds were slighted to create causeways over its ditch. There is no sign of formal ritual abandonment deposits in the Wall forts, though, perhaps suggesting they were simply mothballed.

Advancing Roman forces are described as 'driving back' their enemies,[167] and Pius was duly acclaimed *imperator* in 142. By then, work was probably underway on his Wall, which ran along the Forth-Clyde isthmus, roughly between modern Edinburgh and Glasgow (Fig. 34). This time, forts were intended from the start, and two were built of stone: Castlecary and Balmuildy. The latter was equipped with masonry wing-walls, implying an expectation to bond it into a stone Wall curtain. In the event, the Antonine Wall rampart was built of turf, earth, and timber, supported on a stone

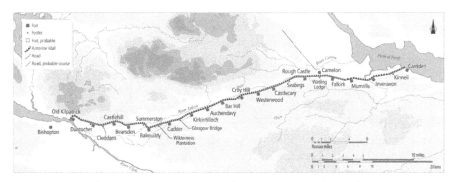

FIGURE 34 *The Antonine Wall as completed. Courtesy of David J. Breeze.*

platform.[168] Impressive stone building inscriptions were also erected, taking the practice of recording the length of curtain constructed seen most prominently at Carvoran to a whole new level. Forts lay at intervals of about 3–5km, but display marked differences in size, with the larger installations interspersed with smaller ones. Whether all of these were originally planned remains disputed, as Gillam influentially proposed six primary forts, with the smaller ones founded following a rethink.[169] Others feel that all, or nearly all, of the forts make most sense as part of a single, integrated Antonine Wall concept.[170] On this score, it may be telling that the full fort sequence is arguably a natural progression from the experimentation with smaller, closer forts during the later phases of construction on Hadrian's Wall. As closer forts cut response times and thereby aid the interception of elusive attackers, they would enable an enhanced low-intensity warfare strategy.

More examples of continuity or innovation are apparent on the Antonine Wall. Perhaps most obviously, its fortlets replicate the basic milecastle plan, and also provide gateways through the frontier. Precisely how regularly these fortlets were positioned is also under debate, but it seems likely they were less rigidly spaced than the original Hadrian's Wall milecastles.[171] This allowed the Antonine Wall fortlets to occupy sensible locations within the landscape, with some positioned near the edge of fort viewsheds, just like turrets 44a and 44b on Hadrian's Wall.[172] Turrets have yet to be definitively proven on the Antonine Wall, but it is plausible they existed. There was no equivalent to the Vallum, though, with individual Antonine Wall posts being protected by their own ditch systems. A counterpart to the Stanegate road and system was also lacking, allowing the Wall rampart to pursue the strongest line through the landscape, without worrying about establishing a visual link south. The absence of an all-weather highway was made good by the construction of a new road known as the Military Way, which linked the Wall posts. Seemingly, the frontier format evolved over time, with, for instance, some fortlet gateways apparently narrowed and many adjacent Wall ditch causeways dug out, reducing the number of crossing points.[173]

To the south, no towns or villas are known to have been founded between Hadrian's Wall and the Antonine Wall, while the highways penetrating Nithsdale and Annandale in south-west Scotland are distinguished by the densest concentration of road fortlets known in Britain, suggesting problems persisted in that region.[174] A failure to build a sustainable occupation would help explain why preparations to abandon the Antonine Wall were underway by 158, meaning the decision was not even tactfully delayed until after Pius' death in 161. Upon evacuation, several forts received what appear to be ritual offerings in their *principia*.[175] A striking example was discovered at Bar Hill, where objects including arrows, coins, an altar, red deer horn, inscription fragments, and columns were deposited in the former well. Such caches have been interpreted as a provincial fusion of Roman, Celtic, and Germanic traditions,[176] providing a broad parallel to some of the religious influences seemingly discernible on Hadrian's Wall.

Creating division

So, what can the earliest years of Hadrian's Wall tell us? The tortuous construction programme reveals how rigorously the original plan was refined as work progressed. Such a convoluted process of trial and error makes one thing clear: the Wall served a practical purpose. If it was an arbitrary statement of imperial power, attempts to finesse it would have been redundant. Instead, we see a radical theoretical concept for border security being progressively rejigged to overcome real-world constraints. The use of long, straight alignments resonates with the view expressed almost 2,000 years later during the Northern Ireland Troubles that such a border would be easier to control (see p. 17), but the Wall builders seem aware that attention to the nuances of the terrain also paid dividends. The correlation between Broad Wall milecastles and important north–south routeways suggests early steps to maximise control over the projected Wall line. This approach again finds parallels in Ireland, where measures were taken to block or tightly control cross-border roads as the Troubles ignited. On Hadrian's Wall, a potential lifespan of just three or four months for Broad Wall construction means there may not have been time to complete every installation whose anticipated value justified early construction. Allowing heightened spacing flexibility following the advent of the Narrow Wall reinforces this sense that the army was sensitive to geography, and appreciated that excessive regularity sabotaged efforts to draw maximum advantage from the landscape. In which case, why did they not simply break with the spacing system outright? Perhaps the explanation is that this flawed but innovative concept was dreamt up by Hadrian himself.

Given that the western portion of the isthmus appears volatile before work on the Wall commenced, it is easy to see how rupturing the status quo could have galvanised local resistance. Although the origins of this western antipathy are unclear, Rome's presence may have inadvertently inflamed longstanding regional tensions, perhaps stemming in part from the geography and associated economies underpinning local lifestyles. Intriguingly, though, the apparent epicentre in south-west Scotland is broadly where Titus Haterius Nepos probably conducted his census in the 90s (see p. 23). If the *Anavionenses* were weakened by having their warriors conscripted into the army just a decade or so before Rome relinquished formal control, it could have destabilised the region with unpredictable results. Perhaps the Wall soldiers reaped what their predecessors had sowed. Uncertainty concerning when precisely Wall construction started remains a significant complication. If early building work did spark fighting in around 121, then the overhaul of the Wall's basic anatomy could have coincided with Hadrian's presence during 122, when the *expeditio* most likely occurred. Alternatively, if work on the Wall only started in the aftermath of an *expeditio* in 122, a subsequent spike in resistance presumably prompted the fort decision. Either way, adding forts and the Vallum seems most easily explained as a response to an abrupt deterioration in the security situation. After all, the milecastle and turret garrisons appear best suited to securing the Wall line, while the fort garrisons present a means to engage more potent threats – perhaps enemies mustering at a distance – or respond rapidly to hit-and-run attacks upon personnel building, patrolling, or supplying the Wall. That Roman soldiers were being targeted while they were vulnerable, rather than within fortifications, would fit with the apparent willingness to reduce the overall milecastle garrison size.

The broadly predictable framework adopted for the Wall allows us to see where the army deviated from standard practice. Superimposing examples of Broad Wall milecastles, abnormally large milecastles, places where milecastle causeways were later retained, additional turrets in a Wall mile, unusually close forts, and large forts on a single map reveals a concentration of special measures in and around the Tipalt-Irthing gap (Fig. 14). The qualities of this natural junction have already been stressed, but it is worth reiterating that the gap acted as an interface between upland and lowland communities. Callwell branded the average uplander a 'naturally warlike character' and 'fighter all the world over'.[177] While this crass character reference must be taken with a pinch of salt, clearly closing a key transhumance route could have prompted repercussions, while the Wall surely also severed a complex ritual landscape. Preventing pilgrims progressing to the probable shrine of Cocidius would have been provocative, even before Bewcastle fort occupied his place of worship. Mineral springs also rise both north and south of the Wall near the gap. Some have been prized for their therapeutic qualities in more recent centuries,[178] and it is conceivable that local communities also associated them with healing. Given this potential for aggravation, there may be a good reason why the Roman army erected what appears to be a victory monument associated with the Wall in the Tipalt-Irthing gap.[179]

As for the Wall's purpose, the original plan seems geared towards restricting opportunities for unauthorised pedestrian access. Although crossings probably remained permissible along the two main highways, passage was presumably subject to customs duties and various checks, while the associated detour would also limit their scope as conduits for day-to-day movement by local inhabitants. Combining this with indications that the milecastle gateways were primarily intended for military traffic suggests a heavy-handed desire to disrupt longstanding patterns of north–south movement. This is most evident in the east, where the distinction between light-touch Stanegate system measures and the fully developed Wall cordon is stark. Of course, it is possible that this was mitigated by more cross-Wall movement being permitted in the east than west, but there is no direct archaeological evidence to support this scenario. Indeed, when access was further tightened in the late 2nd or early 3rd century, the eastern, central, and western sectors seem to have been treated identically. If the Wall was calibrated to clamp down on north–south movement, though, it raises a crucial question: why?

The answer may lie in the descriptions of barbarians being 'dispersed' on the reconstructed Jarrow inscription, or driven back during Pius' advance into Scotland.[180] In both cases, adopting such language, rather than boasting of the annihilation or surrender of Rome's foes, hints at elusive enemies that were hard to defeat decisively. It also suggests these combatants were distinguished from the general population of provincial Britons. Even so, as modern states frequently blame internal dissent on malign manipulation by external actors, any notion that guerrillas operating in Roman Britain did not include homegrown malcontents must be questionable. Once the Wall was operational, it would effectively sever any resistance groups to the south from men and materiel sent by northern sponsors or sympathisers. At the same time, guerrillas within the province would be denied access to safe havens beyond the sphere of Roman control. In short, the Wall would be an excellent means to ensure that resistance within the province withered and died. Any Irish leaders bent on mischief could still send weapons or warriors via the Irish Sea, but the Roman forts running down the west coast would make landing such aid a risky enterprise. Naturally, this scenario is speculative, but the build-up of soldiers emphasises that whatever the precise nature of the problem, Rome was pursuing a military solution to it.

5

A New Normal

War and Peace

In AD 158, a member of the *VI Victrix* legion cut twenty-four characters into a Hadrian's Wall facing stone, commemorating fresh work on the frontier (Fig. 35). Our anonymous informant – perhaps going by the initials S F – added a detail that no other centurial stone is known to disclose: a date. This testifies that three years before the death of Antoninus Pius, measures were in hand to relinquish the emperor's signature conquest of southern Scotland and return to Hadrian's Wall. So far as we know, Pius' strategy had been a purely military one, with the stick of occupation unaccompanied by the carrot of *civitas* capitals or tangible benefits for local groups. This failure to entice a sufficient proportion of the population is

FIGURE 35 *The 158 centurial stone. After RIB.*

presumably what doomed the Scottish enterprise. We do not know what proved the final straw, but local resistance was surely a factor.[1] The manpower demands associated with simultaneously holding the Antonine Wall and refurbishing Hadrian's Wall probably compelled the new governor, Julius Verus, to bring detachments of the VI Victrix and XX Valeria Victrix back from Germany. Sadly, though, an inscription commemorating movement of these troops was liberally endowed with errors and over-abbreviation, making its meaning unclear.[2]

Soldiers tasked with returning Hadrian's Wall to operational order faced an intimidating to-do list. The 158 centurial stone testifies to some Stone Wall elements needing renovation. Although its findspot is uncertain, the western end of Wall mile 9 presents the strongest candidate,[3] potentially signifying Antonine work at milecastles or turrets directly north of the lowest reliable 19th-century Tyne fords at Newburn. Early refurbishment efforts there would fit with the area being judged significant, matching the implication of milecastle 10 apparently being fast-tracked for construction when the Wall was first built. In the west, if most of the Turf Wall was indeed left standing at the end of Hadrian's reign, this was now about 35 years old and in need of replacement. Instating its stone successor probably saw sailors and civilian corvées conveyed to the frontier once more, presumably because manning the Antonine Wall left the available military labour pool shallow. Seven or eight centurial stones from the stone rebuild of the Turf Wall are notable for specifying the distance built, with some of these stones presumably assignable to late Hadrianic work, and the others conceivably Antonine.[4] Among the latter, one seemingly names the Brigantian civitas, and two the classis Britannica. A fourth, found at Drumburgh, is exceptional for giving a personal name – Vindomorucus – but no associated military unit or civitas.[5] Perhaps this omission was due to the work party comprising locals that were subject to military jurisdiction, rather than belonging to a formal civitas. If so, they may have been levied from the Wall's hinterland. A stone very similar to that of Vindomorucus was found at Housesteads fort,[6] hinting that a nearby stretch of Wall curtain either needed extensive renovation or languished incomplete at the end of Hadrian's reign.

New pivot holes were inserted in the milecastles to restore their gateways, while the Vallum seems to have been reconditioned, with accumulated silt probably dug out and heaped on the berm, creating a 'marginal mound'.[7] Most of the Vallum causeways were also eliminated, with only a handful retained opposite milecastles. A new element is also traditionally dated to this period: a metalled Roman road known as the Military Way, which occupies the secure strip between the Wall curtain and Vallum.[8] Although dating roads is tricky, the Military Way could well be a product of the advantages of an all-weather service road being demonstrated on the Antonine Wall. This is not to suggest that the curtain and Vallum corridor was devoid of traffic during the Hadrianic period, though. We have seen that in places the army tolerated unsurfaced highways in Britain for decades, and this strip surely furnishes another example.

Given the scale of the task, it may have been several years before Hadrian's Wall was a viable barrier and the Antonine Wall could be abandoned. At that point, the magnificent stone inscriptions commemorating construction of Pius' barrier in Scotland seem to have been formally taken down, with a number reduced to fragments, and at least some buried in pits.[9] Similarities to the broken dedications sometimes discovered in abandonment deposits within fort *principia* suggest a ritual dimension. For all the wasted effort in Scotland, the return to Hadrian's Wall ushered in a fascinating era. The 142 years from the cutting of the 158 centurial stone to the close of the 3rd century seemingly saw a cycle of violence following the return from the Antonine Wall eventually level off into an era of relative peace.

Crossing the line

It was not long before problems were brewing. The *Historia Augusta* discloses that 'war was threatening' early in Marcus Aurelius' reign (161–180), who responded by sending the governor Calpurnius Agricola against the Britons.[10] Inscriptions record construction or worship under his auspices at Carvoran, Vindolanda, Corbridge, and Ribchester,[11] suggesting the unspecified threat involved the northern frontier zone. This has been proposed as the moment when resistance in south-west Scotland finally received its comeuppance and was 'snuffed out'.[12] While this would explain why very few milefortlets and seemingly no towers on the Cumbrian coast were reoccupied following the return from the Antonine Wall, an alternative explanation is possible. The number of posts shadowing the shore was arguably always excessive to combat incursions by boat, so decommissioning most of the cordon may owe more to an injection of common sense than the suppression of south-west Scotland. Retaining the western coastal forts certainly indicates that military oversight of the coast remained essential. What the *Historia Augusta* does imply, though, is that the frontier forces pulled off an intelligence coup. As the Roman military generally responded to attacks rather than launching pre-emptive strikes,[13] taking countermeasures in Britain before the blow fell suggests the Wall's unusually sophisticated information-gathering apparatus was being put to good use. A sequel probably followed in the early 170s, when we are told 'war threatened' once more.[14] Forewarned was forearmed, and the next major military convulsion to grip the northern frontier would expose the cost of being neither.

Soldiers did not only have human adversaries to fear during this era, though. During the mid 160s, military operations in Parthia had the disastrous side-effect of ushering a virulent disease, known as the Antonine Plague, into the Roman empire,[15] where outbreaks continued into the reign of Marcus Aurelius' successor, Commodus (176–192). Responses to this public health emergency included religious measures, and one expression of this may occur at Housesteads fort, which produced a dedication to 'the gods and goddesses according to the interpretation of the oracle of Clarian Apollo'.[16] The Apollo of Claros, in modern Turkey, is known to have issued oracles concerning the plague, and the Housesteads text is among eleven similar but widely distributed inscriptions. One comes from Ravenglass fort in the northern military zone, another occurs as far south as Morocco, and these dedications may reflect official acts to ward off the disease.[17] It is not clear whether the plague reached Hadrian's Wall, or if this was just a precaution. But if the frontier zone did succumb, those living to the north may have had cause for gratitude concerning the degree of division the Wall created. Indeed, these groups may even have been emboldened if fears of plague disrupted routine Roman military activity in the frontier zone.

The 180s heralded what Dio nominated as the 'greatest struggle' of Commodus' reign.[18] To appreciate this catastrophe, we must turn to another post-Antonine-Wall innovation: a chain of outpost forts beyond the Wall's eastern sector, running along Dere Street into south-east Scotland. Here, history repeated itself, with the army attempting to hold a River Tweed crossing by retaining the fort at Newstead, just as they did during the 1st-century retreat from Scotland (Figs. 36 and 37). Newstead was held by a detachment of the *XX Valeria Victrix* and an auxiliary *ala*, creating a combined heavy infantry and cavalry force capable of packing a powerful punch. To the south lay forts at Cappuck, High Rochester, and Risingham, before Dere Street crossed the Wall just north of Corbridge. This arrangement

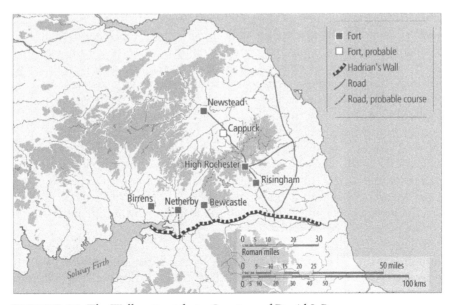

FIGURE 36 *The Wall outpost forts. Courtesy of David J. Breeze.*

FIGURE 37 *The site of Newstead fort (visible as a parch mark in the foreground) beside the River Tweed. Credit: John Reid.*

is sometimes envisioned as a means to project military power into eastern Scotland,[19] but a desire to hold Dere Street may in part stem from the double-edged sword engineered roads represent. Once built, they offer accelerated mobility to all, especially if left unsupervised. This vulnerability may have been exploited to devastating effect in the 180s disaster, when 'the tribes . . . crossing the wall that separated them from the Roman legions, proceeded to do much mischief and cut down a general together with his troops'.[20] Dio's account implies a full-blown invading army and serious loss of life. Damage to the forts at Halton Chesters, Rudchester, and Corbridge, close to the Wall's intersection with Dere Street, can be dated to this broad period and has been tentatively linked to enemy action.[21] If so, we are seeing a major problem in the east for the first time, and a logical inference is that the attackers' passage south was eased by the Roman highway.

Neat though this scenario is, it is unlikely to tell the whole story. Dio specifies enemies from beyond the Wall, but the *Historia Augusta* states that 'provincials in Britain . . . attempted to cast off [Commodus'] yoke'.[22] Assuming this refers to the same episode, it implies insurrection spread within the province, and there are signs south-west Scotland got stuck in, too. An inscription from Mainz records that the *II Augusta* legion, based in South Wales, received a new commander in the mid 180s.[23] Was his predecessor the 'general' killed in action? While the home fortress of the *II Augusta* lay in the west (*Isca* on Map 1), the legion could easily have been deployed to fight in the north-east or north-west. However, a curious altar found 2km from the probable site of milecastle 69 – which was well-placed to provide passage north via an Eden ford marked on 19th-century maps –

was dedicated by the legate of the *VI Victrix*, giving thanks for 'successful achievements beyond the Wall'.[24] A legion based in the east at York was, then, operating in the far north-west, while the euphemistic text could commemorate some kind of punitive raid. Although the altar cannot be securely linked to the 180s invasion, it is broadly dated to the reign of Marcus Aurelius or Commodus and so presumably relates to either reprisals following western transgressions during the chaos, or an earlier pre-emptive strike during Marcus Aurelius' reign.

By 184, the crisis seems to have passed, and Commodus adopted the title *Britannicus Maximus*. But with victory came a reckoning. If the order of events given by Dio is accurate – the enemy crossed the Wall and then defeated a Roman force – it suggests the frontier was taken by surprise.[25] What went wrong? It is possible that losses during the plague had impaired the army's effectiveness. Even if the Wall forces had avoided infection, they were presumably weakened by withdrawals to bolster forces on the Danube after fighting in the 160s and 170s, as Rome's enemies took advantage of the Empire's woes. It seems, though, that the soldiers who survived the 180s debacle in Britain blamed changes to the command structure, and were incensed to the point of mutiny. Their initial response was to try and set up a new emperor, but their chosen candidate declined what must have appeared a fatal appointment. Instead, the army in Britain sent a deputation of 1,500 infantry – a force capable of making their feelings very clear – to Italy, where Commodus allowed them to lynch the official responsible and his family.[26] As with all major military convulsions, those enslaved, displaced, bereaved, maimed, traumatised, or impoverished during the turmoil would inevitably have borne the consequences for decades. In that regard, the human suffering ensuing from the invasion will have long outlived the duration of the fighting.

It would be helpful to know the status of the Dere Street outpost forts on the eve of the invasion. Newstead was abandoned at some point in the 180s,[27] and it has been conjectured that the others were too.[28] Whether Newstead was given up before the assault, thereby aiding its success, or as part of a treaty concluding hostilities is unclear. We know that an accord of some kind was broken *c.* 197, and this may have been a post-conflict peace treaty negotiated *c.* 184.[29] Finds from the Newstead *principia* suggest evacuation of the fort was conducted in an orderly, though perhaps also anxious, fashion. James Curle excavated its well in 1905, discovering an inscription fragment, altar to Jupiter, penannular brooches, chain links, chain mail, a shield boss, coins, a Samian cup base, a quern stone, iron knives, arrowheads, animal bones, leather, deer horn, a bucket base and rim, masonry, and more.[30] The inscription fragment and riot of circular objects are already familiar elements of apparent ritual deposits. Deer antler is a more selective ingredient, but one study of pit deposits has proposed that when combined with querns it relates to the aftermath of crisis events.[31] Either way, the assemblage superficially looks to be a fine example of the *principia* abandonment deposits found in several forts and arguably mimicked in a low-key way at milecastle 50 TW. But the Newstead well also contained less predictable, and less palatable, components: a human skull and skull fragment, and a human skeleton.

We have already seen how representations of heads or the real thing could be deposited in military – and civilian – contexts, seemingly perpetuating ritual headhunting traditions. The human skeleton in the Newstead well is more shocking. Lying firmly within what otherwise resembles the product of a formal military de-consecration ceremony, it is natural to wonder whether this individual could also represent an offering. If so, we are seeing human sacrifice during a Roman military ritual. Such a proposal will provoke incredulity from some, but we must beware double standards: it is mainstream to wonder if individual bodies within some Iron Age pits in Britain could be sacrificial victims, for instance,[32] while it is suspected that various Roman-era bog bodies from northern Britain were offerings.[33] The Newstead skeleton was described as 'crushed among the debris of building material',[34] and weighing down bodies with stones is sometimes associated with burial alive.[35] This form of human sacrifice could occur in Republican Rome, where on one occasion it followed the devastating defeat at the Battle of Cannae in 216 BC.[36] Possible human sacrifice is not the only abnormal ritual activity Newstead can stake a claim to. Over 100 pits or wells have been found in and around the military base, although the significance of their sometimes eye-opening contents remains fiercely contested. Since Curle's excavations, three explanations have gained credence: an exceptional concentration of ritual deposits, routine rubbish disposal, or the site being destroyed by either victorious 'barbarians' or retreating Romans.[37] On this score, several pits associated with the fort defences have convincingly been interpreted as closure deposits, casting them as counterparts to the contents of the *principia* well.[38]

Many of the Newstead pits hold material paralleled in apparent offerings elsewhere, including both full-size wheels and a miniature amulet version, querns, representations of heads, and actual body parts. Curle found human remains on sixteen occasions in the classic locations of pits and ditches. Examples include the skulls of an infant, a child, and four males, one bearing near-parallel cuts above the eye sockets.[39] Most extraordinary, though, was pit 17, which lay in the fort annex and Curle believed received its fill in the late 1st century AD. There, an adult female dwarf was interred with leather circles, pottery, iron implements – including a saw with a deer antler handle – and animal bones. Curle felt that 'How [she] came to lie in a pit beneath the bones of nine horses is a problem of which no solution can be hoped for'.[40] This cannot be routine rubbish disposal, and sacrifice has been suspected.[41] The selection of a dwarf is suggestive, as sacrificial victims sometimes display physically unusual traits. The simplest explanation is that here, too, lies a human offering in a military context, while a third skeleton found upright with a spear in a pit may be similarly explained. Given the parallels with crisis events, perhaps this activity can be linked to the fort twice holding an outer line following a retreat. Maybe this military reverse explains a willingness to resort to taboo rituals, or perhaps such savagery was tolerated as a means to spread terror among Rome's enemies. But either way, the quantity of Newstead pit deposits may well relate in some way to the disturbing consequences of sustained exposure to brutal, unpredictable combat.

Foundations for the future

In the west, the outpost fort at Birrens was also seemingly abandoned in the 180s,[42] but its counterparts at Bewcastle and Netherby were apparently retained (Fig. 36). Perhaps, then, the situation temporarily reverted to that broadly prevailing after the fort decision, with an outpost screen in the west, but not the east. In other regards, later-2nd- and early-3rd-century activity on the frontier was firmly laying foundations for the future. This is the era when we get the first solid evidence for forts holding garrisons that remained resident in the 4th century. Such longevity illustrates both how an army devised for mobile warfare ossified in the frontier zone, and the care with which specific units were assigned to particular locations. Breeze, for instance, has drawn attention to the forces positioned near highways leading north in the vicinity of Hadrian's Wall. In the west, forts at Brougham, Papcastle, Old Carlisle, and Stanwix held cavalry *alae*, while three more are similarly situated in the east at Binchester, Chester-le-Street, and Halton Chesters, allowing them to deploy north (or south) rapidly (Map 2). This arrangement has been associated with a sweeping review following the 180s invasion,[43] but some units kept their existing digs. The *cohors I Aelia classica* occupied the coastal fort of Ravenglass by 158, for instance, while the *cohors I Tungrorum* might have been the original garrison of Housesteads fort.[44] Both units remained resident in the 4th century.

Change was also underway along the Wall curtain in the late 2nd and early 3rd century. On the Antonine Wall, several fortlet gateways appear to have been narrowed, while many causeways issuing from them were eventually dug out.[45] This revision was also applied to Hadrian's Wall, where north milecastle gateways appear to have received less use following the return from Scotland. Ultimately, these portals were narrowed or even fully blocked, while most causeways across the Wall ditch at milecastles were eliminated. This does not seem to have diminished the importance of the posts themselves, as many milecastle garrisons appear to have been increased at around this time. All known early single, small barrack blocks were either replaced or extended, with several posts seemingly making full use of the available internal space for the first time. Presumably their garrisons were also increased, perhaps in many cases bringing them close to the rough figure of thirty-two soldiers that may have been the original intention for the milecastles.

FIGURE 38 *Turret 41a, after being levelled, with a blocking wall in its recess.*

By contrast, some turrets seemingly languished little used following the return from the Antonine Wall,[46] and many were subsequently levelled. This turret cull was most brutal in the central sector, where no turrets between 29b and 44a inclusive are known to have survived (Fig. 38). As at milecastle 50 TW, there are sometimes signs of possible abandonment offerings. A quern was inserted at the north-east junction between the turret and Wall curtain at turret 39b, for instance, while a burnt deposit containing a disc brooch – with parallels at Newstead – was found in an identical position at turret 33b.[47] Some milecastle gate towers were also demolished around this time, with elements of one at milecastle 79 potentially becoming part of a ritual deposit.[48] Placating the gods could not plug reductions in surveillance coverage ranging from 9% to 34.5% along some stretches of Wall, though.[49] One inference is that interest in ensuring small groups did not slip across the curtain unobserved had diminished. Levelling most central-sector turrets may acknowledge that the curtain and crags were sufficient to halt parties reliant on horses or vehicles. But reducing observation coverage also suggests that insurgents slipping into or out of the province on foot were no longer an overriding concern.

There are signs of a similar policy shift near Wallsend fort. Originally, the berm obstacles there commenced over 60m west of the fort, presumably because its presence sufficed to deter incursions. In the early 3rd century, more obstacles were installed – surely sometime after the originals had decayed – but the new set only covered the area immediately adjacent to the fort: precisely where obstacles had originally been judged unnecessary.[50]

While this can be explained by an extramural settlement developing beside the fort, failing to renew the earlier obstacles speaks of a new objective. Rather than persisting with the original goal of hindering people trying to sneak over the curtain some distance from the fort, the new aim was apparently to harden the defences of the military base and associated settlement. This might seem a natural precaution following the 180s invasion, but the apparent delay of around two decades before the obstacles were installed suggests a new danger was concentrating minds. If so, the anticipated threat seems to have graduated from small groups infiltrating across the curtain to direct attacks on military posts.

Developments at several forts, including founding a new, small one at Newcastle, support this reading. Although Newcastle fort can only be broadly dated to the late 2nd or early 3rd century, a Severan date is considered credible.[51] It lay just 3⅔ and 2⅓ Roman miles from the neighbouring forts at Wallsend and Benwell respectively, fitting with the move towards smaller, closer forts arguably apparent during the later phases of Hadrianic construction. The neighbouring Westgate Road milecastle may also have been abandoned at around this time,[52] hinting that it was effectively swapped for the fort to boost the garrison at the northern end of *Pons Aelius* bridge. Severan building inscriptions dating to *c.* 205–207 from the eastern outpost forts at Risingham and High Rochester reveal that if they had been abandoned in the 180s, they were reinstated now.[53] More inscriptions dating to this general period record work at Benwell, Chesters, Housesteads, and Birdoswald,[54] testifying to wide-ranging renovations along the frontier.

Could these revisions be broadly contemporary with the elimination of the turrets? Our dating is frustratingly imprecise – and the turrets may have been levelled in waves rather than just one go – but a clue comes from the treatment of the northern alcoves where the turrets were recessed into the Wall curtain. These recesses were filled with blocking walls (Figs. 22 and 38), allowing the curtain – and any wall-walk – to continue uninterrupted across the former turret site. Crucially, these blocking walls were constructed to match the width of the adjoining curtain. In some cases, this was Narrow Wall, but in others it is what is known in specialist speak as Extra Narrow Wall. This is 2m wide or less, typically associated with hard white mortar, and traditionally attributed to rebuilding under the emperor Septimius Severus (reigned 193–211). Pottery found just outside two levelled turrets would also fit with early 3rd-century demolition.[55] Major renovations along the Wall could also help explain why some ancient sources erroneously credit Severus with building it. Perhaps, then, turret demolition occurred sometime around 207, when a graffito indicates that a quarry in the vicinity of the Wall was active,[56] and the fort inscriptions reveal wider refurbishment underway. By then, the frontier was already spiralling towards its next bout of open warfare.

Dio furnishes valuable details about life beyond the Wall during Septimius Severus' reign. A people called the Maeatae reportedly lay directly to its north, with the Caledonians living beyond them. A passage seemingly relating to 197 states that the Caledonians had broken their promises to Rome. If this was taken as an augury that further hostilities beckoned, it may have provided a catalyst for overhauling the Wall system. As Severus' priorities lay elsewhere, Rome was compelled to 'purchase peace from the Maeatae for a large sum', with this largesse also buying back a few captives.[57] That cash bribes formed part of Roman diplomacy is indicated by the distribution of hoards containing silver denarius coins in Scotland. Fascinating work by Fraser Hunter is illuminating the role such donatives played in Roman meddling in local politics far beyond Hadrian's Wall. The policy seems to commence in the late 2nd century, before dropping off sharply prior to the mid 3rd century.[58] At first, groups in north-east and central Scotland appear to have been targeted, before the pattern shifted to favour communities living closer to the Wall, particularly in south-east Scotland. Rather than dishing out denarii evenly, Rome seemingly sought to empower some groups and isolate others. As there was no local source of silver, cultivating an appetite for it created leverage. Local elites who grew dependent on access to this commodity became vulnerable to threats to turn off the tap. The shifting distribution of hoards suggests Rome made good on such ultimatums, but destabilising these communities may have paved the way for a ferocious new enemy to rise: the Picts.[59] If so, Rome would come to rue this catastrophic by-product of its botched diplomacy.

Dio relishes sketching out the sordid squalor that passed for life among the Maeatae and Caledonians: 'Both tribes . . . possess neither walls, cities, nor tilled fields, but live on their flocks, wild game, and certain fruits . . . They dwell in tents . . . they are very fond of plundering'.[60] We must beware of hyperbole here, as permanent settlements certainly existed north of the Wall, such as a local settlement at Huckhoe, which has produced 3rd-century pottery, and the hill-town of Traprain Law. Yet change was in the air, and Traprain Law is exceptional as a thriving centre in south-east Scotland during the 3rd and 4th centuries. The nearby hillfort at Broxmouth, for instance, had existed for centuries, before being abandoned sometime between the Roman army's withdrawal from the Antonine Wall and the end of the 2nd century.[61] Many other settlements appear to have been extinguished at around this time,[62] and in some regards the reduction in archaeologically visible settlements appears eerily reminiscent of the Northumberland coastal plain farmsteads a generation or two earlier. Indeed, Dio's account is fascinating for fitting with the implications of the environmental evidence from that region. An absence of plant regeneration following the apparent abandonment of the coastal plain farmsteads would be accounted for if pastoral groups were using the land and living in hard-to-detect temporary encampments. Yet if there is a kernel of truth in the lifestyle Dio discloses, it was surely a product of Roman interference. But for the Wall, there is no reason to believe that the mixed farming regime on the Northumberland coastal plain would have collapsed. To put it another way, the impact of

Hadrian's Wall and the Antonine Wall potentially helped nudge some communities towards the desultory existence Dio describes.

What of the south? Study of rural settlement reveals that 'by the end of the 2nd century AD sites to the north and south of the Wall appear to have experienced strikingly different fortunes'.[63] Farmstead numbers within Roman Britain probably dipped a little from their 2nd century high, but overall they were holding up well. Villas appear in north-east England during the 2nd and 3rd centuries, pointing to growing prosperity for some, with a probable outlier at Old Durham lying within 22km of the Wall. Intriguingly, this trend is not echoed in the north-west. Although there is good evidence for traditional-style rural settlements flourishing into the 3rd or 4th centuries, the region seems devoid of villas.[64] This is merely one of many ways in which the west appears more conservative. Another example concerns larger breeds of cattle introduced by the Romans. Traces of such livestock occur from the 2nd century at several forts in the north-east, but apart from a few possible 3rd-century examples at Carlisle, the breed is not known in the north-west.[65] Perhaps this scarcity is a product of an unsuitable climate, or even the vagaries of the supply chain. Forts certainly did not enjoy equal access to commodities. In the 3rd century, for instance, exotic products such as Rhineland and Gaulish mortaria, Campanian wine amphorae, and even Black Burnished Ware 2 pottery are concentrated towards the eastern end of the Wall. In the west, mortaria manufactured at Carlisle only spread about as far east as Great Chesters fort. Certain coin issues are likewise most common in the east.[66] All of this strongly implies that many goods arrived via a port at South Shields, and the closest forts were creaming off the best gear. Even so, hints of an instinctive resistance to Roman-style lifestyles in the west fit well with signs of longstanding resistance of a more martial kind.

Open hostilities erupted in Britain once more while Severus was still in Italy, but in 208 the imperial family arrived for what proved to be the emperor's final war. Striking changes to three frontier forts occurred at around this time (Fig. 39). South Shields was reorganised, with the garrison barrack blocks and *principia* shoehorned into the southern part of the fort, while twenty-two granaries were crammed into the remainder, creating a major supply base. Rare imperial lead sealings that were once affixed to official goods have been found at the site, so it seems reasonable to link this with logistical preparations for a campaign.[67] A more enigmatic change occurred at Vindolanda, where the fort platform was replaced with regular rows of stone roundhouses, possibly under the watchful eye of a small military post. Many theories have been floated about the occupants of these roundhouses, which may have been prisoners, refugees, hostages, levies working on the Wall, or North African troops in Severus' force. Recent work has emphasised the paucity of artefacts from the roundhouses, and that the occupants' diet was not a conventional military one.[68] Farther east along the Stanegate, the fort gutted at Corbridge around the time of the 180s invasion made way for two legionary compounds within what seems to be a developing

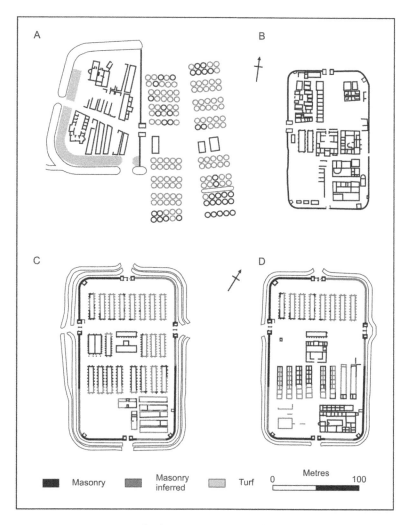

FIGURE 39 *Severan (A) and 4th-century (B) Vindolanda, and Severan (C) and 4th-century (D) South Shields. After A. Birley 2019b, Breeze 2006.*

town. Severus probably launched an invasion from there, as two series of huge marching camps – 67ha and 54ha in size – suggest an advance up Dere Street, a Tweed crossing at Newstead, and campaigning north-east beyond the Gask Ridge.[69] Dio says that the Britons once again refused battle, using guerrilla methods to slay directly or indirectly 50,000 of Severus' force – surely an exaggeration. After coming to terms, the Britons revolted once more, and a sickening Severus snapped, infamously ordering his soldiers to kill everybody, before dying himself in York in 211.[70] The war died with him.

So far, the story since the return from the Antonine Wall has been one of serious fighting more or less once a generation. This pattern breaks after Severus. Although there was probably more turmoil than generally assumed in the 3rd century (p. 7), this era appears comparatively peaceful. What changed? One popular supposition is that Severus inflicted such severe casualties on northern groups that it took the best part of a century for them to recover and regroup. But another factor was also in play. A milestone erected near Penrith in 223 announced that it was 19 miles from the *civitas Carvetiorum Luguvalio*, revealing that a *civitas* capital for the *Carvetii* now existed at Carlisle. We do not know when this was founded, but a Severan date is generally considered most likely.[71] This may have been the first time in around a century that direct military rule – as exemplified by the *centurio regionaris* – was ceded to a civil entity. Given that the establishment of a potential market at Caerwent broadly coincided with the collapse of Silurian resistance (see p. 39–41), it may be telling that the northern frontier fell quiet at around the time a *civitas* capital was established in what was surely another trouble spot. It has been speculated that Corbridge also achieved formal civic status around this time.[72] Modern counterinsurgency strategies hinge on using military force to secure space for a political solution, so conceding a level of autonomy for local communities may have worked wonders for regional security. If restoring some self-determination to the *Carvetii* – and potentially to local communities at Corbridge – helped to draw the sting from resistance within Roman territory, it might even help explain why so many turrets and milecastle gate towers were junked: the risk of succour or sanctuary for southern insurgents was no longer a pressing concern. If so, this is also likely to have generally eased relations with communities north of the Wall, although low-level, guerrilla-style attacks from that quarter probably still occurred sporadically. Degrading the Wall's surveillance capability could also have created opportunities for raiding, but the curtain would still have presented an appreciable obstacle to bands on horseback. Equally, without access to a gateway, carrying away any quantity of plunder would pose a challenge.

All quiet on the north-west frontier?

It would be appropriate if founding a formal town at Carlisle, and perhaps Corbridge, helped usher in an era of relative peace, as the greatest story on the Wall in the 3rd century is that of the fort extramural settlements. These are often styled *vici* or military *vici*, after a type of Roman community known as a *vicus*. This term was applied to settlements that were not grand enough to be towns, but nevertheless had their own council, and therefore a measure of autonomy. Whether or not the settlements that developed outside the Wall forts achieved this status remains debated, but the evidence seems good. Inscriptions referring to the *vicanorum* at Housesteads and *vicani Vindolandesses* at Vindolanda indicate that *vici* existed there (Fig. 40).[73]

FIGURE 40 Vicus *earthworks outside Housesteads fort.*

Most extramural settlements associated with the Wall forts probably have their origins in the Hadrianic period, while the earliest dated extramural building at Maryport was perhaps founded in the 130s (Fig. 41).[74]

The military *vici* reached their greatest size and sophistication in the 3rd century. At Housesteads, for example, the original Hadrianic *vicus* lay on low ground south of the Vallum. It only migrated to the immediate environs of the fort in the late 2nd or early 3rd century. This relocation was once blamed on the imaginary flood of violence in 197 conjured by the Wall-periods framework (see p. 10), but it is now thought that a more literal inundation was to blame. A cooling of average temperature by about 1°C in the 150s ushered in a wet spell, with the rising water table making a more elevated position appealing.[75] Elsewhere, at sites like Benwell, military *vicus* buildings eventually spread over the back-filled Vallum, suggesting this earthwork could now be safely dispensed with. Perhaps, then, the Vallum ceased to be judged necessary at roughly the same time numerous turrets were levelled, fitting with a major rethink about the Wall's scope.

For much of the Roman Empire, the 3rd century was a difficult time. Emperors' life expectancies grew shorter, while civil war, rebellion, usurpers, and invasion became familiar complaints. The Empire also faced economic turmoil, which it was poorly equipped to tackle, and perhaps even understand. This is well illustrated by the debasement of the denarius coin, which formed the backbone of the Roman currency system, and had a value that depended as much on its silver content as its notional face value. In 192, a denarius contained approximately 70% silver, while by 270 its successor

FIGURE 41 *The sprawling military* vicus *outside Maryport fort, revealed by geophysical survey. Courtesy of David Taylor.*

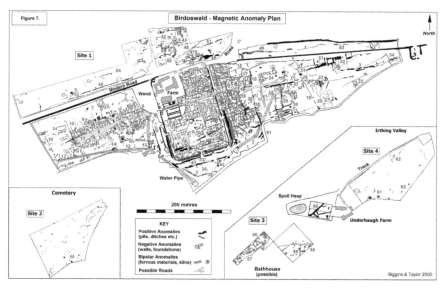

FIGURE 42 *A geophysical survey of Birdoswald fort and military* vicus. *The concentration of structures directly east of the fort might suggest the presence of an annex; structures are also visible to the north of the fort. Courtesy of David Taylor.*

coin, the *antoninianus* had dropped to under 2% silver.[76] Against this litany of woes, Britain is traditionally believed to have fared rather better than the near-Continent. Although Roman Britain also dabbled in rebellion, breaking from the official empire at least twice in the 3rd century, there are grounds to believe it was generally a safer place to be. One reflection of this relative calm may be that after Vindolanda fort was rebuilt following the Severan interlude, a stretch of rampart and gate towers was allowed to deteriorate until they collapsed, forcing rebuilding work in 223. Something similar potentially occurred at Chesters in 221.[77]

Another possible sign that the Wall zone was comparatively calm comes from evidence for small numbers of military *vici*-style buildings and/or field systems established directly north of some Wall forts, on the 'barbarian' side of the curtain. The limited dating evidence for these structures remains a stumbling block, but Paul Bidwell plausibly assigns two buildings from Wallsend to sometime within the first three-quarters of the 3rd century. Traces of activity have also been found north of Newcastle, Benwell, Chesters, Birdoswald, and Stanwix forts. This includes potential 3rd-century farming activity at Benwell, while geophysical survey at Birdoswald showed probable military *vicus* buildings spilling north of the Wall (Fig. 42).[78] There, the number of structures suggests that those bold enough to colonise this more exposed terrain amounted to a tiny minority, but their presence fits with a fragile sense of security. By contrast, though, defended annexes were certainly or probably thrown up around portions of several fort extramural settlements lying to the south of the Wall. Fortified enclosures certainly existed at Wallsend – where it has a 3rd-century date – and Housesteads, while something similar can perhaps be seen directly east of Birdoswald fort on the geophysical survey,[79] and at Vindolanda. Such measures have been interpreted as a response to a palpable threat, but these forts are also among those definitely or possibly hosting irregular military units in addition to their regular garrison during the 3rd century (see p. 114). These irregular units may have been accommodated outside the forts, perhaps helping to explain the defended annexes. Beyond the Wall, there is scant sign of extramural settlement associated with the outpost forts at Bewcastle and Risingham, while possible candidates at Birrens and High Rochester once again occupy a defended annex.[80]

At least some *vicani* followed in the grand tradition of frontier settlers down the ages by taking a relaxed approach to law and order. A tavern outside Housesteads fort turned up loaded dice, while moulds for minting counterfeit coins were also unearthed in the *vicus*. Remains of two individuals stashed beneath the floor in the backroom of another apparent tavern have traditionally been associated with an attempt to conceal a more serious crime. One of them had been stabbed with enough force to leave part of a sword tip lodged in their chest, seemingly making a verdict of murder irresistible. As the victims appear to be a man and woman, the killing has been described as 'the earliest incident of "domestic violence" in British criminal history'.[81] However, only one of the bodies was 'comparatively complete', with the other reduced to a 'few fragments'. Although full details were not published, an accompanying plan shows this second body as merely a skull placed on or in a pit.[82]

The presence of a skull associated with a pit provides a striking parallel to the evidence for ritual activity we have already encountered, but it is not such a comfortable fit with a rushed attempt to conceal a crime. Under that scenario, why would both bodies not be complete? Instead, the treatment of the corpses seems more easily explicable as ritual murder, which is to say sacrifice. Proving sacrifice as a motive is difficult, but excessive violence has been identified as a common feature of such acts,[83] which might explain the broken blade. A handful of potentially comparable examples occur in both civilian settlements and military bases along the Wall. One, from Carlisle, is dated to the 3rd century, and concerns a man who received horrifying head injuries before being pitched into a well,[84] which contained additional deposits bearing some resemblance to those at Newstead. The possibility that sacrifice was a motive for the body parts in the Vindolanda ditch has also been mooted (see p. 88–89), though with the caveat that 'there is no specific evidence ... to support this scenario'.[85] Perhaps such acts were exceptional responses to crisis events of some form on Hadrian's Wall.

Plenty of less extreme ritual activity was also underway in the settlements. An altar found near Wallsend mentions a priest who presumably lived in the military *vicus*, while a priestess of Hercules of Tyre was active at Corbridge.[86] Places of worship certainly existed within or close to the military *vici*, with the finest example presented by the boggy valley directly west of Carrawburgh. This held a mithraeum, a shrine to the nymphs and *genius loci*, and Coventina's Well, where a wealth of offerings were made at a spring. The god Mithras was imported by the army from the east, while Coventina was either a local goddess or brought by soldiers from Spain or Gaul. The style of her shrine certainly finds parallels on the Continent.[87] At Housesteads, examples of smaller shrines were found among *vicus* buildings, such as that containing a sculpture of the *Genii Cucullati* – three hooded gods – with an offering of 3rd-century coins.[88] Excavating a military *vicus* building at Maryport yielded a broken altar and two fragments of pipe-clay Venus figurines. The combination of a face-pot fragment and a model cauldron in a pit within the dwelling's backlot has also been taken as potential votive activity.[89] Further pits contained portions of querns, although naturally this does not prove that a hole was initially dug for ritual purposes, as wells or latrines may have received closure deposits. Circular pottery tokens were also found at the property, with the overall range of potential ritual material perhaps reflecting a rich medley of Roman, Celtic, and local superstitions.

Naturally, places of spiritual significance were not restricted to the settlements, and – probably much like local communities – there was Roman interest in the region's abundant watery places. One fine example is a fragment of a 2nd- or 3rd-century silver patera handle – perhaps once used for making libations – showing Minerva presiding over a sacred spring, while a pilgrim drinks its healing water.[90] This was found in a hoard at Capheaton, which is about 2km from the Devil's Causeway Roman road, 12km from the Portgate – where Dere Street crossed the Wall – and 10km from Great Whittington, where Iron Age and Roman metalwork has been detected in a boggy setting (Fig. 32). More examples of potential Roman-era deposits occur at boggy sites both north and south of the Wall, while altars to Latis, the Celtic goddess of marshland, are known from Birdoswald and near Burgh-by-Sands forts.[91] A deposit from Whitfield Moor,[92] just south of the South Tyne valley, combines cauldrons in the local style with a Roman patera, suggesting a fusion of traditions. As both cauldrons and patera could play a role in ritual activity, either offerings to Latis or – perhaps more likely – the cautious disposal of surplus sanctified material might be suspected. Taking such precautions seems strange to modern eyes, but ancient views on the disposal of sacred objects have been likened to ours regarding radioactive waste.[93]

Military *vici* were practical, as well as spiritual, places. Retired veterans often seem to have settled outside the last fort they served in, while soldiers' partners, children, and slaves probably lived in these settlements. Study of finds from within and without the fort at Vindolanda shows that objects with potential female associations, such as beads, bracelets, and hairpins, are far more common in the *vicus* than the fort during the 3rd century.[94] Economic opportunities may also have drawn some local people seeking a new lifestyle. As well as the taverns and – almost certainly – brothels calculated to appeal to bored soldiery, a range of retail opportunities would have been on offer. Strip buildings are common in military *vici*, and were set gable-end to the road, creating street frontage for commercial premises or workshops, with domestic space to the rear. There are signs that some military *vici* had a metalworking quarter, while textiles, pottery, and even cheese were produced.[95] At Housesteads, the *vicus* occupants seemingly enjoyed access to higher quality glass vessels than the fort personnel,[96] indicating that some of these wheeler dealers grew comparatively wealthy. Even so, the preponderance of buildings suited to entrepreneurial activity rather than luxury elite residences indicates that the commercial opportunities presented by the garrison underpinned the military *vicus* economies.

Manufacturing in military *vici*, or at least outside forts, brings us to a curious kind of pottery known as Housesteads ware. This has been securely identified at Birdoswald, Vindolanda, Burgh-by-Sands, and – naturally – Housesteads. It seems to date primarily to the 3rd century, and is found concentrated in areas outside, rather than inside, the fort defences. The pottery is also distinguished by being handmade, rather than wheel-turned like standard Roman pottery. Its closest parallels can be found in what is now the northern Netherlands, which back in the 3rd century was free Germany, beyond Rome's Rhine frontier. An irregular military unit raised there is known at Housesteads in the 3rd century: the *cunei Frisiorum*. A second, the *numerus Hnaudifridi*, may also have originated in the region. As the pots were made from clay local to the Wall zone, it seems likely that these soldiers – or their families – continued to produce pottery in their traditional style.[97] At Birdoswald, these pots were concentrated to the south of the fort, where there was less evidence for Roman-style material culture, prompting the suggestion that this area became a numerus fort for an irregular unit.[98] The possibility that these units were in some way associated with external annexes has already been discussed. As the two irregular formations at Housesteads probably comprised cavalry, while the resident *cohors I Tungrorum* was an infantry unit, they would have created a well-balanced military strike force. This might suggest a move away from the forts holding individual components of a much larger army, in favour of them becoming bases for forces that were versatile in their own right.

A more widespread shift in frontier culture involves a gradual tailing off of inscriptions on dedication slabs and altars over the course of the 3rd century. The last great spike comes in 213, and perhaps served as an expression of gratitude to the emperor Caracalla, after he extended Roman citizenship to freeborn provincials in 212. Following the 250s, inscriptions are very rare, depriving us of a major source of information.[99] Some probable 3rd-century examples do, though, shed interesting light on the region. One is a statue base from Vindolanda, referring to Gallic citizens.[100] As the Fourth Cohort of Gauls is recorded at the site in the 3rd and 4th centuries this may not seem especially notable. However, the vagaries of auxiliary recruitment have been discussed, and this suggests that some members of the unit were still recruited from its notional homeland. A series of altars probably dating to the 260s, and seemingly associated with milecastles directly west of the Tipalt-Irthing gap, are also instructive. These invoke the probable local warrior god Cocidius, and in one case apparently also the Genius of the Wall, perhaps indicating the dedicators desired supernatural assistance in combat conducted on or near the Wall. Given the modest size of the milecastle garrisons, a possible explanation is that low-level guerrilla attacks were once again being launched from the north.[101] It is not unknown for soldiers in combat zones to develop a heightened interest in religion, and so it may be significant that Birdoswald, in the same sector as these milecastles, has purportedly produced more 3rd-century altars than other Wall forts.[102]

Another development as the 3rd century wore on is a reduction in the number of fort gateways. Although some were seemingly blocked during the Hadrianic period, walling-up gateways becomes more common over time, although its precise nature varies from fort to fort. Sometimes, only one of the two portals at each major gateway would be walled-up, reducing rather than terminating access. In other cases, both passages would be blocked, with knock-on effects for the circulation of traffic through the fort interior. As such, access points seem to become gradually more restricted. One reason for this might be that less and less people were using the gateways. An important change within the forts, which will be discussed in more detail in the next chapter, is a new style of barrack accommodation. This seemingly emerges in the first half of the 3rd century, at forts such as Vindolanda and Wallsend, and continues to be built into the 4th century.[103] The resulting structures are typically referred to as 'chalets' by specialists, but any image this conjures of alpine splendour is misleading. Although the chalets were generally built as freestanding structures, rather than the adjoining rooms found in earlier barracks, there are clear similarities in style. Rows of chalets tend to occupy the same footprint as their predecessors, for instance, although there were less individual buildings than rooms in the original barrack blocks (Fig. 43).[104] It is generally accepted this points to a reduction in garrison size, but by what margin remains contentious.

One constant, was that bodies of soldiers, veterans, or their families would be destined for the fort cemeteries (assuming they did not form one of the potential ritual killings discussed above). Although these cemeteries have been comparatively little explored, we know that burial traditions on the frontier were slightly out of step with those farther south, as cremation rather than inhumation remained dominant. Like the military *vici* these cemeteries had – on the basis of the pottery used for cremation urns – developed since the 2nd century. Work at Birdoswald revealed that only a minority of cremations were placed in such receptacles, amounting to just nine out of forty-eight burials within one portion of the cemetery. Of these, a pair of urns containing the remains of a child about five years old and a

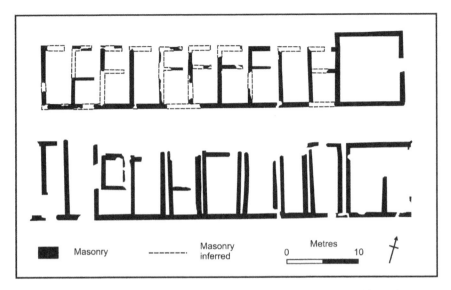

FIGURE 43 *Second-century barracks (above) and their probably 4th-century chalet replacements (below) at Housesteads. After Crow 2004.*

20- to 40-year-old woman were particularly interesting. The woman's urn also contained rings and a portion of chain mail, providing another incidence of a fascination with circular objects. Some burials showed signs of being marked with mounds or gravestones.[105] A fine collection of the latter has come from the frontier zone, with many bearing names or personal details that suggest the deceased came from or traced descent to groups living outside Britain. Limited investigation of a cemetery outside Beckfoot fort indicates burials probably ceased around the end of the 3rd century. There are suggestions, though, that memorial rites continued into the 4th century.[106]

The military *vici* also appear to vanish abruptly in the late 3rd century, sometime around 270. What caused this sudden reversal in their fortunes? Britain was buffeted by significant political and military events in the second half of the 3rd century. It twice ceded from the 'official' Roman Empire, once in 260–274 as part of the Gallic Empire, and then again from 286–296, under the usurpers Carausius and then Allectus. On the second occasion, it was an invasion by Constantius Chlorus that returned Britain to the imperial fold. While the first episode seems a good general fit with the military *vici* dating, there is no other reason to believe that reasserting Roman control spelled decisive change to settlement patterns along the northern frontier. Alternatively, decreased unit sizes and debased coinage might have so diminished soldiers' purchasing power that the military *vici* were no longer economically viable.[107] It does seem likely that seeking a cause specific to northern Britain is to look in the wrong place. Breeze has noted there are signs of extramural military settlements disappearing at around the same time on the Continent.[108] He wonders if a natural catastrophe, such as the Cyprian Plague, which is attested elsewhere in the empire during this era, could be to blame.[109] What the abandonment of the military *vici* meant for the nature of life within the forts will be discussed in the next chapter.

The times they are a-changing

The later 2nd and 3rd centuries are crucial for understanding Hadrian's Wall. Not only was the frontier reconfigured to remove some of its original hallmarks – such as the regular cordon of turrets – but a cycle of generational violence seemingly also gave way to an era of relative peace. It is naturally tempting to wonder whether these two phenomena could be linked. Some turrets were seemingly levelled in the early 3rd century, and extensive work is certainly attested along the Wall in the years around 207. It is conceivable – though by no means certain – that other amendments such as the narrowing of the milecastle gateways, elimination of many associated ditch causeways, and perhaps even downgrading of the Vallum were broadly contemporary. If so, three developments are observable: the garrisons along the Wall were less able to detect low-level incursions on foot, it became more accessible from the south, and less accessible from the north. These alterations would fit with greater stability emerging to the south of the Wall, and an increased expectation that problems would arrive from the north. Given that the *civitas Carvetiorum* is believed to have been founded in the Severan period, while Corbridge also took on a more urban character at around this time, both political and military measures were potentially in play. Perhaps, then, granting a greater degree of autonomy to local groups had a calming effect on the Wall's southern hinterland. Even so, it is probable that trouble still flared there from time to time. Ironically, if the Wall was reconfigured to face a growing threat from the north, this may have been neutralised by Severus' campaigns a few years later, leaving some modifications redundant.

As the 3rd century wore on, the military *vici* flourished, often outgrowing in size the forts that spawned them (Figs. 41 and 42). To the south of the Wall, military *vicus* buildings could overlie backfilled stretches of the Vallum, while to the north small numbers of structures colonised ground immediately beyond the curtain. Unlike the Vallum, though, there is no sign that the Wall curtain was judged obsolete and levelled to accommodate new development. Instead, military control measures seemingly still hinged on a continuous linear barrier. While founding buildings north of the Wall implies there was a period – or periods – when such a venture did not seem prohibitively risky, there are also grounds to assume that low-level guerrilla attacks mounted from north of the Wall still occurred intermittently. The series of altars probably dating to the 260s and likely to have come from milecastles west of the Tipalt-Irthing gap would fit with this. The earlier appearance of irregular cavalry units might, too. It is not unknown for groups seeking to stamp-out insurgencies to recruit practitioners of similar combat from elsewhere, in the hope that their knowledge of its methods will bring success. Mounted warriors hailing from beyond the Roman frontier in free Germany could well be expected to bring some familiarity with the dark arts of guerrilla warfare.

The apparent 3rd-century inscription referring to Gallic citizens at Vindolanda suggests that some regular army units also continued to look overseas for at least some of their manpower. Various examples of potential ritual deposits would also support continued contact with traditions that flourished on the near-Continent. These include the wheel-associated sky god's shadowy traces, which are present on the Wall in greater quantities than is generally appreciated, but still pale in comparison to those from France and the Rhineland. Equally, the fondness for depositing body parts – especially heads – near defences or in pits, probably reflects a continued respect for either traditional Celtic or local ways. The presence of querns in deposits ranging from the Newstead pits and Hadrian's Wall turrets to a Maryport military *vicus* building might point to increasing local recruitment or at least influence. Querns are, after all, a widespread marker of apparent ritual activity in local farmsteads. However, Roman-era pit deposits containing querns and generally bearing a marked similarity to those discussed here are also known in France, Belgium, and Germany, making both local and continental influences plausible.[110] Cadavers or body parts in pits also occur in these regions, including instances – some accompanied by horses or displaying signs of ultraviolence – associated with Roman military sites. Although these bodies are often explained away as burials, the presence of individuals within what otherwise resemble offerings has raised suspicions they could be sacrifices.[111] Unlike the corpse within an apparent formal *principia* abandonment deposit at Newstead, though, the examples from Hadrian's Wall may have been a product of rites perpetrated covertly. Even so, acts of devotion by soldiers and military *vicus* dwellers on Hadrian's Wall could stray some distance from what we now consider to be 'Roman' behaviour.

6

The Long 4th Century

An End and a Beginning

Change was afoot as the 4th century dawned. Once, Rome's soldiers were primarily divided between the legions and the auxiliaries. But a force designed for conquest looked increasingly obsolete in a world where simply securing the Empire's edges tied down innumerable soldiers. The distinct challenges thrown up by seeking to hold existing territory, rather than seize more of it, were acknowledged by restructuring the army into two new branches: the *comitatenses* and the *limitanei*. Of these, the *comitatenses* served as mobile field armies, which had the flexibility to deploy in response to enemy activity, wherever it occurred. Meanwhile, their comrades in the *limitanei* were tasked with holding the frontiers. These soldiers have traditionally been seen as inferior, partially because they were paid less, but the *limitanei* were still regular troops and this stereotype is probably unfair.[1] Reorganising the army was among several important reforms distinguishing the late Roman period from what came before. The Empire was also split in two, with emperors reigning in both the east and west, while civil and military careers became separate. No longer were military units commanded by a succession of ambitious aristocrats in post for three or so years before – hopefully – ascending the career ladder. Instead, these positions became the preserve of professional soldiers. Because such changes began to be formalised after Diocletian became emperor in 284, with further refinements following under his successors, notably Constantine (reigned 307–337), scholars often talk about a 'long' 4th century. This runs from 284 through to the final collapse of imperial control in Britain *c*. 409,[2] presenting us with the final act for Hadrian's Wall in the Roman period.

Although the Wall's nature means we are primarily concerned with the *limitanei*, field army members were probably present in the wider frontier zone. Fifteen late Roman burials, some furnished with the flashy crossbow brooches and belt fittings signalling either military or administrative status during this era, were found at Scorton near Catterick and may have been members of the *comitatenses*. Isotope analysis of nine of them revealed that six were probably brought up on the Continent, showing migration still occurred.[3] By contrast, it is generally assumed that during the 4th century the vast majority of *limitanei* were recruited relatively locally. Indeed, one new measure to aid recruitment was making military service a hereditary obligation.[4] There are no certain examples of 4th-century soldiers' names from Hadrian's Wall, but in its southern hinterland Binchester fort has produced a list of probable garrison members preserved on a brick. Twenty-three names were Latin in style, while only four were overtly Celtic.[5] Assuming these lads were locally born, and had not changed their names upon entering military service, the simplest explanation is that the soldiers' fathers were veterans. Units becoming obliged to draw on a diminished geographical spread for their needs is a repeated theme of the 4th century. Goods that were once ferried in from southern Britain or the Continent were increasingly eclipsed by more local alternatives. Long before the end of Roman Britain, the frontier zone was evolving into something new.

Continuity and change

Study of Hadrian's Wall during this period owes much to a document known as the *Notitia Dignitatum* or 'register of offices'. Sure enough, it provides a list of key civil and military posts in both the eastern and western empires. Both the precise purpose of this document and – most importantly for us – the date of the information it itemises remain disputed. Candidates for when the portion covering the western empire was pulled together include 395, with some later amendments, or 420 – after Britain had been lost to the Empire, but perhaps before the imperial authorities accepted this reality.[6] Among the military commands is the *dux Britanniarum* or duke of the Britons, who presided over the *limitanei* in the Hadrian's Wall frontier zone. According to the *Notitia Dignitatum*, these forces include the *VI Victrix* legion, still at York, thirteen units in northern Britain, and sixteen units designated *item per lineam valli* or 'along the line of the Wall', with a scribal error perhaps omitting a seventeenth entry.[7] Either way, the Wall units are familiar from the 2nd or 3rd centuries (Table 1). This reveals a remarkable degree of stability, with old friends like the *cohors I Tungrorum*, which might have been the original Hadrianic garrison at Housesteads, still in residence during the twilight of Roman Britain. Six further units are also catalogued, mostly on the Cumbrian coast, of which five were once again longstanding cohorts.[8]

One curiosity concerning the units commanded by the *dux Britanniarum* is that the longevity of the Wall and Cumbrian coastal garrisons was not matched by those in the hinterland. Rather than presenting familiar names, the thirteen units listed after the *VI Victrix* bear brash late-Roman stylings, such as the *supervenientes* or 'surprise attackers' at Malton. This particular epithet emphasises how times had changed, as this staple tactic of guerrilla warfare, which Tacitus found so repugnant in the 1st century, was now deemed a worthy appellation for a Roman army unit. More significantly, this rash of new late Roman formations implies that at some point the earlier units manning the hinterland forts disappeared.[9] The root cause of this presumably involves fighting of some kind, and several candidates exist.

Renovation work along the Wall once again provides an overture to frontier warfare. Two building inscriptions dating to 297–305 are known, one – fragmentary – from Housesteads, and another from Birdoswald.[10] The latter furnishes our last detailed account of Roman building operations, telling us that the cohort 'restored the commander's house, which had been covered with earth and fallen into ruin, and the headquarters building and the bathhouse, under the charge of Flavius Martinus, centurion in command'. Although such dedications tend to aggrandise the work at hand, there is no reason to doubt that this restoration followed a period of neglect. That refurbishment efforts were not restricted to the forts is suggested by milecastles yielding a greater proportion of coins from the period 294–318 than is normal.[11] Fragments of earlier ornate architecture, inscriptions, and tombstones were sometimes reused to patch up essential structures. Examples of such recycling date back to at least the 3rd century, but the military's maintenance needs increasingly saw them cannibalising their own monuments. Gratuitous acts of architectural display could still occur, though, with South Shields fort receiving a trendy new 'cruciform' internal street arrangement – complete with a plush commanding officer's house – sometime between 286 and 318 (Fig. 39). Examples of this layout are rare in Britain, but there is a famous example at Palmyra in Syria. As a unit of Tigris boatmen from Mesopotamia probably moved into South Shields at this time,[12] they may have brought a taste for the style with them. If so, the *limitanei* were still receiving transfusions of migrant manpower.

The latest possible date for the Birdoswald building inscription – 305 – coincides with a new Roman offensive in the north. Constantius Chlorus, whom we last met bringing Carausius and Allectus' breakaway state to heel in 296, returned to Britain as emperor to wage war against a new enemy that appears in the literature around this time: the Picts. On this occasion Chlorus was joined by his eldest son, Constantine, and it seems likely that south-west Scotland was once again in Rome's sights. Fighting in this region would explain how a gold crossbow brooch that was a gift from the emperor Diocletian in 303 ended up in Erickstanebrae, Dumfries and Galloway.[13] Despite Chlorus celebrating victory, in July 306 he followed Severus' example and expired in York. His troops duly acclaimed his son, Constantine, emperor, although imperial politics meant he had to content himself with the lesser rank of Caesar. Eusebius mentions Constantine campaigning in Britain early in his reign, although this might be a garbled recollection of his original acclamation following Chlorus' conflict.[14] Either way, we are told that Constantine 'campaigned against the land of the Britons and those who dwell at the very Ocean where the sun sets'.[15] This reference to the setting sun – assuming it is not a literary flourish – fixes the fighting in the west, matching the implications of the Erickstanebrae brooch. Two hundred years after a border began to coalesce on the Tyne-Solway isthmus, south-west Scotland was seemingly still a source of trouble.

Regardless of how many campaigns were waged by Chlorus and son, they seem unlikely to explain the disappearance of units manning the hinterland forts. If these formations were annihilated during the fighting, could the units arranged *per lineam valli* really have escaped intact? The same goes for any unrecorded barbarian invasions: it would be strange if the Wall and coastal units survived, while the hinterland forces were destroyed wholesale. Instead, it seems likely that the absent units were redeployed elsewhere, probably by a commander gambling that the Wall and coastal forces were temporarily sufficient to secure the region. If so, the discrepancy apparent in the *Notitia Dignitatum* is presumably a product of the lethal rivalry colouring 4th-century imperial politics. One plausible scenario is that the hinterland units – as well as those in the northern outpost forts – were withdrawn during the lead up to Constantine's final showdown with the emperor Maxentius at the Battle of the Milvian Bridge, near Rome, in 312. Zosimus states that Constantine's victorious army included forces 'collected from Britain'.[16] Constantine credited this triumph to another power destined to flourish as the 4th century progressed: Christianity. Back in Britain, assigning new garrisons to the hinterland forts suggests that holding them remained necessary to ensure long-term security. This is supported by a potential 4th-century tombstone from Ambleside, which seemingly commemorates a father and son 'killed in the fort by enemies',[17] testifying to the existence of bold adversaries. By contrast, the outpost forts north of the Wall appear to have been judged dispensable and permanently abandoned in the early 4th century.[18]

How substantially the hinterland units swelled the ranks of Constantine's army would have depended on how severely their strength was depleted over the course of the 3rd century. We have seen how the emergence of chalet barracks suggests that the overall number of soldiers in individual units was falling. The 'long' 4th century brings more examples of such buildings. Perhaps the most famous is at Housesteads, which has played a central role in discussion concerning the purpose of this accommodation (Fig. 43). One influential theory is that each chalet block formed 'married quarters' for an individual soldier and his family after the military *vici* were abandoned. This reading, though, implies that garrison strength was slashed from a paper strength of 800, to just 70–100 soldiers. Although such a savage reduction is seemingly supported by surviving documents from the East, which imply the existence of 100- to 200-strong cohorts and *alae*, these numbers are inferred rather than stated.[19] Another, more serious obstacle to the chalets acting as family homes is that some predate the abandonment of the extramural settlements, while those at Housesteads were installed about three decades after the adjacent *vicus* seemingly disappeared. Just like its predecessors, then, the Housesteads chalets seem best understood as a new style of barrack block rather than purpose-built homes for former *vicus* dwellers. If individual chalet blocks held eight or so soldiers, the Housesteads garrison may still have numbered about 600, just 200 lower than its 2nd-century heyday. That, though, leaves the question of where the partners, children, and slaves once populating the military *vici* had gone.

The thriving urban centres at Corbridge and Carlisle offer one possible answer. If reduced garrison sizes, depreciating wages, and increased reliance on payment in kind had crippled the economies sustaining the military *vici*, it would make sense for their inhabitants to relocate to larger, more prosperous settlements.[20] One complication is that now service was hereditary, soldiers' sons were entered on the unit register and for much of the 4th century could draw rations,[21] so having them live some distance away would needlessly complicate logistics. Equally, one curious feature of some chalets is that they have shuttered frontages, reminiscent of the military *vici* strip buildings. At Vindolanda, the structures overlying the 3rd-century barracks in the north-west portion of the fort seemingly included workshops, shops, domestic housing, and open yards.[22] Here, then, elements of the *vicus* do appear within the fort. Finds also support the presence of women in unprecedented numbers at some point in the 4th century. Although seeking to determine gender on the basis of particular types of artefacts is risky, studying the patterns of hairpin loss at Vindolanda supports a radical change in the intramural demographic. During the 3rd century, only 12% of seventy-six hairpins were found within the fort. In the 4th century, all fifty hairpins came from within its ramparts.[23] While this presents a neat solution to where the *vicus* facilities went, uncertainties remain. Hodgson accepts that women and children may have been living in centurions' quarters from the 3rd century, but contends there is no sign of them elsewhere in barracks/chalets until the late 4th century.[24]

Another example of military *vicus*-style activity appearing within forts involves spreads of low-denomination coins. These have been detected in front of the headquarters building at Newcastle and Carlisle, and just within the west rampart at Wallsend and Vindolanda. Such a phenomenon can be explained as small change lost at markets held inside these forts. The coins suggest that either market activity peaked around 330–350,[25] or that money was less frequently used in transactions thereafter. At Newcastle fort, a type of pottery known as 'Local Traditional Ware' was found in notable – but still modest – quantities. Such pottery was made in the local Iron Age style and occurs occasionally along the Wall from the 2nd century onwards. Analysis indicates two sources of fabric, one from near South Shields fort, and the other probably between the rivers Wear and Aln. Not only does the pottery from Newcastle fort show that traditional techniques survived into the 4th century in the Wall's hinterland, but the quantity of material would fit with members of these local communities participating in its markets. A case for a degree of rural continuity can also be made in the west, where sites south of the Wall with probable or certain prehistoric origins such as Durranhill and Ewanrigg survived into the late 4th century.[26] That said, some farmsteads are also known to have been abandoned by this period. In

Newcastle, purchasers of Local Traditional Ware need not have been swayed by its rustic charm, as by the mid 4th century the pots were 'as serviceable as many of the other coarser types of pottery that reached the fort'.[27]

Patterns of supply were certainly shifting. As we have seen, earlier procurement could expose different forts to different produce from different sources. Even so, pottery manufactured in southern Britain or the Continent still arrived in some quantity. Imports from Gaul, Germany, and the Mediterranean almost completely ceased during the late 3rd or early 4th century, with only small numbers of amphorae arriving from overseas thereafter. Even so, plenty of pottery was still being shipped in from southern Britain, with some limited production in the north-east. This balance was upended over the course of the 4th century. At the western end of the Wall, BB1 pottery remained the most common form of coarse ware until *c.* 350. But throughout the frontier zone, local producers – especially groups based in east Yorkshire – were strengthening their grip on the military market. By the late 4th century, their supremacy verged on a monopoly. When this produce stopped reaching the Wall is unclear, but it was probably in the 5th century.[28] This switch from long-distance to regional supply is symptomatic of the military garrisons becoming increasingly rooted in their environs, with coins representing one of the few commodities still routinely arriving from overseas.

An increasing reliance on local procurement also changed how space within forts was used. One development that must have contributed to the sights and smells of garrison life was industrial activity spreading beyond the workshops of earlier centuries to colonise other spaces suited to the task. At Newcastle, a metalworking furnace was inserted into a former granary, while evidence for metalworking was also encountered in the Housesteads headquarters building.[29] This pragmatic reimagining of the ritual and administrative heart of the unit speaks volumes about the waning symbolism of 2nd-century power architecture. External bathhouses also fell out of favour, with new suites appearing within the fort walls.

By now, 2nd-century fortifications were obsolete throughout most of the Empire, and some Wall fort defences received attention. At Housesteads, additional towers sprouted along the rampart, while small platforms may have supported artillery pieces.[30] Even so, no Wall forts are known to have been upgraded with the high ramparts bristling with bastions favoured elsewhere. This omission has led to the zone being branded 'stable', 'relict', and even a 'backwater'.[31] On the west coast, though, Lancaster was rebuilt with a state-of-the-art rampart, while Maryport apparently received projecting bastions on its seaward side. Seemingly, then, these coastal garrisons were judged more deserving of improved defensive architecture. Indeed, some Wall forts ultimately began to revert to an earlier phase of development when portions of masonry elements collapsed in the very late 4th or 5th century. These were patched up with turf, earth, or timber substitutes, presumably due to a shortage of skilled masons. At Housesteads, for instance, three gateways and a tower were rebuilt in timber, while a fallen length of rampart was replaced in turf.[32]

Comparable changes can be detected in a handful of milecastles and turrets. Milecastle 35, on Sewingshields Crags, seems to have become a metalworking depot, with earlier artefacts stockpiled there for recycling.[33] Very late timber repairs to masonry structures are also known. The latest surviving level inside turret 44b, which commanded the eastern edge of Walltown Crags, produced masses of large nails associated with a coin of 364–378. Its excavator concluded that 'a great portion of the upper part of the turret must have been constructed of wood',[34] an interpretation that fits perfectly with what we now know about late measures to keep fort defences viable. Two further examples are offered by milecastles 51 and 52, which contained south gateways that were probably rebuilt using pairs of massive timber posts. This is once again explicable as a measure to keep them operational during the dying days of Roman Britain. As turret 44b and milecastles 51 and 52 occupy the flanks of the Tipalt-Irthing gap,[35] conspicuous measures to control this natural junction can be detected over the course of some two centuries. Farther afield, the absence of fallen debris among later 4th-century layers beside the Wall curtain near Wallsend fort fits with continuing efforts to keep this element serviceable.[36] Such steps suggest that the curtain – or at least lengthy stretches of it – remained important to military control strategies.

Conspiracy theory

The British security situation deteriorated in the 360s. At the start of the decade we are told that 'savage tribes of the Scots and Picts, who had broken the peace that had been agreed upon, were laying waste the regions near the frontiers'.[37] Worse followed in 367, when a crisis known as the 'barbarian conspiracy' unfolded. Raids by Franks and Saxons targeting Gaul, and Picts, Attacotti, and Scots striking Britain brought devastation and suspicions of collusion. In Britain, one high-ranking Roman commander was slain and another, by the name of Fullofaudes, was 'cut off by enemy ambush'. Fullofaudes was a *dux*, and therefore quite possibly the *dux Britanniarum* responsible for the Wall zone. His fate is not clear, but potentially he, too, was killed.[38] Meanwhile, the attackers were 'ranging widely and causing great devastation' as far south as London, while scores of surviving Roman soldiers aggravated the catastrophe by deserting. In response, a force perhaps 2,000-strong under the command of Theodosius – the father of a future emperor with the same name – was dispatched from the Continent.

By the time Theodosius arrived, the enemy forces had splintered and were seeking out booty. To restore the situation, his soldiers adopted tactics once considered borderline banditry. They 'secured beforehand the places suitable for ambushing the savages', rather than – so far as we can tell – fighting set-piece battles. This approach proved provident and, after the danger had passed, Theodosius is credited with protecting 'the frontiers with watch-posts and defence works', and disbanding a group referred to as the *areani*.[39] Its members reportedly ranged far and wide to gather information, making it likely they were a late incarnation of the Wall's intelligence-gathering apparatus. If so, they expose an inherent danger of such outfits, as the *areani* were reportedly turned by the enemy and bribed into betraying Roman secrets. That assumes, of course, they were not simply singled out as a convenient scapegoat for a spectacular military catastrophe.

Although we do not know whether the 367 invaders directly targeted the Wall garrisons, or sought to bypass them, the killing of one senior Roman commander, and ambushing of another, emphasises that the attackers were powerful enough to inflict serious losses. There is no sign in the written sources that the Roman forces in Britain could have salvaged the situation without aid from overseas. If securing booty was the attackers' principal aim, attempting to bypass the Wall garrisons would have an obvious appeal. Theodosius' strengthening of the frontier defences may be relevant here. There is no sign of major upgrades to the Wall, but a chain of fortifications was raised along the north-east Yorkshire coast at around this time. These small installations are recognisable as a variant of a fortification type popular on the Continent and comprise stout stone towers set within high masonry ramparts boasting projecting bastions.[40] Creating such a cordon could fit with the 367 conspirators simply sailing past the Wall and landing to its south.[41] One complication is that the garrisons of these new coastal stations are unlikely to exceed about eighty soldiers, which would leave them well-suited to counter small-scale incursions, but powerless to repulse a full-blown invasion. They do, though, perfectly match the implication of the western coastal forts at Maryport and Lancaster: it was securing the shore that warranted heightened protective measures during this era. Even so, this developing threat may be partially attributable to Hadrian's Wall curtailing overland raiding so effectively it incentivised striking by sea.

Religious practices were also changing during the final decades of Roman Britain. At Corbridge, temples were torn down after 370, with elements reused in the road.[42] Offerings at Coventina's shrine seemingly cease sometime around 388, while broken fragments of superstructure were reportedly found in her well,[43] which would fit with a deconsecration ceremony analogous to those sometimes found in fort headquarters buildings. This suppression of longstanding ritual sites can presumably be attributed to Christianity. With occasional exceptions, official tolerance for the religion had grown since Constantine's victory at the Milvian bridge. In 391, an edict made sacrifice illegal and closed the temples.[44] The degree to which Christianity penetrated the Wall communities remains unclear, and some see the military garrisons as bastions of the old gods.[45] However, the evidence for a military uptake of Christianity seems reasonably good. A few overtly Christian objects have been found, perhaps most obviously those bearing the *chi-rho* emblem. This device superimposes the first two Greek letters for *Christos* and is sometimes set within a circle. On such occasions it evokes a six-spoke wheel, which would surely have elicited knowing smiles from

FIGURE 44 *Pits that once held the timber uprights for an enigmatic monument at Maryport.*

any remining adherents of the Celtic sky god. Recent excavations at Maryport revealed a cluster of graves, some of which might have a Christian origin. These lay near an enigmatic concentration of large pits, many of which contained earlier altars reused as packing to support sizeable timber uprights for some sort of monumental structure erected during the twilight of Roman control (Fig. 44). As this complex occupied the highest point of the local topography, it was presumably intended to be as visible as possible.[46] Churches are suspected within South Shields, Housesteads, Vindolanda, and Birdoswald forts, while Christian-style gravestones are known at Vindolanda and Maryport.[47] Although these memorials probably date to the century or so after the end of Roman Britain, if Christianity was being practised by the descendants of fort garrisons, it seems reasonable to propose that the religion took root during the Roman era.

Magnus Maximus, an important commander in Britain and possibly another *dux Britanniarum*, is known to have been baptised in 383. He is also credited with successes against the Picts and Scots, but in 383 was proclaimed emperor by his troops. Maximus initially proved a proficient usurper, and successfully took Gaul and Spain, before invading Italy in 387, where he was captured and executed. It is likely that his continental adventures were powered in part by troops withdrawn from Britain.[48] Thereafter, pressure on the island continued to mount. In around 398, reinforcements were sent against perils including a sea that 'foamed with hostile oarsmen'.[49] Less than a decade later, the army in Britain mutinied in 406 or 407, setting up a succession of usurpers as the situation on the Continent steadily deteriorated. In around

409, it was either invaders from beyond the Rhine frontier or perhaps even a desire to remove unwelcome military units brought in by the army that sounded the death knell for Roman Britain. Zosimus records that they 'made it necessary for the inhabitants of Britain and some of the nations among the Celts to revolt from Roman rule and live on their own, no longer obedient to Roman laws. The Britons therefore took up arms, and braving danger for their own independence, freed the cities from the barbarians threatening [or billeted in] them'.[50] While this passage implies that Roman Britain came to a neatly defined end, archaeology demonstrates the reality was less clear cut.

Rather than the Wall garrisons being withdrawn and the forts abandoned around 409, evidence for continued occupation is mounting. The classic sequence was teased out at Birdoswald during Tony Wilmott's trailblazing 1987–1992 excavations. There, important changes to the two fort granaries began *c.* 350, when the subfloor spaces in the southern structure were filled in, while its northern counterpart collapsed at around this time. That the refurbishing of the southern granary marks a shift from storage to high-status activity is implied by what is probably either a foundation or abandonment deposit: a gold earring, glass ring, and silver coin of 388–395, found near hearths. The last two continue the round objects theme, while the earring is hexagonal, but features a decorative scheme vaguely evocative of wheel spokes. Sometime afterwards, a new floor surface was laid on top, before the south granary was seemingly abandoned in favour of a timber building inserted into the shell of the northern granary. This was, in turn, superseded by a sizeable timber hall, which stood on postpads (Fig. 45). Wilmott observed that the adapted granaries are explicable as venues where the unit commander could address his troops, while the final timber edifice resembles an early medieval chieftain's feasting hall. The chronology fits this, with the adapted southern granary probably not abandoned until 420, the first quasi-timber structure lasting to perhaps 470, and the timber hall standing until 520 or later. This puts us over a century beyond the end date of Roman Britain. Crucially, though, no break in occupation was detected at the fort. Instead of marching away, the Roman garrison seemingly stayed put, gradually mutating from a regular army unit into an early medieval warband.[51]

The centre cannot hold

The Wall changed immensely over the course of the 4th century. Failure to upgrade the military posts with cutting-edge new defences left them resembling relics from a bygone era. But inside, change was underway. Fort layouts designed to reinforce a hierarchy stretching all the way to the emperor, and hold storage and workshop facilities commensurate with sophisticated long-distance supply lines, were morphing into something new. Ruined or redundant monumental architecture could be quarried to patch

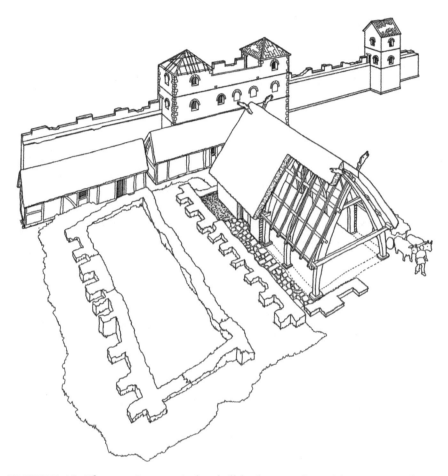

FIGURE 45 *The post-Roman timber hall built at Birdoswald. Courtesy of Tony Wilmott.*

humdrum but essential structures, such as defences and roads, or surrendered to industry, thereby helping to tackle the immense logistical challenges associated with becoming more self-sufficient. This shift surely involved local producers in the vicinity of forts supplying more goods for the military market, suggesting close links with rural communities. Currently, we can only see hints of this, but in the west, it is likely that some late Roman sites south of the Wall were successors to longstanding settlements with prehistoric origins. In the east, the endurance of Local Traditional Ware also supports a degree of continuity. A chronic reduction in overseas imports, and indeed products from southern Britain, robbed Wall life of a distinctive facet over the course of the 4th century. Yet transitioning to regional supply probably enabled soldiers to weather the early-5th-century turmoil. Rather than the end of Rome's financial and material support forcing an abandonment of the forts, local suppliers offered a lifeline. In turn, the protection fort garrisons could extend provided an incentive for rural producers to nurture this relationship.

Severing links with Rome spelled fundamental change for existing power structures. No longer were unit commanders beholden to a distant *dux*, probably based in York, who was in turn just another cog in the imperial hierarchy. Instead, individual unit commanders would have had greater autonomy than ever before. Even this development, though, seemingly has its roots in the later 4th century. If the refurbishment of the southern granary at Birdoswald was designed to create a venue where a commander could address his men, it marked an important shift from the arrangement in previous centuries. Once, such gatherings occurred in the headquarters building, beside the unit shrine and the trappings of imperial power. The new arrangement at Birdoswald would have increased the focus on individual commanders. By this reading, the eventual shift to a timber feasting hall symbolises how regular military commanders gradually transformed into early medieval chieftains. The end of Roman authority over the Wall, then, was not accompanied by an evacuation of the heavily armed soldiers manning its forts. Instead they remained, to become part of the region's future.

7

The Mythmakers

From *Limitanei* to Legend

As Roman Britain slipped into the past, communities of *limitanei* and their families still clung on in the Wall forts. In the 30 years since the Birdoswald excavations, traces of 5th-century activity have been found with sufficient frequency that it now seems continued occupation – for an unclear duration – was the rule, rather than the exception.[1] In many ways this should be unsurprising. Rome had lost direct control of Britain numerous times in the past, but always reasserted its authority sooner or later. It may have been many years before the realisation that the Empire was gone for good sank in. Even the end of cash payment need not have been decisive, as fresh coin issues become rarer in the archaeological record in the later 4th century. The latest coin known from the immediate vicinity of Hadrian's Wall was found at the enigmatic site of Great Whittington and minted 406–408.[2] The arrival of money seems to have slowed to a dribble long before then, though, as the *limitanei* were forced to focus evermore keenly on fort environs for their needs.

An end to cash shipments poses a problem for modern archaeologists, as activity along the former frontier becomes harder to date with any precision. This is compounded by the scarcity of new – rather than recycled Roman – artefacts dating to the immediate post-Roman period. Other than a few distinctive brooches, there is very little that can be confidently assigned to this period, while buildings have also proven difficult to detect. This scarcity is one of the reasons why the period was once known as the Dark Ages, a term that somewhat underplayed the cultural achievements of the era. This epoch has since been generally rebranded as the early Anglo-Saxon period, reflecting the migration of Angles and Saxons into Britain, which seemingly shaped its post-Roman destiny. Nowadays, the term Anglo-Saxon is also attracting criticism for being insufficiently inclusive. Like 'Roman', 'Briton', and 'Celt' it is retained for convenience here, but must be understood to encompass many different groups, rather than solely Germanic immigrants.

This chapter will not, though, seek to provide a full political history of the region. Instead, it focuses on activities involving the Wall in the first millennium or so following the collapse of Roman Britain, especially its status as a ready source of building material. But the monument was not just being exploited to raise new structures, as memories of its role proved fertile ground for mythmaking.

Fall and rise

We have seen how evidence from Birdoswald indicates that the military garrison gradually transformed into an early medieval-style warband. That the regular army unit did not march away *c.* 409, leaving a vacant fortification for others to occupy, fits with what we know about 4th-century recruitment. Now that service was hereditary, many of the *limitanei* soldiers were surely born in the Wall zone, and so the region was their 'home'. Equally, their status as trained professional soldiers must have been particularly valuable in what was surely an uncertain time. If our societies were to collapse tomorrow, it is easy to see how having friends in a nearby military base might be an advantage. The question concerning Hadrian's Wall is how long the former army units and their descendants held on. The apparent feasting hall in Birdoswald could plausibly have been standing in 520, while a probable Christian gravestone written in Latin from Vindolanda may have been cut *c.* 500.[3] By then, it has traditionally been assumed that groups descended from established Roman or local communities were sharing the region with new incomers.

Anglian settlers seem to be present in the region from the mid to late 5th century. The scale of continental immigration is currently a source of considerable debate, though, with some arguing that the number of arrivals was no greater than in previous centuries, while others prefer an 'elite takeover', whereby Anglian incomers usurped leadership of pre-existing local communities, prompting a selective uptake of Germanic styles.[4] Scientific analyses promise a way forward here, but this work is still in its infancy. What is certain, is that material culture and burial rites cannot be used to distinguish between recent settlers (or their descendants) and members of longer established communities. In the former Wall zone, the Picts and Irish will also have remained influential actors. Two important Anglo-Saxon kingdoms arose in the eastern part of the region: Bernicia, which stretched to the north, and Deira to the south. These were united in the 7th century to create Northumbria, a kingdom that expanded west and north to carve out a territory stretching from the Forth to the Humber, and the North Sea to the Irish Sea. This placed the Wall's ruins at the heart of an extraordinary political, religious, and cultural powerhouse.

South Shields fort is reputedly the birthplace of a 7th-century king of Deira, and so by then was presumably an Anglo-Saxon royal possession (Fig. 46).[5] Other forts may also have served as power bases for influential

FIGURE 46 *The Roman fort at South Shields, beside the mouth of the Tyne. Credit: Nick Hodgson/Tyne and Wear Archives and Museums.*

leaders as the new Anglo-Saxon order consolidated its grip. The Roman name of Great Chesters – *Aesica* – potentially survived as *Ahse*, a district existing in the late 7th century.[6] Equally, St. Cuthbert, Bishop of Lindisfarne, was famously shown a functioning Roman fountain at Carlisle in 685. Corbridge, meanwhile, developed a new core about 1km from its Roman precursor, a shift easily explained by proximity to a suitable ford after the Roman bridge collapsed, and went on to host a slave market in the early Middle Ages.[7] These urban sites probably fared rather differently to most Wall forts, though. Corbridge and Carlisle may have remained permanently occupied down to today,[8] whereas the absence of modern population centres overlying most of the Wall forts emphasises they were abandoned at some stage.[9] From this perspective, the lingering significance of South Shields – perhaps attributable to its port – potentially makes it the exception, rather than the rule. Equally, eastern river valleys have been pinpointed as the focus for early Anglo-Saxon activity.[10] Although this picture may be skewed by the relative archaeological visibility of settled arable farmers compared to mobile upland pastoralists, if accurate it placed the forts in a peripheral position. So, what happened to their former garrisons?

A fascinating perspective on the final days of the Wall is provided by Gildas, a preacher who wrote a polemic entitled *De Excidio Britonum* or *the Ruin of Britain*, probably in the early to mid 6th century. Little is known about Gildas, but his tract is especially valuable for furnishing the first account of the Roman occupation from a British perspective. In Gildas' narrative, which is studiously vague on dates, names, and places, Roman Britain ended in around 383 when Magnus Maximus departed for Gaul, taking Rome's soldiers with him. After the Scots and Picts wreaked havoc, the Britons beseeched Rome for help, and 'a legion' was duly dispatched to force back the attackers. The Britons were instructed to raise a rampart, but it proved ineffective because they built it of turf. Once more the Britons were attacked, and once more they petitioned Rome for relief. The Empire came to the rescue again, by both land and sea, and this time their forces stayed long enough to help the 'wretched inhabitants' build a stone wall. This stretched from sea to sea, and incorporated several towns within its course. After informing the Britons that henceforth they were on their own, the Romans withdrew. The Britons manned the Wall, but were 'too lazy to fight, and too unwieldy to flee . . . they sat about day and night, rotting away in their folly'. Some came to a sticky end at the hands of the Scots and Picts, while the remainder ultimately 'abandoned the towns and the high wall'.[11]

Given the discussion of the Wall's use over the last few chapters, the idea that it was built after the end of Roman Britain by returning Romans and their former British subjects can be dismissed as literally incredible. Nowadays, such a basic blunder casts considerable doubt over the remainder of Gildas' account, which has been cast as 'a moral tract . . . not a factual history' and 'bloodcurdling religious rhetoric'.[12] Others, though, have observed that as Gildas rages against those who peddle falsehoods, wilfully departing from the truth would somewhat compromise his message. By this reading, Gildas was – by and large – doing the best he could with the materials to hand.[13] What those sources were, is an interesting question. Gildas states he relied more on 'foreign tradition' than 'literary remains from this country',[14] and access to a greater or lesser number of Classical texts has been deduced from his content. Knowledge of the ancient author Orosius has been proposed, for example, although he plainly attributed a wall to Severus, so why would Gildas ignore this? One possibility is that Gildas was also drawing on British oral legends.[15]

As far as the Wall is concerned, once you leave aside the matter of its construction, many of Gildas' claims tally with what we know. It is not outrageous that the Britons might remember the usurpation of Magnus Maximus as the end of Roman Britain, especially if he led scores of British-born fighting men to their deaths in Italy. These events do seem broadly to initiate the death spiral leading to what we view as the collapse *c*. 409. Equally, references to Roman reinforcements after Maximus' fatal expedition tally with hints in the Classical sources that troops were sent around 398, and even that their operations had a naval dimension (see p. 127). The mobile 'legion' could be a field army, while accounts of Britons manning the Wall might reflect British perceptions of the *limitanei*. After all, these soldiers were presumably predominantly born in the region. Although the 'towns' are clearly Wall forts, many potentially did resemble towns as much as military bases following their 4th-century transformation. Finally, Gildas seems well aware of something that modern scholars only really grasped after Wilmott's excavations at Birdoswald: the Wall forts remained manned beyond the end of Roman Britain. It is also interesting that while Gildas describes defenders being slain by spears, he gives the impression that ultimately the forts were abandoned by choice, rather than overrun. As for Gildas' dating of the Wall, this allowed him to credit it to a Christian Roman Empire, while its loss could be blamed on the incorrigibly sinful Britons. Both implications advanced his moralising agenda. Would, though, Gildas have risked ascribing an inglorious end to the Wall forces, if many of the Wall forts were still occupied by descendent communities when he wrote c. 540?

A small, but conspicuous quantity of Anglo-Saxon material is known from the forts. Leaving aside South Shields, because of its possible royal connection, finds or activity occur at Wallsend, Newcastle, Benwell, Chesters, Vindolanda, and Birdoswald, as well as Corbridge and Carlisle. Some of this seems to be in the form of grave goods, such as two later 5th- to 6th-century brooches from Benwell, which would not necessarily mean the forts were still occupied. Binchester fort, south of Hadrian's Wall, may be instructive here. An apparently mid-6th-century burial was inserted into the ruins of a bathhouse, before a larger cemetery was established in the 7th century.[16] It is wondered if this contained descendants of the fort community, perhaps alongside some incomers, with the site potentially remaining significant until Bishop Auckland was founded 3km away in the 11th or 12th century.[17] A 7th-century brooch from Chesters and 9th- to 10th-century belt strap ends from Vindolanda prove activity,[18] but not whether this accompanied permanent settlement or fleeting visits.

Newcastle fort reputedly housed a monastery known as Monk Chesters, and there are possible signs of post-Roman structures preceding the establishment of a cemetery within its ramparts during the late 7th century.[19] Farther upstream, a 7th-century royal villa known as *Ad Murum* has been assigned to Walbottle on the strength of place-name evidence,[20] which would mean the vicinity of the key Tyne fords at Newburn was once again singled out for special treatment. Bewcastle may also have housed a monastery, and a stunning, probably 8th-century, cross still stands within the former fort (Fig. 47). This may even represent a conscious effort to re-sanctify and appropriate an enduring Romano-British cult site.[21] Even so, the general rule of thumb is that evidence for unbroken occupation becomes weaker over time. While there are compelling signs that activity continued in many forts well into the 5th century, this becomes patchy in the 6th century, and sparse in the 7th century.[22] Perhaps some forts well situated for settlement remained population centres for centuries, while less amenable locations were abandoned in favour of more convenient sites.

Abandonment of some forts by the 7th century fits with a new use being found for them. During the second half of that century, the kingdom of Northumbria burnished its Christian credentials by establishing a network of religious establishments. Of particular relevance are the monastic house at Jarrow, founded in 681, and the church at Hexham, built in the 670s.

FIGURE 47 *The Bewcastle Cross.*

Both employed reused Roman stone. Jarrow monastery seems to have primarily sourced this from Wallsend, which probably formed part of its endowment and fits with South Shields being off-limits as a royal concern.[23] At Hexham, stonework in the surviving Anglo-Saxon crypt presents an architectural jumble, sourced from monuments including Corbridge Roman bridge, a nearby mausoleum, and Chesters fort. The labour-saving gains from recycling Roman material were considerable, and it has been estimated that three-quarters of the effort expended on building masonry structures comes from quarrying material.[24] However, a deeper motive also seems to be in play. These buildings would have been the grandest raised in the region since the Roman period. Bede, a monk based at Jarrow, mentions such stone churches were described as being built in 'the Roman manner'.[25] As such, the powerful Church of Rome in 7th-century Northumbria was consciously building in what was seen as a Roman style, courtesy of genuine Roman material. This must have sent a powerful message to the local populace that the heirs of Rome were at hand.

Myths and measurements

Bede is most famous for writing his *Ecclesiastical History of the English People*. This, too, can be read as a vehicle to assert the pre-eminence of the Church of Rome in England.[26] It was probably completed in 731, and once again provides a potted history of Roman Britain. Bede draws heavily on Gildas, as well as Classical authors – especially Orosius – and his own observations to provide a revised account of Hadrian's Wall. This time, its origins are placed earlier in the Roman period, with Severus credited as the author of the huge earthwork running to the south of the Wall curtain. Bede calls this the Vallum, gifting it the name it still bears today. In other regards, though, Bede largely followed Gildas' lead and recounts how attacks by Scots and Picts following Rome's departure prompted appeals for help. A legion duly drove back the attackers, allowing the Britons to build a turf wall. Bede specified it stretched between Peanfahel and Alcluith – Kinneil and Dumbarton – identifying it as the Antonine Wall. When this was overrun, the Romans returned again, and helped to install a stone wall near Severus' Vallum: 'at public and private expense and with the help of the Britons, they made a famous wall which is still to be seen. It is eight feet wide and twelve feet high, running in a straight line from east to west'. The Britons held the Wall 'with dazed and trembling hearts', but after abandoning it were 'torn in pieces by their enemies like lambs by wild beasts'.[27]

Despite repeating Gildas' error concerning the date of the Stone Wall, Bede has often won plaudits from modern scholars. He has been lauded as 'a scholar and a scientist, an educated and trained mind' and there is no doubt that his inclusion of dimensions for the Wall curtain was precocious.[28] Bede probably gained first-hand experience of this at Wallsend, and allowing for the vagaries of the Anglo-Saxon foot, his measurements amount to a curtain 2.24m wide by 3.36m high.[29] Despite this authoritative touch, Bede's account cannot be considered wholly objective. His *Ecclesiastical History* opens with a dedication to King Ceolwulph of Northumbria, whom Bede had sent an earlier draft for approval. Unsurprisingly, Bede's text also tends towards promoting Northumbrian rulers at the expense of those in the kingdom's great contemporary rival: Mercia.[30] This bias has seen his work branded 'little short of propagandist'.[31] Certainly, Northumbria was – naturally – an autocracy, and a time-honoured approach for such entities to achieve and retain legitimacy is by making their existence look natural and uncontroversial.[32] Bede's work can also be viewed in that light. He insinuates that Northumbrian supremacy is divinely sanctioned,[33] while his reference to the Antonine Wall has the side-effect of emphasising that the Romans swept the Picts and Scots from southern Scotland, handy for a kingdom whose northern boundary lay on the Forth. Equally, stressing that the Britons were slaughtered when they stood alone, but could build marvels when guided by a benevolent foreign power that had converted to Christianity, must have held a certain contemporary resonance.[34] In that regard, Bede's history is a natural companion to the building of churches in the 'Roman style', because it casts the English as Rome's heirs. Ceolwulph was doubtless pleased.

Given that the favour of the Christian god was presented as integral to Northumbria's success, the new ecclesiastical establishments could even be seen as perpetuating the Wall's protective purpose. If so, it is ironic that Northumbria's religious houses ended up as targets. Jarrow was raided by Vikings in 794, emphasising the arrival of a new threat, which would go on to subsume part of Northumbria's territory in a Viking kingdom centred on York. After Northumbria was broken apart, the next major political rupture to impact on the Wall seems to be the Norman subjugation of the region in the 11th century. This ushered in the emergence of a contested border between England and Scotland, where rivalries occasionally flared into full-blown border warfare, while a violent reiver culture flourished. Although the Anglo-Scottish border ultimately solidified to the north of the Wall line, the former barrier still bolstered England's spiritual and martial security concerns within this debatable land, by providing stone for churches and castles.

Lanercost Priory presents a fine example of a new foundation, which was established in around 1169, on land recently taken by the English crown from the Scots. Not only did the priory make extensive use of Roman stone, but the Wall also defined part of the northern edge of its estates. This led to a situation in which the Wall curtain was largely robbed out, only to be reinstated in a more modest guise during the 14th century to mark the boundary. A nearby Wall turret may also have been retained as a watchtower or beacon.[35] That such posts could be desirable is indicated by an apparently 14th-century tower built into the curtain at Steel Rigg, where its command of the terrain contrasts with the compromised plots occupied by the regularly spaced Roman turrets. The Wall also offered suitable positions to station militia known as the night watch, who kept an eye out for signs of danger. In the 16th century, their watches included the Wall from Carrawburgh to the North Tyne, as well as a stretch near Heddon.[36] A 1542 report on the border defences is valuable for specifying areas where the 'thieves' were striking from: Liddesdale, Tynedale, Gilsland – a district running west from within the Tipalt-Irthing gap – and Bewcastle.[37] It is surely telling that all four locations can be linked to areas where the Roman military seemingly took particular care to achieve security. Conceivably, then, the geography and local economies underpinning 16th-century border raiding and skirmishing were also of relevance in the Roman period.

Secure residences were unsurprisingly popular in turbulent times, and a number of castles were built on or near the Wall. One, at Thirlwall, was raised beside the Tipalt Burn, in the early 14th century. It lay on the eastern flank of the Tipalt-Irthing gap and was built almost entirely out of recycled Wall stones (Fig. 48). In the 16th and 17th centuries, some less affluent residents built bastle houses, which resembled towers and had ground floor

FIGURE 48 *The ruins of Thirlwall Castle.*

space where cattle were secured overnight, while the families slept on an upper level. The remains of one can still be seen built into the south gateway of Housesteads fort. More modest structures also took root in the ruins of the Wall, including temporary quarters for shepherds whose livestock grazed the uplands as summer pasture. Such structures are known as shielings, and were usually modest affairs. Several 14th- to 16th-century examples lay near milecastle 39, while the memory of such seasonal boltholes lingers in place names like Sewingshields and Winshields.[38] Other buildings benefitting from recycled stone include Britain's first purpose-built gaol at Hexham in 1330, and Newcastle Castle. All told, around thirty-six ecclesiastical buildings and over thirty fortifications either certainly or probably contain(ed) Roman stone. Little wonder, then, that it has been claimed 'no other ancient monument in the British Isles has had such an impact on the adjacent landscape'.[39]

Mural controversies

With the exception of an account of the Wall in Nennius' 9th-century *Historia Brittonum*, which serves up a confused collation of Gildas and Bede,[40] until recently it was thought that little more of substance was said on the subject until the dawn of serious antiquarian interest in the late 16th century. William Shannon has punctured this perception by combining written accounts and maps to demonstrate that the Wall's renown remained undimmed. Extraordinarily, the oldest surviving detailed maps of Britain all mark Hadrian's Wall. Four were created *c.* 1250 by Matthew Paris, a monk based in St. Albans, and are conventionally referred to as A-D (Fig. 49). As these were compiled to aid journey planning, and provide little in the way of extraneous detail, it is perhaps surprising that Hadrian's Wall – and, on maps A and B, the Antonine Wall – made the cut. Shannon attributes this to a 'nationalist pride in the island of Britain', and in particular the Wall's testimony to 'our heroic

FIGURE 49 *Matthew Paris map 'A', c. 1250, showing Hadrian's Wall and the Antonine Wall. Credit: The British Library.*

national past', but it probably also reflects the Wall's significance for conceptualising space within the island. Map D is notable for identifying the Wall as the *murus pictorum* or Picts' Wall. This appears to be the earliest known appearance of a name that entered common parlance in England.[41] The first copperplate map of the British Isles, which was produced in Rome in 1546, also features the Wall. It appears as shattered ruins, complete with gateways, perhaps suggesting some knowledge of its fabric. Even more intriguing is an Anglo-Saxon world map dating tb *c.* 1025–1050, which is several re-drawings distant from a Roman original. Near a wavy line that may or may not represent Hadrian's Wall are two nonsense words that seem to read *marin pergis*. Shannon proposes that this is a botched rendering of words on the original Roman map: *murus pictis* or Pict's Wall.[42] If so, this was presumably its late Roman name, while the inclusion of a named enemy would mirror the coastal defences of south-east Britain being entered in the *Notitia Dignitatum* as the *litoris Saxonici* or Saxon shore. As stoking fear of malignant outsiders is another time-honoured tactic for states looking to reinforce their authority, the name Pict's Wall would have a ready appeal to both the late Roman Empire and England while its northern border was in flux.

One 14th-century writer based north of the Wall favoured a different name. John of Fordun compiled his blend of fables, often called the *Scotichronicon*, in the 1380s. He states that the land of Scotia once commenced at the Wall, and draws heavily on Bede when describing it. Fordun does, though, take an especial interest in how the monument fared immediately after the Britons defending it were defeated by the Scots, Picts, and Irish: 'Thus they speedily summoned the peasantry, with whose hoes and mattocks, pickaxes, forks, and spades, they all, without distinction, set to work to dig broad clefts and frequent breaches through the wall, whereby they might everywhere readily pass backwards and forwards. From these breaches, therefore, did this structure take its present name, which in the English tongue is Thirlitwall'.[43] It seems telling that in England the Wall became widely known after the enemies it kept at bay – the Picts – while a Scottish writer employed a name emphasising the slighting that broke its power as an obstacle. Today, the name is specifically associated with Thirlwall, the castle and hamlet in the Tipalt-Irthing gap. The Wall does appear as the *Thwertner Dyke* in a 1290 legal matter concerning Heddon-on-the-Wall, though, suggesting a similar name once enjoyed wider currency, although not everyone has been convinced it meant what Fordun claimed.[44]

A key development in Hadrian's Wall studies was the 15th-century publication of the surviving Classical sources in more readily accessible print editions. Caesar appeared in 1469, Tacitus in 1470, and crucially – as it identifies Hadrian as the Wall's builder – the *Historia Augusta* in 1475. This was picked up by Hector Boece, who appears to be the first surviving post-Roman source to credit Hadrian with a British wall, albeit in turf. Boece's work was published as the *Scotorum Historia* in 1527, and it was followed by Polydore Vergil's *Historia Anglica* in 1534. Vergil stressed that the *Historia*

Augusta credited Hadrian, rather than Severus, with the first Roman wall in Britain. This should have been an important step forwards, but instead the opportunity was squandered. Shannon argues that prejudice meant both Boece and Vergil were considered deeply suspect from an English perspective, because they were Scottish and Italian respectively.[45] Vergil was accused of spreading papist deceit, while Boece's work was excoriated with a tart 'what lies he wrote'.[46] This last was penned by John Leland, who was Henry VIII's librarian. Leland undertook a lengthy tour of Britain and visited at least part of the Wall in around 1539, gathering additional details from a local informant. Sadly, Leland died before concluding his write-up, and there is a gap in the manuscript at the beginning of a section on the Wall, indicating that he planned to insert further material.[47] Despite this loss, Leland's record of observations made in the field paved the way for future studies. Scholars were finally preparing to pick up the gauntlet laid down by Bede's precocious record of the Wall curtain's dimensions 800 years earlier.

Creating knowledge

At first sight the story of the Wall in this era is one of loss, both of knowledge and the monument's physical fabric. The accounts of Gildas and Bede show that the Wall's true origins had been forgotten, while the remains of Roman structures were targeted by powers looking to cement their writ in the north. But these intellectual and engineering endeavours also emphasise the Wall's continuing relevance. For Gildas, the failure to hold the Wall helped explain the world he lived in, while Northumbria exploited both architecture and history to draw parallels with Rome. Bede could state that the Wall was already famous in the 8th century, and its renown helps explain its presence on 13th-century maps drawn up by a monk based in St. Albans, and a 16th-century map printed in Rome. If the monument was considered an irrelevance it would have simply been left off, like sundry other archaeological sites. Its existence also provided a focus for concepts of England and Scotland, with some 14th-century marine charts still placing the border on the Tyne-Solway line.[48] But if mythologising and plundering the monument seem an unlikely prelude to its scientific study, the seeds of modern understanding of the Wall lie in these acts. Attempting to whittle the fact from the fiction in Gildas and Bede would ultimately lead to our current knowledge of the Wall, aided by Roman inscriptions that survived in the fabric of later buildings.

8

Wall Renaissance

Evidence from the Earth

The year 1586 heralded one of the most influential books ever to contemplate Britain's past. William Camden's *Britannia* sought to set knowledge of ancient affairs on a surer footing by stripping away the accretions of mythology and folklore (Fig. 50). Written in Latin – readers had to wait until 1610 for an English edition – the book set a new benchmark for study of Britain's heritage. Camden's coverage of what he calls the *Murus Picticus* or Picts Wall has often seen him credited as its first true antiquarian.[1] Even so, Camden did not initially have first-hand experience of the monument, and instead presented a skilful blend of several sources, including Leland's still unpublished manuscript, a letter written by one Christopher Ridley, reputedly belonging to a family from Willimoteswick near Haltwhistle,[2] and information set down by John of Fordun. Camden was equally judicious in his treatment of the ancient sources, managing – just about – to reconcile the Classical authors with Gildas and Bede. While shoehorning these conflicting accounts into a broadly coherent narrative was a triumph of ingenuity, it can be viewed with hindsight as the hallmark of a subject in desperate need of an injection of fresh evidence. Fortunately, the very publication of *Britannia* helped achieve this. It excited such interest that collecting inscribed stones became fashionable. In some cases, details were fed back to Camden, informing future editions.[3] This marks the beginning of a new approach to studying Hadrian's Wall: routinely using evidence won from the monument to deliver fresh insights. The journey from antiquarianism to archaeology had begun.

Reading the monument

Camden's chronology for Hadrian's Wall varied across different editions, but they all depended on the Romans moving between the Clyde-Forth and Tyne-Solway lines with dizzying alacrity. His first attempt started with Agricola garrisoning the Clyde-Forth isthmus, before Hadrian withdrew to

FIGURE 50 *William Camden. Credit: Rijksmuseum, Amsterdam (Public Domain).*

the Tyne-Solway line and built a barrier. Here, Camden employs phrases from the *Historia Augusta*, but not just the section explicitly relating to Britain. Instead, he mixes in a passage crediting Hadrian with a timber palisade, which probably refers to the barrier he installed in Upper Germany.[4] Antoninus Pius was back in Scotland to erect his Wall, before Severus retreated south and built the Vallum. Severus Alexander marched his men back to the Antonine Wall and then returned to the Vallum, which remained the outer line until Theodosius reoccupied the Antonine Wall after the barbarian conspiracy. The Picts and Scots eventually broke through, and a legion was dispatched to aid the Britons, who helped build a stone wall on the line of Severus' Vallum.[5] In later editions, Camden demonstrated an awareness of the importance of setting Hadrian's Wall within the wider context of the frontiers of the Roman Empire and his succinct statement of their role remains apposite: 'Along these limits or borders, souldiors lay garisoned in time of peace within Frontier-castles and cities: but when there was any feare of waste and spoile from bordering nations, some of them had their field-stations within the Barbarian ground, for defence of the lands: others made out-rodes into the enemies marches, to discover how the enemies stirred, yea, and if good occasion were offered, to encounter with them before they came to the Limites'.[6]

In 1599, Camden remedied his earlier omission and visited the Wall. He demurred from exploring its whole course, famously detouring south at Carvoran to avoid the 'ranke-robbers' still populating the central sector.[7] Camden's observations appeared in subsequent editions of *Britannia*, and he assured readers that he had not swallowed any of the 'fabulous tales of the common people concerning this wall'.[8] A few, though, had already slipped in via Christopher Ridley's letter, including a splendid story about a brass tube set within the Wall curtain, which allowed soldiers in the various posts to speak to each other.[9] No such device existed. Distinguishing fact from fiction on Hadrian's Wall can still be a treacherous business, although in this case Ridley's insistence that payments for the upkeep of the tube were still made to 'some gentilmen in Northymberland', perhaps provided a clue something was awry.[10] Camden also followed an increasingly well-worn path by anchoring contemporary concerns in the Roman past and thereby claiming them as the natural order of things. In this case, an ancient pedigree was invoked for feudalism, while a thinly veiled subtext of English civilisation versus Scottish 'barbarity' was developed.[11] Camden's interest in the landscape was pioneering, though, and he endorsed the notion of northern enemies crossing the Wall in the Tipalt-Irthing gap – where there was no obstructing watercourse to the south – before his 1599 inspection.[12] This insight was presumably influenced by a reading of John of Fordun.

Camden's observations of contemporary life in the north are also illuminating. He notes that in Gilsland 'you mey see as it were ancient Nomades, a martiall kinde of men',[13] who travelled into the uplands between April and August as part of the annual cycle of transhumance. This district stretched west from within the Tipalt-Irthing gap, and if Hadrian's Wall had once disrupted the movement of similarly 'martiall' men, it would help explain why special measures were adopted thereabouts. Camden's view also chimes with Callwell's crass generalisation that uplanders are 'fighters'.[14] Place names referencing shielings show that transhumance was widespread in the central sector, but taking advantage of the Tipalt-Irthing gap would make sense. If livestock panic while crossing a ford they can be drowned, so there is an incentive to drove via a place where north–south passage was possible without gambling on a river crossing. Farther east, Camden observes that the inhabitants of Tynedale and Redesdale 'breed noteable light horsemen',[15] and it is just such a threat that the Roman cavalry manning Chesters fort, in the North Tyne valley, would be ideal to counter. In south-west Scotland, it is recounted that 'This Nithsdale, together with Annandale, breeds a warlike sort of people, but infamous for their depredations. For they dwell upon Solway, a fordable Arm of the Sea, through which they often made excursion into England for booty'.[16] It is also in Annandale and Nithsdale that we find the densest concentration of Roman fortlets along roads in Britain, while the former valley is where Titus Haterius Nepos is believed to have undertaken his census of the *Anavionenses* in the AD 90s, potentially destabilising the wider region. A readiness to strike across the Solway certainly resonates with the siting of Bowness fort opposite the lowest fording point on the Solway, which lies close to the mouth of Annandale (Fig. 27). It cannot be stressed enough that these generalisations prove nothing about Roman Britain. But they do fit the implications of the archaeology.

Two individuals accumulating Roman inscriptions during this period are worthy of note. John Senhouse assembled the nucleus of what is now the oldest collection still in private hands, which is on display in the Senhouse Museum, Maryport.[17] He also hosted Camden during his 1599 tour. Meanwhile, Reginald Bainbrigg described diggings that yielded two inscriptions at Castlesteads fort in 1601, thereby producing the first detailed account of an excavated structure on the Wall.[18] Camden died in 1623, but *Britannia* outlived its author, with later editors updating the text to greater or lesser effect. At the same time, hesitant steps towards what we now recognise as the bread and butter of archaeology accelerated as the 17th century gave way to the 18th. This was aided by a shift in the contemporary circumstances of the border. In 1704, Nicholas Armstrong, who briefly owned Housesteads fort and hailed from a clan of notorious horse thieves, was hanged and his brothers dispersed.[19] This is often taken as drawing a line under the reiver era. Shortly afterwards, the Treaty of Union between England and Scotland in 1707 brought a new political dynamic to the region. This concord may explain why English references to the ancient frontier less frequently namedrop the old enemy beyond, beginning to favour the 'Roman Wall' instead.[20]

In 1708 and 1709, Robert Smith capitalised on the new stability to improve on Leland's and Camden's treatments of the Wall, by compiling 'the first continuous description of the Roman frontier works' from Stanwix to Wallsend.[21] When Smith's account was published in the 1722 edition of Camden's *Britannia*, it also introduced scholarship to a local term that found favour: Mile-Castles.[22] John Leland's *Itinerary* was finally published in 1710, while six years later John Warburton presented the first detailed map showing the Wall's course, and in 1725 the distinguished antiquaries William Stukeley and Roger Gale toured the *murus*. The following year saw the release of Scottish antiquary Alexander Gordon's *Itinerarium Septentrionale*, for which he surveyed both Roman walls, and numerous intervening sites. Gordon captured the spirit of the age by asserting that the role of 'Archiology, which consists of Monuments, or rather Inscriptions' is 'to prove demonstratively those Facts which are asserted in History'.[23] The idea that it might tell us something new was not yet entertained. Gordon also courted controversy by holding that the scale of the fortifications testified to Scottish valour: 'there can be no greater Proof of the Scots never having been conquered, than the very Roman Walls themselves, built as Fences against their Hostilities: Which, while there is a Stone of them remaining, will be undeniable Monuments of the Valour and Prowess of that Nation'.[24] Despite this being no more than a natural inversion of the English civilisation/Scottish barbarity subtext propagated by the likes of Camden, it proved provocative.[25]

English scholars indignant about Gordon's claims were doubtless relieved when John Horsley released a more detailed survey – *Britannia Romana or the Roman Antiquities of Britain* – just six years later in 1732. This extraordinary achievement remains an essential reference work for Wall scholars, because it includes a detailed account of the visible remains, backed up by maps, plans, and sections. The Wall's evolution remained a significant stumbling block, though, and Horsley produced what was destined to be the last great theory before the truth cut through. Horsley credited Agricola with the forts, Hadrian with the Vallum, and Severus with the stone curtain. Sadly, he allowed this interpretation to colour the section drawings. In order for Hadrian's Vallum to form a sensible barrier, Horsley needed the so-called marginal mound to be a rampart. As we have seen, in reality this may have been upcast from ditch cleaning, but Horsley's illustrations present it as a far more pronounced obstacle. Such liberties aside, the success of Horsley's survey can be gauged from later antiquaries not seeing the need to attempt a new synthesis.[26] The potential of illustrations was demonstrated again in 1741, when Susanna Maria's diggings in Castlesteads bathhouse resulted in the first diagram of an excavated Wall structure.[27] Four years later, though, the 1745 Jacobite uprising brought the Wall's ancient purpose to the fore once more – with disastrous consequences.

The union between England and Scotland had made some view Hadrian's Wall as an irrelevance, or even an impediment to a healthy relationship between the two countries. One anonymous pamphlet released in 1708 argued that talk of 'the Picts-Wall . . . must be quite obliterated, in order that Great Britain may enjoy an undisturb'd UNION'.[28] Ironically, it was a violent disturbance in the union that took this notion of obliteration one step farther. Jacobite forces loyal to Charles Edward Stewart captured Carlisle in 1745, but were repulsed from Newcastle. When British units under General Wade sought to counterattack from Newcastle, they were thwarted by winter weather rendering the roads impassable beyond Hexham. Wise after the event, one Cumberland antiquary wrote that using the rivers Tyne and Eden alongside garrisons at Newcastle and Carlisle, together with about 6,000–7,000 troops between Hexham and Brampton, should have been sufficient to deny the Jacobites' passage.[29] Although the troop numbers are generous, in other regards this resembles a reprise of what the Romans seemingly

FIGURE 51 *The B6318, running directly over the Wall curtain as it approaches Eppies Hill.*

attempted with the Stanegate system. Another antiquary declared himself vindicated: John Warburton. He claimed that his earlier Wall map was intended to persuade the authorities to refurbish the Roman road and thereby ensure that modern military manoeuvring could be conducted unfettered. After the Carlisle debacle, Warburton's case seemed unanswerable. Sadly, rather than renewing the Stanegate, the authorities elected to build a new Military Road. For much of the 40km stretch west of Newcastle this would be built on and out of the Wall curtain. It is now the B6318 (Figs. 30 and 51).

Some have argued that the new road was a good thing, protecting underlying stretches of the Wall from later ploughing. At the time, however, Stukeley was horrified, and petitioned a royal contact to try and have the road rerouted, but it was to no avail.[30] It is certainly difficult for anyone who cares about the Wall to read descriptions of long stretches being dismantled and its masonry pulverised into road metalling. Although this demolition was perpetrated without any formal attempt to record what was destroyed, information from various inscribed stones was at least salvaged from the devastation, among them the 158 centurial stone described at the beginning of chapter 5.[31] More losses were to follow. Several private landowners took their lead on how to deal with Roman antiquities from the national authorities and levelled monuments on their own land. Equally, the line of the Wall was now more accessible than it had been since the Roman era. Stone from those elements not buried beneath the road could be easily carted away, while this increased accessibility also encouraged new development. If earlier centuries had seen recycled Roman stone concentrated in ecclesiastical buildings and fortifications, the 18th and 19th centuries brought a democratisation of this resource. Increasing numbers of farms and houses incorporated Wall masonry in their fabric, while in the 1870s part of South Shields fort was put on public display as the People's Roman Remains Park, with surplus stonework fashioned into a giant rockery.[32] In some cases, such material was not even sourced directly from the Roman remains: 19th-century cottages at Thirlwall won their Wall stones from the ruins of the medieval castle.[33]

Once again, Wall scholars must content themselves with important new inscriptions as a consolation prize. Two examples,[34] almost certainly taken from milecastle 38 in the 18th century, proved crucial for the next breakthrough. In 1840, John Hodgson made an incisive case for Hadrian being responsible for the Wall in a 173-page-long footnote within his *History of Northumberland*.[35] His judicious weighing of the evidence, not least milecastles being integral to the Wall and the associated implications of the stones from milecastle 38 naming Hadrian, is held to have 'changed the whole course of events and transformed the study of the Wall'.[36] Just because Hodgson had hit on the truth, though, the case was not closed. Hodgson built a detailed argument supporting his conclusion, but the matter continued to provoke strong passions. The Society of Antiquaries of Newcastle upon Tyne, which had been founded back in 1813, provided a forum where the arguments could be rehearsed. Debate was still ongoing when the Cumberland and Westmorland Antiquarian and Archaeological Society was set up in the west in 1866 – 21 years after Hodgson's death – but by now his supporters held the upper hand. In part this was because of the emergence of persuasive new evidence, but Hodgson also found a vocal and influential champion in the form of John Collingwood Bruce (Fig. 52).[37]

Bruce's involvement with the Wall came about by pure chance. In 1848, he planned to visit Rome, but revolution stalked the streets of numerous European cities, persuading him to look elsewhere for his summer holiday. Denied the opportunity to peruse the vestiges of empire at its former heart, Bruce turned instead to its northern edge. An expedition ensued in June, with Bruce accompanied by his 14-year-old son, the brothers Charles and Henry Richardson – who provided an artistic record of the excursion – and a groom. Along the way, the party were hosted by influential local landowner John Clayton, whose enviable property portfolio ultimately ran to five Roman forts and many miles of the Wall. These were protected from robbing, but sometimes 'restored'. Clayton had been digging in Chesters fort, which was conveniently located in his front garden, since 1843. The two men would go on to have a long association. After Bruce completed his trip, he gave a series of talks in Newcastle. The watercolours he used to illustrate them made an impression on his audience, who were surprised to discover such extraordinary Roman ruins lay close at hand.[38] By popular demand, Bruce led a return visit in 1849. This is now regarded as the first in a series of tours that have become known as the Pilgrimages of Hadrian's Wall. Although Bruce was angling for an encore in the 1850s, the second Pilgrimage did not follow until 1886. Thereafter, a pattern was established that every decade Wall specialists of the day would lead a tour of the Wall. The two

FIGURE 52 *John Collingwood Bruce, leaning on an altar to Jupiter Optimus Maximus, incorporating wheel emblems. Credit: Tyne and Wear Archives and Museums.*

world wars forced intermissions, and after the second the Pilgrimage was brought back in line with the original and held in 1949. Otherwise, the tradition has held and it is believed to be the longest running archaeological tour in the world.[39]

The 1849 pilgrims were able to inspect a recently cleared Wall post, as John Clayton's workmen had exposed the milecastle on Cawfields Crags in 1847–1848 (Fig. 1). Doing so yielded another fragment of a building inscription naming Hadrian, and Clayton observed in a letter to the Newcastle antiquaries that the remains 'tend to confirm the conjecture of our late lamented friend and secretary, the Rev. John Hodgson'. If the work at Cawfields helped nudge one problem towards a resolution, though, it also ushered in a major new conundrum. A postscript succinctly added that 'a massive gateway has been found in the Murus . . . forming the northern wall of the Castellum . . . There is a similar gateway, or entrance, into the Castellum on the south side'.[40] As we have seen, the reason for these paired gateways remains a fruitful source of debate.

Other important developments include Henry MacLauchlan's detailed survey of the Wall between 1852 and 1854, while in 1862 the Ordnance Survey began issuing high-quality maps of the region. Sadly, stone robbing continued, including for field walls enclosing the uplands, but digging into the ruins for the sake of seeing what was there also gradually grew more common. Not everyone encountering their Roman past was gripped by this new spirit of enquiry, and Robert Bell recalled in 1852 how it had been 'the custom of the superstitious on the line of the Wall, in our neighbourhood, either to pound the slabs or altars, bearing inscriptions, into sand for their kitchens, or to place them in the foundations of houses, or stone walls, because they considered them unlucky; calling them witch stones'.[41] Building was not the only business booming in the region. As the industrial revolution gathered steam, so too it presented a new way to burnish Britain's credentials as Rome's heir. As one antiquary put it, 'we might almost imagine . . . that the walls, roads, and bridges of the Romans are in some fashion the parents of the great engineering achievements of the present century'.[42]

Bruce proved the perfect person to communicate the advances of the age and the work of Horsley and Hodgson to a wider audience. After publishing a weighty tome known as *The Roman Wall* in 1851, he distilled its essence into a handy wallet-book, perfect for those wishing to explore the monument. Like the Pilgrimage, this innovation has stood the test of time, and the *Handbook to the Roman Wall* is currently in its 14th edition.[43] Bruce was extraordinarily successful in raising the profile of the Wall's remains, although as he grew older his views hardened and he would brook no disagreement about their interpretation. It was later observed that 'there were "young bloods" at Newcastle only waiting till Dr. Bruce died to awake the slumbering problems of the Wall'.[44] They got their chance in 1892. This has been described as the 'crucial year',[45] though not because of Bruce's passing, but rather J.P. Gibson's excavation of turret 44b that same year (Fig. 3). While digging, he distinguished between different layers of activity preserved within the turret, producing what can be described as the first scientific report of an excavation on the Wall.[46] Further advances followed, with the Turf Wall both predicted and then discovered in 1895, briefly raising the spectre of a stone Severan wall succeeding a turf Hadrianic edifice once more. Digging overseen by pioneers like Francis Haverfield and Elizabeth Hodgson sought to establish what order the various Wall components were built in, while Gibson entered a fruitful partnership with F.G. Simpson. The explosion of information forthcoming since then has been discussed at length in the preceding chapters of this book. We have, like the sky god's wheel, come full circle.

To protect and present

While discussing 20th-century archaeological theorising would be re-treading old ground, it would be remiss not to consider some of the wider issues relating to the monument. Perhaps the most obvious is its preservation. While the Wall had been quarried for building materials since at least the 7th century, a new threat emerged towards the end of the 19th century in the form of large quarries extracting whinstone from the very ground the Wall stood on. A quarry at Walltown destroyed turret 45b soon after it was discovered in 1883, while extraction at Cawfields began to eat away the environs of milecastle 42. Although scheduled ancient monuments had been protected since 1882, this did not extend farther than their physical footprint and took no account of the wider landscape setting. A scheme to open another quarry at Melkridge, south of the Wall, led directly to the 1931 Ancient Monuments Act, gifting ministerial power to implement planning schemes and pay compensation. Straitened public finances in the aftermath of the 1929 Wall Street crash left extraction at the existing quarries underway, but in 1938 the problem came to a head once more, as the Walltown quarry prepared to obliterate turret 45a. Compensation persuaded the company to dig farther east, although this still meant sacrificing a length of curtain. The outbreak of the Second World War focused attention elsewhere, but in 1943, F.G. Simpson alerted the Ministry of Works that a noted viewpoint overlooking milecastle 42 was at risk. Happily, a compromise was thrashed out, involving copious compensation and a scheme to quarry southwards and downwards, thereby protecting the remainder of the Wall.[47]

As tourist numbers grew, bringing an economic dividend for the region, more of the Wall was unearthed for public inspection. Once exposed, the masonry needed to be consolidated – often involving the application of a mortar and stone cap, as well as repointing the facing stones – to protect it from harm inflicted by the weather or over-eager visitors. In the 1960s and 1970s, conservation work saw magnificent stretches of the Wall cleared at sites such as Cawfields, Walltown, and Willowford. Sadly, despite the advances that had occurred in the excavation of archaeological *sites*, the Wall curtain was still seen as just a wall. The soil shrouding it was dug away by Ministry of Works workmen, and there can be no doubt that irreplaceable information went with it. But the loss would have been much worse without the personal interest of Charles Anderson, a Ministry of Works mason who was involved with the Wall for almost four decades. Anderson kept notes and took photographs, creating an invaluable record of his work. He also became captivated by the mysteries of the curtain, noting oddities such as some fallen stones cleared from Willowford being rather larger than those in the standing curtain.[48] Some unwanted tumbled masonry from Walltown found its way into a new structure, when it was used to build the first full-scale reconstruction of the Wall curtain and a turret at Vindolanda in the 1970s (Fig. 53). Elsewhere, surplus stones from an excavation at Housesteads were used to build a bungalow in 1970, while the Wall curtain reconstructed near Wallsend fort in 1997 also incorporates some genuine Roman facing stones.

One instruction issued to the ministry workmen engaged at Cawfields was that only definite Roman material should be consolidated. Where there was any doubt, the remains were to be discretely lowered.[49] This brings us to a crucial point concerning how the Wall archaeology is presented to the public. As we have seen over the last two chapters, activity in the region – or

FIGURE 53 *Reconstructed curtain and turret at Vindolanda.*

even specifically on the Wall – did not suddenly cease at the end of the Roman period, leaving unsullied ruins for future generations to enjoy. Quite apart from stone robbing, people lived or worked in the shell of many former military posts. There is the apparent royal activity at South Shields, the possible monasteries at Newcastle and Bewcastle, farms in many forts or milecastles, and even a milking shed in milecastle 39. Visitors will find fewer traces of such activity today. Part of a bastle house still projects from the south gate of Housesteads, a shieling remains nestled in the curtain just east of milecastle 39, and farm buildings still stand in Birdoswald, for instance, but traces of numerous post-Roman structures have been removed. For many years, even the Roman era was routinely rewound, to present the public with traces of what seemed to be the original workmanship. As the Roman Wall became specifically associated with Hadrian, so too visitors expected to encounter *his* Wall. The result is an incongruous hybrid, as Wall sites are simultaneously presented in a semi-original yet ruined state.[50] Naturally, at no point prior to these sites being prepared for tourist display did they ever look anything like this. Still, the result is no odder than any other reimagining of the region's imperial legacy to meet contemporary needs over the 1,600 or so years since the end of Roman Britain.

The international value of Hadrian's Wall was recognised in 1987, when it became a UNESCO World Heritage Site (WHS). Since then, it has become a component of a pioneering transnational WHS, known as the Frontiers of the Roman Empire. This came into being when the Upper German and Raetian Limes achieved WHS status in 2005, and it is hoped that the remainder of the Roman frontier systems operating between roughly 100 and 200 will ultimately follow suit. In terms of heritage, then, Hadrian's Wall is being set in its international context once more. Greater connectivity along the line of the Wall was also achieved when the Hadrian's Wall Path National Trail opened in 2003. Although the National Trail deviates from the course of the Wall in places, it has created an environment in which it can be experienced as a continuous monument, rather than a succession of individual museums and heritage sites that visitors dip in and out of. This new way to enjoy the Wall has proven popular, which in many ways makes for a fitting conclusion to a chapter that has demonstrated how much has been gained from investigating its physical remains. In areas with sensitive archaeology this means that great care must be taken, though, if we are to avoid loving the Wall to death.[51]

The Age of Wall wanderers

The centuries following the publication of Camden's *Britannia* have seen an explosion of knowledge about the chronology of Hadrian's Wall, and perhaps more importantly the different sorts of lives lived in its shadow. On one level, Camden's treatment of the Wall stands as a testimony to the futility of trying to reconcile ancient written sources in an evidence vacuum. On another, Camden signposted the way forwards, by considering the wider network of Roman frontiers, evidence freshly won from the monument, and the interaction between the Wall and its landscape. Subsequent scholars demonstrated ever more clearly just how much could be learned from increasingly close scrutiny of the archaeology. This was rewarded with an explosion of information over the course of the 20th century. Comparing knowledge in Camden's day with what is available now presents the greatest possible tribute to the innovative thinkers and workers that have probed the mysteries of the Wall. In the 19th century, Bruce demonstrated the merit of making the results available to the widest possible audience. Today, visitors can engage with the Wall in ever more ways, be it by visiting sites and museums, walking the National Trail, participating in archaeological fieldwork, delving into the literature, or taking Newcastle University's online course. The Wall has transitioned from a largely closed military zone to a mass tourist destination, without ever losing its relevance.

9

Romancing the Stones

A Media *Murus*

The preceding chapters have considered the physical impact of the Wall on its hinterland, alongside wider attempts to fashion political identities. But there is another strand to the Wall's legacy: its cultural impact. One commentator has observed that 'As far as I know, the wall does not have a great literary history, in that few poets, playwrights and dramatists have been moved to embrace it in their work'.[1] Despite this downbeat assessment, the monument has inspired creative endeavours for as long as it has existed. These range from gaudy ancient trinkets to the modern pop-culture behemoth that is *Game of Thrones*. While musing about the Wall's cultural contribution would have been a digression from the central thrust of the previous chapters, this aspect is key to understanding how the monument has been perceived over time. Comprehensive treatment is impossible here, so instead a selection of examples will be examined to illustrate how the monument has been presented, and what sort of messages it is used to convey.

Vallum visions

We have already seen that the Wall itself was a vehicle for artistry in the Roman period. Phalli, wheel emblems, Celtic heads, and other images were probably intended as a form of magical protection (Figs. 9 and 10). But the Wall was not just a canvas to adorn with imagery, and the monument was almost certainly inspiring art in the Roman period. Given that some soldiers seem to have venerated a Genius of the Wall, it is entirely possible that one or more of the fragmentary sculptures found in the frontier zone depicting what seem to be genii wearing mural crowns sought to personify the Wall's guardian spirit.[2] Indeed, even in the narrow genre of genii, art can tell its own story. A statuette from Carlisle dedicated to the genius of a military century wears a mural crown, and bears an unusual cornucopia. Rather than overflowing with fruits and symbolising plenty, it appears to hold a pine cone, symbolising mourning and death. Both the mural crown and pine cone are seen as oddities,[3] but walls and mortality could well have been a particular preoccupation on the frontier, especially in its western sector.

A more literal representation of the Wall may grace a group of *paterae* or skillets that carry text naming some western-sector forts. The most famous example is the Rudge Cup, which was found not on Hadrian's Wall, but deposited in a well in Wiltshire in 1725. This receptacle originally bore enamelled decoration resembling a stylised wall, with crenelated turrets rising at regular intervals (Fig. 54). It was once described as 'the only contemporary representation of the Roman Wall known to have survived to our times'.[4] As both the 'turrets' and the gaps between them also feature crescent emblems, it has been wondered if the resemblance to a wall is coincidental. Even so, the regularly spaced Wall turrets must have been a distinctive feature, making it a plausible motif for vessels commemorating the frontier. Perceptions of the towers that proliferated in Northern Ireland during the Troubles are a reminder of the powerful psychological impact such structures can have (see p. 16).

A comparable patera was found at Amiens in 1949, while the incomplete Hildburgh Fragment, reportedly purchased in Barcelona, and a piece from Bowers Gifford and North Benfleet display a similar decorative scheme. The Ilam Pan offers a variant by naming forts and probably also the Wall,

FIGURE 54 *The Rudge Cup. From Horsley 1732.*

but featuring flamboyant enamelled Celtic-style decoration (Fig. 19). As enamelling is a particularly British trait, these cups were conceivably produced by a workshop combining local and Roman artistic traditions. Only Bowness-on-Solway, Stanwix, and Castlesteads forts are named on all three pans bearing complete or near-complete texts, which might indicate the workshop lay nearby one of them. If the Ilam Pan does refer to the *vallum Aelium*, it suggests manufacture in the Hadrianic period, as the barrier was seemingly more commonly known as simply 'the vallum' in later eras.[5] These vessels are generally seen as souvenirs, indicating that from the very beginning 'Hadrian's Wall was something special, a place to remember'.[6]

Following the Roman period, the earliest surviving representations of the Wall have already been discussed, as they comprise either lines on maps or attempts to convey the contemporary state of the ruins. One map does, though, feature a charming touch. It was drafted by William Hoyle to accompany a two-volume series of poems published by Michael Drayton in 1622 and called *Poly-Olbion*. This compendium features a personification of the 'Pictswall', who gives an account of his life, which involves setting several of Camden's assertions to verse, including the apocryphal speaking tube. Hoyle's map features personifications of rivers, hills, and towns, as well as what seems to be Pictswall himself, idling beside the *murus*.[7] Showing the Wall in this fashion mirrors the Roman belief in its spiritual identity, while emphasising its enduring status as a major landscape feature.

A hint of magic in the landscape is also apparent in some of the local folklore. Happily, John Collingwood Bruce did not share Camden's aversion to such material, and sprinkled it through the first edition of what would become the *Handbook to the Roman Wall*. There, alongside descriptions of the archaeology, readers could enjoy an account of a shepherd stumbling upon King Arthur's spellbound court, and a haunted house.[8] In the latter case, Bruce assures readers that shepherds still believe the spirits of murder victims are manifest as flickering lights. Such tales of supernatural happenings in wild country neatly counterpoint the increasingly scientific approach to the archaeology. The Wall has inspired poetry as well as ghost stories, and Bruce also included Sir Walter Scott's 1797 verse 'To a Lady, With Flowers from a Roman Wall', which contrasts the romantic ruin with its former status as a place of conflict. To achieve this, Scott draws a parallel between the flowers clinging to the ruins, and the warriors he imagined scaling the curtain:

> Take these flowers, which purple waving,
> On the ruined rampart grew,
> Where, the sons of freedom braving
> Rome's imperial standards flew
>
> Warriors from the breach of danger
> Pluck no longer laurels there:

They but yield the passing stranger
Wild-flower wreaths for beauty's hair.

While Scott conjures a beguiling sense of nature conquering a crumbled empire, the 18th and 19th centuries brought increasing interest in reimagining the Wall's original state. An early example occurs on Jan Goeree's 1707 engraving (Fig. 55), which appears as a frontispiece in *Les Delices de la Grand' Bretagne et de l'Irlande.*[9] This rendering takes several liberties with reality, by showing what seems to be an ashlar curtain behind which loom mountains that are forbidding and fictitious in equal measure. While such dramatic contrivances have proved popular, the false ashlar render found at Denton suggests the Romans themselves were not above trying to make the curtain more visually imposing (see p. 63).

In 1857, William Bell Scott completed a remarkable painting known as *Building of the Roman Wall* (Fig. 56). It is the first of eight compositions at Wallington Hall in Northumberland, and was commissioned by Sir Walter and Lady Paulina Trevelyan to illustrate the region's history from the Roman era to the Industrial Revolution. The painting helpfully specifies that 'The Romans cause a Wall to be built for the protection of the south'. On this occasion the landscape is recognisable, with Crag Lough and then Winshields

FIGURE 55 *Goeree's 1707 engraving. Courtesy of Richard Hingley and Christina Unwin.*

Crags visible in the background. The Wall in the foreground is out of place, though, and based on a stretch at Walltown, about 10km to the west. Scott shows the Wall simultaneously under construction and attack, with a small band of northern archers seeking to impede progress. The construction team reflects knowledge of the disparate origins of the Roman army. One legionary is seemingly of African descent, while an auxiliary soldier sports a Phrygian cap, signifying eastern origins. Some Britons aid the troops in their endeavours, but one group of locals is lazing about having a brew-up as a legionary centurion gesticulates at them. In a nod to contemporary Wall studies, John Collingwood Bruce has leant his features to an auxiliary soldier, while it is possible that the centurion's face belonged to local landowner and murophile John Clayton. A subtext of civilisation and barbarism is written in the heavens, with blue sky breaking through to the south, while storm clouds gather in the north.[10]

FIGURE 56 *William Bell Scott's* Building of Hadrian's Wall. *Credit: The National Trust.*

This powerful composition seems to tap into the zeitgeist of contemporary British experiences of imperialism. Completion of the painting in June 1857 coincided with the early stages of a rebellion in India, which broke out the preceding month. Scott's patrons were personally touched by the violence, as the daughter of Sir Walter's sister was among the civilians slaughtered at Cawnpore. As Richard Hingley has pointed out, in December 1857 a newspaper editorial contrasted British and Roman policy, viewing the latter's practice of sending soldiers recruited from one province to serve in others as an enlightened measure ensuring that security did not depend on soldiers being willing to kill their relatives and countrymen. While Scott's painting cannot be a reaction to events playing out as it neared completion, his emphasis on soldiers drawn from many origins collaborating to protect southern Britain perfectly matches these contemporary concerns. In that regard, *Building of the Roman Wall* could be taken as a recipe for how an empire can prevail against local resistance and indolence.[11]

Imperial undercurrents are also discernible in another celebrated Wall-inspired work. Rudyard Kipling's 1906 *Puck of Pook's Hill* is a collection of children's tales that probably still furnishes the Wall's most famous foray into fiction – at least in a recognisably 'real-world' form. The story revolves around two children that inadvertently summon a magical being – Puck – who introduces them to a succession of historical characters, including a centurion in the Roman army by the name of Parnesius, who was raised on the Isle of Wight. Kipling was born in India, and so a child of the Empire. His experiences seem to have coloured his account of Hadrian's Wall – a monument that he also had first-hand experience of – and his description of the Roman frontier zone has been characterised as 'an analogy for the British imperial North-West frontier in India and for concerns about the potential state of decadence in the British empire'.[12] Despite, or perhaps because of this, Kipling manages to evoke a convincing – if not archaeologically accurate – frontier zone: 'Just when you think you are at the world's end, you see smoke from East to West as far as the eye can turn, and then, under it, also as far as the eye can stretch, houses and temples, shops and theatres, barracks and granaries, trickling along like dice behind – always behind – one long, low, rising and falling and hiding and showing line of towers. And that is the Wall!'[13] Kipling's focus on the towers when introducing the barrier offers a potential literary equivalent to the Rudge Cup decoration.

Puck of Pook's Hill features numerous elements that have become tropes of Wall fiction. Early on in the narrative, Parnesius recalls his father stating that 'To [save Britain], we must keep the Painted People back ... if your heart is set on service, your place is among men on the Wall'.[14] The implication is clear: the Wall stands between civilisation and chaos. To reach the Wall, Parnesius undertook a 20-day march from Pevensey on the south coast of Britain. Although Kipling describes the landscape becoming wilder as the soldiers progress north, the Wall is still cast as a boundary between two ways of being: 'There are no adventures South the Wall', Parnesius remarks at one point.[15] But despite this apparent success in creating order, Kipling provides a nuanced picture of the military presence, describing the town shadowing the Wall as 'long like a snake, and wicked like a snake', while most of the officers were posted there as penance for past transgressions.[16] Kipling slightly exaggerates the scale of the Wall, giving it a height of 30 feet,[17] but an accompanying drawing by H.R. Millar goes farther, showing a soaring edifice topped by cranes or catapults (Fig. 57). The multi-cultural nature of the Wall community is also noted, while a more

'And that is the Wall!'

FIGURE 57 *H.R. Millar's take on the Wall in* Puck of Pook's Hill. *From Kipling 1906.*

unusual touch is a sympathetic portrayal of the Picts, who are described as caught between the Romans to the south and 'Winged Hats' to the north. Parnesius' presence is set in the 4th century, and he is ultimately tasked with holding the Wall while Magnus Maximus siphons off soldiers to fight on the Continent. Sure enough, the fate of civilisation soon hangs in the balance.

There are many more examples of the Wall being portrayed as distant and/or exotic. Both ideas had already been employed in an imaginary journey to the frontier presented alongside other meditations on the murus in R.H. Forster's *The Amateur Antiquary*, published in 1899. A similar scenario plays out in Rosemary Sutcliff's 1954 novel *The Eagle of the Ninth*, when the protagonists travel north to encounter both the Wall, and a ribbon of 'wine shops, temples, married quarters, and markets' along the road running parallel to it. Once again, the Wall is presented as a true barrier: 'This was the great Wall of Hadrian, shutting out the menace of the north'.[18] Such a role is made even more explicit in the 2011 cinematic adaptation, which features the line 'No Roman can survive north of the Wall alone'. Indeed, the film follows in the footsteps of the 1707 engraving by briefly showing imaginary mountains looming beyond the barrier, although this time to the north.

Even terse allusions to the barrier can convey this sense of a distant, multicultural place. A collection of Miss Marple stories published by Agatha Christie in 1932 as *The Thirteen Problems*, for example, features a mystery with a decidedly archaeological flavour. It is set on the edge of Dartmoor, and involves a grove that one character believes was dedicated to the Phoenician goddess Astarte. By way of explanation he states simply that 'There is, I believe, one known Grove of Astarte in this country – in the North on the Wall'.[19] W.H. Auden explored the separation that went hand in hand with such cultural mixing in 'Roman Wall Blues', a 1937 poem that features the bleak line 'I'm a Wall soldier, I don't know why'. The 2017 science-fiction graphic novel *Hadrian's Wall* also slots into this tradition. There, Hadrian's Wall is the name of a survey ship that is manned by a multinational crew and orbiting a remote planet. This heavenly body is incapable of sustaining human life, but harbours a deadly secret that seeming leaves Hadrian's Wall as the last hope to save civilisation on Earth. In a subversive twist, though, the crew's sacrifices are undercut by a discovery that the nature of this threat has been deliberately exaggerated.[20]

When it comes to fantasy re-imaginings, the great ice edifice protecting Westeros in *Game of Thrones* is currently the most renowned of the Wall's alter egos. George R.R. Martin's inspiration for this reportedly came from a 1981 trip to the central sector of the Wall at Housesteads.[21] At first sight, the Westeros wall is a far cry from its real-world counterpart, as it comprises an artificial ice barrier standing almost 700ft high, and crowned with cranes and catapults. Yet many of the key themes of Wall fiction are present, including Jon Snow and Tyrion Lannister's lengthy journey to reach the barrier. There, they find the Night's Watch, a band of desperados and misfits tasked with shielding the realm from northern terrors. We are told the wall itself exudes a sense of *'This is the end of the world'*.[22] Dust has coated the ice over the centuries, leaving it a pale grey colour that sparkles in the sunlight, not unlike some stretches of the real Wall. The notion of a dizzyingly high curtain topped with strange contraptions shares similarities with H.R. Millar's vision of the Wall in *Puck of Pook's Hill*. Martin's wall is already ancient when the events of *Game of Thrones* play out, making its nearest real-world equivalent the medieval night watch mounted on stretches of the ruined Roman works (see p. 138). We learn that the Westeros wall once comprised nineteen strongholds. Just three are still held, and even there the garrisons have been gravely reduced in strength. Just like the medieval Wall, then, its fictional counterpart seems to be losing its original purpose. One remarkable aspect of *Game of Thrones* is its impact on how some visitors experience Hadrian's Wall. Videos of people swearing the fictional Night's Watch oath amid the real Roman archaeology have been posted on YouTube,[23] while English Heritage deployed 'Watchers on the Wall' at four of its sites in 2019, to answer visitor queries as the final season of the HBO drama aired.

Given the fictional emphasis on the Wall being experienced as part of a journey, it is perhaps unsurprising that the monument has spawned various factual travelogues. The first was penned by William Hutton, who undertook a journey of 601 miles on foot at the age of 78 in 1801. Given this commitment, he was understandably contemptuous to realise that 'Many had written upon the subject; but I could discover, that very few had even seen it'. The result is part observation, part anecdote. While we cannot naysay Hutton's boast that he was perhaps 'the first man that travelled the whole length of the Wall' since the Roman period, he was off the mark to add that he would probably be 'the last that will attempt it'.[24] The National Trail has catered for this widespread desire since 2003, but the Wall is also a highlight of Britain's first official long-distance footpath: the Pennine Way, which opened in 1965. Indeed, when renowned fellwalker Alfred Wainwright critiqued its course, he felt that continuing the path into the Cheviots missed a trick by eschewing 'as its thrilling finale, the exciting arrival at the Roman Wall'. Wainwright also wryly describes 'an affliction known as Wall Fever, which besets visitors to these old fortifications and results in enthusiasm and imagination, and a passionate urge to discover more'.[25] Hunter Davies' *A Walk Along the Wall* was published in 1974, and excelled at setting the Wall within the living, breathing communities existing along its length. A more recent example catered to those communities, by documenting the exploits of a troupe of actors walking the Wall, pausing to perform a play at nine venues along its course.[26] The play itself concerned a (fictional) attempt to install a monorail and transform the Wall into a theme park, presenting a satirical take on how new generations keep the past relevant.

Meditations on how the past rubs along with the present are a theme of several recent works. *All Along The Wall*, for instance, is a 75-minute performance created by eight songwriters, poets, and musicians in 2010. Their work has been released as a live album, and grapples with the Wall's sometimes conflicting modern resonances. Great fun is had updating Roman-style blessings and curses, and probing Hadrian's motivation. Pride in an internationally famous monument is evident, and the performance is also notable for bringing female perspectives to the fore, with the song *Dear Friend* written from the viewpoint of a soldier's daughter, who laments 'I have nothing in common with those fighting men'. The group do not shy away from delving into the barrier's darker side, by tackling the misery that walls have left in their wake through the ages. Questions about where our appetite for division will end also feature in a recent poem by Daljit Nagra entitled 'Hadrian's Wall', which ponders whether the barrier's modern heirs can be found in passports and the 'Great Firewall of China'.[27]

Poking fun at attempts to interpret the Wall or using it to satirise political projects present more offshoots from its study. In 1869, a cartoon in *Punch* lampooned members of a 'learned society' inspecting 'a Roman Wall' that lies imperceptible amid a cultivated field.[28] Just over a century later, Scott Dobson took aim at 'Messrs. Horsley, Stukely, Brand, Hutton, Lingard, Hodgson, Bruce – and in the 20th century particularly, Professors Richmond and Birley'. He wrote 'Nice lads all of them – but far too keen on the Romans', before laying out a spoof alternative history for what he called the Geordie Wall.[29] The 2019 Pilgrimage embraced the whimsical side of Wall studies with the *Borderline Funny* exhibition, which showcased a collection of cartoons casting an irreverent eye over the frontier. This inspired a strip in the children's comic *The Beano*, which reimagined longstanding adversaries Dennis the Menace and Walter in a Roman setting.[30] A problem from more recent centuries was projected back in time with them, when Hadrian's tribune Walterus discovered that work on the Wall was behind schedule because a local Celt was pilfering the masonry to build his house.[31] Rather more barbed gags have been generated by the Wall's status as a shorthand, albeit inaccurate, for the Anglo-Scottish border. During Scottish devolution in 1997 and especially the 2014 independence referendum campaign, a rich seam of satire imagined the Wall's reinstatement. When it comes to using the Wall as a vehicle to express dissent, though, once again the Romans got there first. A graffito cut into a quarry face reveals one worker's resistance to some or other enterprise by stating simply 'I, Daminius, did not want (to do it)'.[32]

Art imitates life?

Considering the Wall's cultural life reveals two motivations for its presence. The first is the Wall's power to convey messages because of its Roman origins, the second is because it was considered notable or dramatic in its own right. An apparent emphasis on regularly spaced turrets on the Rudge Cup, for instance, could be a visual metaphor for the Wall imposing order.

William Bell Scott, by contrast, seemingly saw the diversity of manpower the Empire mobilised as the key to imperial stability. When it comes to fiction, the tradition of presenting the Wall as a distant bulwark against the forces of chaos echoes the words of ancient authors. While Procopius' 6th-century description of a realm beyond the Wall wreathed in 'pestilential air' strains credibility, this broad scenario is integral to the plot of the graphic novel envisioning Hadrian's Wall as an orbiting spaceship. But just as Classical authors could take liberties with reality, so too we can question the authenticity of some common features of the Wall's fictional reimagining. Rather than it being manned by the dregs of the army, for instance, a personal acquaintance of Hadrian served as a commander at Maryport fort, and there is no sign that a Wall posting proved a barrier to a successful career. As for the veracity or otherwise of the greatest Wall trope, we have already seen that the true threat posed by Rome's northern foes remains the stuff of lively scholarly debate.

10

Long Division

The Many Lives of the Wall

Following a book-length account of how successive generations found ways to make the Wall relevant to them, a cynic might feel it is little wonder that this volume has emphasised guerrilla warfare and the barrier's impact on local communities. After all, the first two decades of the 21st century have laid bare the devastating impact irregular resistance can have on technologically advanced armies, while also bringing more than their fair share of anxiety about changing border controls. From that, it is only a short step to suspecting that rather than offering objective assessments of the evidence, the theories advanced here are simply the latest example of present concerns being projected onto the Roman past. On that score, it will surprise no one to learn that this is not what I think has happened. But it does seem appropriate to add that the first steps towards the interpretation of Hadrian's Wall offered here were taken in a University of Nottingham undergraduate dissertation, which was submitted in the summer of 2000: long before counterinsurgency and borders leapt up the news agenda. Hadrian's Wall would also be far from unique as a massive military response to nimble tormenters. A recent project dedicated to Lawrence of Arabia and the Great Arab Revolt in the First World War, for instance, contrasted the trench systems and strongpoints constructed by regular Ottoman soldiers, with the scatter of British-issued munitions left by their agile opponents: 'Asymmetrical warfare seems to leave asymmetrical imprints: a highly visible regular army confronting a shadowy, flitting, almost invisible enemy'.[1]

Our inability to see an obvious enemy poses perhaps the greatest challenge to interpreting Hadrian's Wall. While the 19th-century discovery of regular gateways in the milecastles initiated a progressive scholarly downgrading of the Wall's military capabilities, which reached its epitome with John Mann's invocation of imperial rhetoric to explain the monument,[2] this seems jarring when considering its peers. If all that was needed was a boundary marker, why not construct a palisade akin to that in Upper Germany? And if the Wall was essentially Hadrian's vanity project, why did so many subsequent emperors keep it manned and maintained? The sustained finessing of the Wall concept during the construction phase was surely geared towards making the system more efficient, but if so, it must have been doing something tangible. Measures that make most sense as a means to clamp down on small-scale pedestrian movement imply that restricting civilian movement was an important part of the Wall's remit. Yet as initially conceived, the scale of the barrier and the quantity of soldiers manning it seem simultaneously excessive to tackle everyday mobility or raiding, and inadequate to repel or even seriously impede a full-blown army. A reasonable inference, then, is that the original anticipated threat lay somewhere between these two extremes. Ancient accounts of military activity in Britain testify to a significant proportion of the fighting involving what is now often called guerrilla warfare, while descriptions of enemies being dispersed or driven back in the vicinity of Hadrian's Wall suggest foes the army struggled to bring to battle and decisively defeat. All of this fits with the supposition that Hadrian's Wall formed part of a low-intensity warfare strategy. As Breeze and Dobson observed, the Wall makes sense as a means to control population movement, but this should be viewed against the backdrop of a largely closed barrier, as an increasing number of scholars suspect.[3]

Despite the important recent work on local communities settled on the Tyne-Solway isthmus, these groups have yet to permeate frontier literature as much as they should. If resistance to the military occupation did take the form of guerrilla warfare, then more modern analogies consistently point to local populations being instrumental to understanding the conflict. Certainly, the risk that the military build-up on the isthmus posed to pre-existing social structures was appreciable. After all, the mere existence of such a force meant that Roman generals rather than local leaders now held the regional balance of power. Equally, mobility would have underpinned many aspects of everyday life for local communities, be it to partake in markets, trade, religious ceremonies, and seasonal gatherings, or because of transhumance. In the world before the Wall, the most notable features of the isthmus were surely watery, given its abundance of rivers, springs, and bogs. Such elements could be viewed as sacred, divine, or perhaps even revered for their healing properties, making access a matter of communal welfare. Given the regional web of connectivity that must have existed, there can be little doubt that establishing the Stanegate system and then – especially – driving a barrier through this landscape risked severing a complex political, working, and religious landscape.

It remains speculative to link the commencement of Wall building with a spike in resistance that prompted both an *expeditio* and the fort decision, not least because it is unclear if work began before or during 122. Either way, there are signs that the army manipulated the construction programme to bring key routeways under control early in the process. This policy is clearest in the natural junction presented by the Tipalt-Irthing gap. Its military significance can be gauged from the environs receiving special attention from the early 2nd century through to the 4th century, while a Roman victory monument seemingly also graced the gap. If the signs that the milecastle gateways were primarily intended for military use are reliable, then it seems inevitable the Wall inflicted major disruption on local interests. Despite this, the overall barrier concept is unlikely to amount to a total block on movement, as north–south passage was presumably still permitted at the major highway crossings. Even so, the sizeable detours required to reach these routes, coupled with the probability that customs dues were levied, may well have made this option impractical for many. The apparent collapse of a settled farming community north of the Wall on the Northumberland coastal plain at around the time the frontier became operational certainly indicates that the new measures had an impact on local groups. If so, the question really boils down to whether these communities appreciated the risk and acted to try and save their way of life, or simply did nothing as it was extinguished.

That some groups chose violence fits with the abrupt decision to add forts and the Vallum to the Wall. The *auxilia* manning these new Wall forts created an unprecedented population density in the region, while also implanting both Roman and more diverse modes of expression. In terms of cult worship, evidence for Classical-style activity appears most common, but other rites were practised. We have concentrated on Celtic influences here, and the gods, superstitions, and traditions most easily paralleled on the Continent, especially Gaul and Germany, suggest that recruits from these regions or their descendants persisted with some old-country traditions. Local influences seem to enter the mix as well, perhaps best exemplified by a stone disc with good parallels in the Iron Age north bearing an apparent Celtic-style wheel emblem, and being deposited in a Roman Wall turret. There are also ambiguous but consistent signs that rituals involving real or substitute heads and – very occasionally – human sacrifice were perpetrated by soldiers or civilians living in Roman posts or settlements. These latter acts may reflect responses to moments of acute stress.

Here, then, lies our answer to what the Wall did. It simultaneously divided some people – specifically those living to the north and south of the Tyne-Solway isthmus – and brought others together. This latter category comprises not only Roman soldiers, dependents, and hangers on, but also the local population south of the Wall. We have seen that some rural settlements display heightened signs of prosperity as the 2nd century wore on, while the widespread presence or imitation of Roman-style pottery implies some kind of relationship between conquerors and conquered. This is also a reminder that local responses to the Roman presence must have varied, seemingly ranging all the way from resistance to collaboration. Such interactions may even have influenced how the Wall fabric evolved. Levelling most turrets, for instance, would have degraded the army's ability to prevent low-level infiltration, while some other components of the Wall system seem to have been hardened. Such measures could signal that a Hadrianic focus on clamping down on small-scale incursions across the curtain and hit-and-run attacks on soldiers while they were vulnerable had graduated to a situation where direct attacks on military posts were feared. As this potentially follows the founding of towns at Carlisle and Corbridge, and therefore enhanced autonomy for local groups, it is possible that the Severan overhaul reflects a reduction in resistance within the Roman province. If the anticipated threat now lay primarily to the north, it would fit with a willingness to build extramural settlement over back-filled portions of the Vallum. The signs are, then, that the Wall really was a catalyst for division, with lifestyles in its northern and southern hinterlands propelled onto different trajectories.

It may be that Severus' fateful war successfully degraded this northern threat, as the subsequent decades are when the Wall concept can stake the strongest claim to paying off. This is the period when it seems most likely that a handful of buildings were constructed directly beyond the barrier at forts such as Wallsend and Birdoswald, suggesting a degree of stability and even optimism. While the bulk of extramural settlements were conspicuously concentrated to the south of the curtain, their growth and vitality – with at least some achieving *vicus* status and a measure of self-governance – showcases the military's contribution as an economic driver, as well as an instrument of force. But it was not to last. Maybe the dwindling size of military units wrecked the economic basis of the military *vici*, or maybe plague took a terrible toll of these frontier communities. Whatever the explanation, the extramural settlements were abandoned and their moment in the sun had passed by the end of the 3rd century. Whether forts now took on some of the former functions of the extramural settlements, and if soldiers' dependents joined them within the ramparts remains contested. Perhaps the situation varied from fort to fort, but there does seem good evidence that during the 4th century the number of women within Vindolanda increased markedly.

Change is certainly a feature of the 4th-century Wall zone. As supply lines that once reached the Continent or southern Britain contracted, so too there was an increasing emphasis on sourcing material locally. These new procurement patterns came with different processing needs, and in places 2nd-century power architecture was repurposed for metalworking and butchery, or even cannibalised to shore up essential structures. Manpower was probably also secured more locally, with soldiering becoming a hereditary profession. In the southern hinterland of the Wall, at least some rural settlements with prehistoric origins survived into the 4th century, while produce from Newcastle indicates that traditional pottery was still being made, and indeed sold at the fort market. It would be fair to observe that there is currently less sign of rural settlement continuity in the Wall's immediate northern environs. Time was also being called on the temples and shrines of the old gods, many of which show signs of abandonment before the end of the 4th century, as Christianity became ascendant. Meanwhile, the fort garrisons were seemingly gradually evolving from military units with a hierarchy stretching to a distant emperor into warbands led by resident chieftains. Excavations at Birdoswald certainly indicate that when the curtain fell on Roman Britain, the soldiers stayed put.

The era previously known as the Dark Ages is also the time when the fate of Hadrian's Wall, and the descendent communities within the forts, is most mysterious. While innovative research has shown that continuity of activity initially seems to be the rule, rather than the exception, the relative paucity of finds and difficulty dating structures leaves the nature of this existence somewhat shadowy. Gildas certainly claimed that some of the forts were held by Britons – perhaps his take on homegrown 'Roman' soldiers – beyond the end of imperial control. If any of the Wall forts were still occupied by descendent communities when Gildas was writing, probably in the early to mid 6th century, he glossed over this point. Certainly, evidence of occupation continuity becomes scarcer over time, and it seems likely that different forts experienced very different fates. South Shields perhaps became a royal possession, while some forts probably housed monasteries, with others robbed of their masonry to build religious houses. This appropriation can be seen as the first concerted attempt to exploit the Wall to cast new powers as the heirs of Rome, in this case both the Anglo-Saxon kings of Northumbria and the Church of Rome in England. It is a claim staked with considerable sophistication by Bede in his *Ecclesiastical History*.

The birth of serious antiquarian enquiry into the monument in the 16th century is seen as setting its study on a more scientific footing. While subsequent centuries saw the emergence of more rigorous methods, it is ironic that the great problem of this era – who built the Wall? – which remained a bone of contention until well into the 19th century, could have been hastened towards resolution by the work of Boece and Vergil. That their opinion was regarded as suspect emphasises the ownership that English scholars took of the monument. While Camden reassured his readers that he had stripped away the fanciful tales concerning the Wall, he developed a subtext setting up the English as the inheritors of Roman civilisation, in pointed contrast to their northern rivals. Gordon touched a nerve when he inverted this narrative with his 18th-century claim that the scale of the Wall was a monument to Scottish valour. While the arrival of more sophisticated recording methods in the late 19th and early 20th century means that we can now interrogate the archaeology reasonably independently of earlier generations' preconceptions about what it all meant, a sense of kinship with Rome can perhaps still be found in England. Given that the education system presents the Romans as 'rather like us',[4] this is hardly surprising.

A degree of tunnel vision is also discernible in many of the Wall's forays into culture. Some of the most celebrated examples were used as vehicles to explore aspects of Britain's own empire, especially William Bell Scott's painting *Building of the Roman Wall*, and Kipling's *Puck of Pook's Hill*. In both cases, the lineage of modern English civilisation was traced to that imported by the Romans. Many of the Wall's appearances in art, literature, and popular culture display Roman sympathies, with the men manning the Wall and their burden as guardians of civilisation taking the limelight. Sir Walter Scott's poem 'To a Lady, With Flowers from a Roman Wall' provides a classic counter-perspective. Such alternative viewpoints, though, typically align with northern enemies rather than occupied local farming communities. We archaeologists cannot be too complacent here. With the exception of pioneers like George Jobey, early antiquarian and archaeological investigation persistently prioritised the Roman remains. This bias is still apparent in the selection of heritage sites presented to visitors along the Wall corridor. Even the fresh information from local rural settlements revolutionising our knowledge of the frontier zone is primarily a product of changes to national planning guidelines, rather than a conscious determination to look farther afield. All the signs are that the solution to the mystery of what Hadrian's Wall did turns on an understanding of local and incoming communities. It is high time that the stories of both conquerors and conquered are embraced as essential to Wall narratives.

NOTES

Chapter 1

1　Tomlin 2018, 102.
2　Breeze 2019a, xvii–xviii.
3　Horsley 1732, 116, 121.
4　Breeze 2014a, 111.
5　Bruce 1867, 73–74.
6　Forster 1899, 11–12.
7　Collingwood 1921a, 4.
8　Breeze and Dobson 1976, 37.
9　Mann 1990, 53.
10　Bidwell 1999, 35.
11　Hodgson 2017, 160–166.
12　*Historia Augusta, Hadrian* 5, 1–2.
13　*Historia Augusta, Marcus Antoninus* 8, 7–8.
14　Dio 72, 8; 76, 12.
15　Procopius 8, 20, 42–46.
16　A.R. Birley 2005, 465.
17　Zosimus 6, 5, 2–3; 6, 10, 2; Bartholomew 1982.
18　Haynes 2013, 285–298.
19　Mattingly 2006, 33–37.
20　Dio 76, 12.
21　*RIB* III 3364; A.R. Birley 1998.
22　*Historia Augusta, Marcus Antoninus* 8, 7–8; *RIB* 589, 1137, 1149, 1703, 1792, 1809.
23　*CIL* XIV, 126; Roach 2013, 105.
24　Breeze 2014a, 12.
25　See Hodgson 1840, 289–290.
26　Allason-Jones 2009a, 149; *RIB* 1064; *CSIR* I 1 248.
27　*T.Vindol.* I 38.
28　*T.Vindol.* II 291, 154, 301, 343.
29　*T.Vindol.* II 164.

30 James 2002, 23–24.

31 Richard Hingley in Proctor 2009, vii.

32 See Hingley 2009, 150.

33 See, for instance, Proctor 2009; Proctor 2012; Hodgson 2012.

34 Breeze 2014a, 85–88.

35 Gibson 1903; Gibson and Simpson 1911.

36 Breeze 2006, 21–22.

37 Hodgson 2008, 11.

38 Breeze 2019b, 54–57.

39 See Hodgson 2008.

40 Bidwell 2005.

41 Simpson 1976, 109.

42 Wilmott 1997.

43 Tacitus *Agricola* 21.

44 Proctor 2012, 170.

45 Garrow and Gosden 2012, 33.

46 A. Birley 2019a, 37.

47 Huntley and Stallibrass 2019.

48 Whittaker 1997, 87.

49 Hodgson 2017, 10.

50 Camden 1586, 464–466.

51 Symonds 2019a, 100.

52 McCarthy 2018, 189.

53 Ferriter 2019, 10.

54 Ferriter 2019, 93–100.

55 G. Carr cited in Ferriter 2019, 94.

56 Symonds 2019b, 41–42. See Hodgson 2017, 39. For Roman counterinsurgency generally see, for instance, Mattern 2010.

57 Iron 2008, 180.

58 C. Powell cited in Ferriter 2019, 106.

59 Iron 2008; Ferriter 2019, 97.

60 McAtackney 2014, 1–15; Iron 2008.

61 Iron 2008, 179.

62 John Scott pers. comm.

Chapter 2

1 Hingley et al. 2018, 285–287.

2   Kristiansen 1996, 138–140.
3   Haverfield 1905, 2.
4   Mattingly 2006, xi–xiii, 3–4, 11.
5   Hingley et al. 2018, 288.
6   Mattingly 2006, 17.
7   Collis 1996, 167.
8   Tacitus *Germania* 29.
9   Haynes 2013, 2, 101.
10 Haynes 2013, 126.
11 Willis 1999, 85–86.
12 *RIB* III 3526; *RIB* 1695, 1142.
13 Haselgrove 2016, 472–480.
14 For instance, Collis 1996; James 1999.
15 James 1999, 17; Strabo 4, 4, 6-4, 5, 1.
16 Haynes 2013, 104.
17 See Haynes 2013, 227–230.
18 *CIL* XI 5213; A.R. Birley 2002, 95–96.
19 Nesbitt 2016, 240.
20 Mullen 2019, 102–105; *CSIR* I 1 247.
21 See Leary 2014.
22 Vyner 2007.
23 Barrett and Boyd 2019, 69.
24 Cunliffe 2017, 127–131, 143–145.
25 Berger et al. 2019.
26 Garrow and Gosden 2012, 41.
27 See Haselgrove 2016, 450, 483.
28 Edgeworth 2011, 122.
29 Caesar *Gallic War* 6, 13.
30 Pliny *Natural History* 16, 249.
31 Cunliffe 2005, 568–569.
32 Haselgrove 2016, 457.
33 Cunliffe 2005, 566–569; Heslop 2009, 4.
34 Croom 2018, 2; Heslop 2009, 7.
35 Merrifield 1987, 50–51.
36 Armit 2012, 7; Haselgrove 2016, 441.
37 Haselgrove 2016, 437.
38 Proctor 2009, 87–90; Hodgson 2012, 201.
39 Jobey 1982.
40 Jobey and Jobey 1987, 188; Taylor 1982, 235.

41 Green 1986, 39–40.

42 Garrow and Gosden 2012, 21–22, 39.

43 Hunter 2015a, 85; Garrow and Gosden 2012, 25–28.

44 Hunter 2015a, 89.

45 Garrow and Gosden 2012, 23–28.

46 Alcock 1986, 118.

47 Alcock 1986, 113.

48 Roberts 2019, 176–177. Roberts associates this with protection against 'dark smelly toilets and their danger to health'. Those frequenting insalubrious modern nightclubs, though, will know that unscrupulous patrons find toilets to be conveniently secluded places where grudges can be settled.

49 Parker 2017.

50 Isserlin 1997, 93–94.

51 Merrifield 1987, 51–52.

52 Strabo *Geography* 4, 4, 5.

53 Armit 2012, 15.

54 Livy 23, 24, 12.

55 Ross 1968, 277.

56 Isserlin 1997, 95.

57 *RIB* III 3185; Tomlin 2018, 63–64.

58 Allason-Jones and McKay 1985, 34.

59 Allason-Jones 2009a, 148.

60 Tacitus *Germania* 43.

61 Mattingly 2006, 214–217.

62 Green 1986, 39.

63 Green 1986, 45–59.

64 Green 1984, 231.

65 Green 1984, 21.

66 See Megaw 1970, no. 185.

67 See *RIB* 1877; *RIB* III 3448.

68 Symonds 2018a, 73–75.

69 Croom 2001, 68; Collins 2020, 292.

70 *CSIR* I 6 339; Allason-Jones in Haigh and Savage 1984, 97.

71 Ross 1974, 104–105; Armit 2012, 34.

72 Allason-Jones 2009a, 148.

73 See, for instance, Symonds 2018a, 75–78.

74 *RIB* 2015; it has been proposed that *vali* could be a contraction of *Luguvalium* (Carlisle), but Hodgson's interpretation of a Genius of the Wall is convincing (2017, 93).

75 Symonds 2020b, 39.

76 Symonds 2018a, 78.

77 Potter 1979, 120.

78 See Proctor 2009; Hodgson 2012.

79 Hodgson 2012, 207–210.

80 Stallibrass 2009.

Chapter 3

1   Caesar *Gallic War* 4, 20–38.

2   Cunliffe 2017, 16–19, 343.

3   Cicero *Letters to Atticus* 89, 7.

4   Mattingly 2006, 72–73.

5   Creighton 2006, 20–27.

6   Haselgrove 2016, 483.

7   Dio 59, 25, 1–5.

8   Cunliffe 2017, 7.

9   Dio 60, 19.

10 Inall 2020, 79.

11 Dio 60, 19–22.

12 Tacitus *Agricola* 12; 20.

13 Zartman 1995, 9.

14 Garrow and Gosden 2012, 71–76.

15 Suetonius 6, 18.

16 Tacitus *Annals* 12, 38–39. For 'guerrilla', see A.R. Birley 2005, 27.

17 Callwell 2016, 15, 39–43.

18 Tacitus *Agricola* 17.

19 Callwell 2016, 114–115.

20 Webster 2003, 219.

21 See, for instance, de Durand 2010, 14.

22 For instance, Tacitus *Annals* 12, 32.

23 Tacitus *Annals* 14, 30.

24 Mattingly 2006, 105.

25 I am indebted to Al McCluskey here. His as-yet unpublished views do not involve 1st-century Wales, but they have influenced my thinking.

26 Symonds 2017, 214–216.

27 Tacitus *Histories* 3, 45.

28 Zant 2009, 5.

29 McCarthy 2002, 50.

30 McCarthy 2002, 37–38.

31 Collingwood 1916, 87.

32 Tacitus *Agricola*, 25–37.

33 Woolliscroft and Hoffmann 2006, 225–234.

34 Tacitus *Histories* 1, 2.

35 Bidwell and Hodgson 2009, 13.

36 For instance, *T. Vindol.* II 155, 168, 343, 226, 659.

37 *T. Vindol.* III 628; A.R. Birley 2002, 80.

38 For instance, *T. Vindol.* II 182, 186.

39 Cool 2006, 129.

40 *T. Vindol.* II 154.

41 *T. Vindol.* II 164.

42 *T. Vindol.* II 344.

43 *T. Vindol.* II 250.

44 Alston 1995, 86–96.

45 *P. Ryl.* II 141.

46 Hartley 1972, 15.

47 See Hodgson 2009a.

48 Symonds 2017, 101–103.

49 Callwell 2016, 115–120.

50 Hodgson 2017, 34–35.

51 Symonds 2020a, 100–104.

52 Gillam 1961, 63–64; Hodgson 2012, 212.

53 Tacitus *Germania* 41.

54 Symonds 2020a.

55 Symonds 2020b, 38.

Chapter 4

1 Summarised in Symonds 2019b, 37–38.

2 Different measuring conventions existed in the Roman world, with *pedes monetales* apparently employed on Hadrian's Wall.

3 Swinbank and Spaul 1951, 228, 231.

4 A.R. Birley 1997, xiv.

5 Tomlin 2018, 101–102.

6 Mann 1990, 53; Breeze 2009.

7 Dio 69, 4.

8 *Historia Augusta, Hadrian* 11, 2.

9   Huntley 2013, 47–48.

10   A.R. Birley et al. 2013; Meyer 2019.

11   Callwell 2016, 254.

12   A.R. Birley 1997, 78.

13   Symonds 2019a, 104–105.

14   E. Birley 1953, 23; A.R. Birley 1998, 302; *CIL* XI, 5632; *CIL* X, 5829.

15   Fronto *On the Parthian War* 2.

16   Dio 69, 13–14.

17   A.R. Birley 1997, 268–276.

18   Dio 69, 13.

19   Breeze 2003.

20   See Abdy 2019, 11, 46–49.

21   See Abdy 2019, 50

22   A.R. Birley 2014, 245–253.

23   *RIB* 2244, 2265.

24   *RIB* 1051b; Graafstal 2012, 133–136; Hodgson 2017, 160.

25   Symonds 2017, 20–21.

26   Symonds 2017, 108–109; Symonds 2005, 73–76.

27   Breeze and Dobson 2000, 41.

28   Cuvigny 2006, 307–308; *O.Krok.* 6.

29   Haigh and Savage 1984, 36; Crow 1999, 127; Hill 2013.

30   Collingwood 1930.

31   Woolliscroft 1989, 7.

32   See Dobson 1986, 9; Breeze and Dobson 2000, 41.

33   See Baatz 2007, 22–23.

34   Woolliscroft 1989; Donaldson 1988; Foglia 2014.

35   Woolliscroft 1989.

36   Bidwell 2008a, 140.

37   Breeze 2014a, 113.

38   Bidwell 2008a.

39   Gibson and Simpson 1911, 420. Bidwell (2018, 157–159) suggests *c.* 3.66m
     for the Broad Wall and *c.* 3.55m for the Narrow Wall.

40   Symonds 2015, 305.

41   Hill 2006, 41.

42   Bidwell and Watson 1996, 23–26.

43   Crow 1991, 59.

44   Bidwell and Watson 1996, 25.

45   Hill 2006, 24; Bidwell 2018, 221–222.

46   *T.Vindol.* II 156; Bidwell 2018, 39.

47 Breeze 2006, 59.

48 Graafstal 2012, 136–138; Hodgson 2017, 64–67.

49 Symonds 2020a, 104.

50 Symonds 2019b, 34.

51 Welfare 2004.

52 Mattingly 1995, 107.

53 Bidwell 2005.

54 Bidwell 2019.

55 Bruce 1889, 196.

56 Allason-Jones 2009b, 221.

57 Collingwood 1929, 143.

58 Jones 1976.

59 Symonds 2017, 121–122.

60 Stevens 1966, 39.

61 Graafstal 2012, 149–151, 159.

62 *RIB* 1634, 1637, 1638, 1852, 1666, 1935.

63 Poulter 2009, 77–79.

64 Breeze 2006, 52.

65 Poulter 2009, 78–79.

66 Breeze and Dobson 2000, 68–70.

67 Bidwell 2018, 45–46.

68 *RIB* 1319, 1320. See Tomlin 2018, 93–94.

69 *RIB* 665.

70 For instance, Stevens 1966, 52, 84; Hodgson 2017, 66.

71 Hodgson 2017, 41.

72 E. Birley 1953, 26–29.

73 Hill 2006, 125; Hill and Dobson 1992, 40.

74 Gibson and Simpson 1911, 401.

75 Symonds 2005, 72.

76 Graafstal 2012, 131.

77 See Vyner 2007.

78 Symonds 2019a, 106–107. The Hexham fords were superseded by a bridge before the Ordnance Survey maps were surveyed and so are not marked on Fig. 14.

79 McCluskey 2018, 161.

80 Bidwell and Snape 2002, 254; Breeze and Dobson 2000, 75.

81 Bidwell and Snape 2002, 259.

82 Eckardt and Walton pers. comm.

83 Heslop 2009, 4–7.

84 Symonds 2013, 67–68.

85 *P.Mich*. VIII 468.

86 Symonds 2019b, 32–34.

87 Breeze and Dobson 2000, 47–55.

88 See Hill 2001; Bidwell 2003.

89 Swinbank and Spaul 1951, 228, 231.

90 Breeze 2017, 34–35.

91 See *RIB* 1550.

92 Symonds 2019a, 111.

93 Orton and Wood 2007, 22–23.

94 McCluskey pers. comm.

95 *RIB* 801.

96 Breeze 2018, 17.

97 Breeze 1972, 89–90.

98 See Symonds 2019c, 54.

99 Woolliscroft 1999, 61.

100 A.R. Birley 1997, 127.

101 Tomlin 2018, 87–90.

102 *RIB* 1340, 1427.

103 *RIB* 1445; Bidwell 2008a, 138.

104 *RIB* 1365.

105 *RIB* III 3376.

106 Compare Stevens 1941, 359 and Fulford 2006, 70.

107 Simpson in Richmond and Gillam 1952, 38.

108 *RIB* 1142; Bidwell 2010, 77–78.

109 *RIB* 946; Tomlin and Hassall 1999, 384–386.

110 Simpson and Richmond 1937, 157–158; Breeze 2006, 198.

111 Breeze and Dobson 2000, 53; Wilmott 1997, 99–100.

112 Callwell 2016, 114–115.

113 Symonds 2017, 115–118.

114 Symonds 2013, 59.

115 Symonds 2019a, 109–111.

116 For instance, Hodgson 2017, 63–69; Graafstal 2012, 155.

117 Breeze 2014a, 59–62.

118 *RIB* 1736.

119 See *RIB* 1550.

120 For instance, Crow 1991, 55; Wilmott 1997, 90–91.

121 *RIB* 1778, 1813, 1814, 1816, 1818, 1820, 1822.

122 Symonds and Breeze 2016, 10–12.

123 Symonds 2020c, 210.

124 Jones and Woolliscroft 2001, 113–114.

125 Symonds 2020a, 105.

126 Wilmott 1997, 99; *RIB* 1909.

127 Welsby 1985, 75.

128 Allason-Jones pers. comm.; Allason-Jones and Jones 1994, 271–272.

129 Bidwell and Croom 2002, 169–170.

130 Huntley and Stallibrass 2019, 87.

131 Collins 2019a, 145; R. Hingley pers. comm.

132 Porch 2013, 52.

133 Austin and Rankov 1995, 10.

134 Breeze 2006, 99–100.

135 Austin and Rankov 1995, 25.

136 Jackson 2016, 152–155, 166–173.

137 Proctor 2012, 135, 169–175.

138 Smith and Fulford 2016, 410.

139 Hodgson 2012, 191–216; Proctor 2009, 70.

140 Hodgson 2012, 218–219; Proctor 2009, 83.

141 Hodgson 2012, 216.

142 For instance, Jobey 1978, 98–99; Reid and Nicholson 2019.

143 Dio 69, 14.

144 Bidwell 2009.

145 Abdy 2019, 47.

146 Koch 2007, map 15a.

147 See Hodgson 2003, 23–34.

148 *CSIR* I 1, 247.

149 Haynes 2013, 127

150 Allason-Jones 1988, 217.

151 Bidwell and Speak 1994, 27.

152 Examples include *RIB* 1877, 1397; *RIB* III 3448; See also *CSIR* I 6, 55.

153 See *RIB* III 3448. Examples of similar symbols include two on a tombstone from the Antonine Wall commemorating Salmanes - a name well attested in the Syrian region - with the emblems perhaps attributable to a Celtic sculptor (see *RIB* 2182).

154 See McCarthy et al. 1982, 85–87; Croom 2018, 178.

155 Green 1986, 46–48.

156 Bidwell 2018, 11.

157 Snape in Bidwell and Speak 1994, 136–137; see Allason-Jones and McKay 1985. I am indebted to Margaret Snape for drawing my attention to this.

158 See Green 1999, 11–13, 16.

159 See *RIB* 1667; Woodfield 1965, 182.

160 Simpson 1976, 99–103.

161 Cunliffe 1995, 76; Craig et al. 2005, 175–176.

162 Buck et al. 2019.

163 E. Birley 1930, 154.

164 Symonds 2018a.

165 Collins 2020, 293-294.

166 See Fronto 'Preamble to History' 10–11.

167 *Historia Augusta, Antoninus Pius* 5, 4.

168 Hanson and Maxwell 1983.

169 Gillam 1975.

170 Poulter 2009, 121–123; Graafstal et al. 2015.

171 Poulter 2009, 121–123; Symonds 2017, 145.

172 Symonds 2020c, 211.

173 Symonds 2018b.

174 Symonds 2017, 81–90.

175 Symonds 2018a, 73–75.

176 Karst 2016, 176.

177 Callwell 2016, 255.

178 Symonds 2020b, 38–39.

179 Breeze 2014b, 62.

180 *RIB* 1051b; *Historia Augusta, Antoninus Pius* 5, 4.

Chapter 5

1 Hodgson 2011, 69–70.

2 Tomlin 2018, 143–145.

3 Hodgson 2011, 66–68.

4 *RIB* 1917, 1944, 1945, 2022, 2053; *RIB* III 3416, 3426, 3429; Fulford 2006, 67–68.

5 *RIB* 2053.

6 *RIB* 1629.

7 Breeze 2015, 17–19; cf. Wilmott 2009, 135–136.

8 Breeze 2006, 89.

9 Breeze and Ferris 2016, 33–35.

10 *Historia Augusta, Marcus Antoninus* 8, 7–8.

11 *RIB* 589, 1137, 1703, 1792, 1809.

12 Hodgson 2017, 105.

13 Austin and Rankov 1995, 12.

14 *Historia Augusta, Marcus Antoninus* 22, 1.

15 *Historia Augusta, Verus* 8, 1–3.

16 *RIB* 1579.

17 Jones 2005; Tomlin 2019, 495.

18 Dio 72, 8.

19 Hodgson 2017, 102–104.

20 Dio 72, 8.

21 See Hodgson 2009b, 32.

22 *Historia Augusta, Commodus* 13, 5.

23 Tomlin 2018, 170–171.

24 *RIB* 2034; Tomlin 2018, 162.

25 Mann 1990, 54.

26 Dio 72, 9; A.R. Birley 2005, 168–170.

27 Hartley 1972, 40.

28 Breeze and Dobson 2000, 134–135; Hodgson 2017, 106.

29 Hodgson 2017, 106–107; Breeze 2019b, 105.

30 Curle 1911, 116–117.

31 Karst 2016, 170.

32 For instance, Green 2001, 145–146; Cunliffe 2005, 568–569.

33 Green 2001, 88–89; Isserlin 1997, 93–94; Taylor 2008, 93.

34 Curle 1911, 114.

35 Taylor 2008, 93.

36 Livy 22, 57, 2–7.

37 For instance, Ross and Feachem 1976; Manning 1972, 243–246; Clarke and Jones 1994.

38 Clarke and Jones 1994, 120; Symonds 2018a, 73.

39 Curle 1911, 380–383.

40 Curle 1911, 111, 120.

41 Merrifield 1987, 51; Green 2001, 159–160.

42 Breeze and Dobson 2000, 134.

43 Breeze 2019b, 102–106.

44 Rushworth 2009, 283; Holder 2004, 56–59; Tomlin 2019, 495–496.

45 See Symonds 2018b, 154. For Hadrian's Wall see Welfare 2000.

46 For instance, Miket and Maxfield 1972, 158.

47 See Simpson 1976, 111; Miket and Maxfield 1972, 156–157. There are many more potential examples.

48 Symonds 2018a, 75–76.

49 Foglia 2014, 42.

50 Bidwell 2018, 86–87.

51 Bidwell and Snape 2002, 253.

52 Harbottle et al. 1988, 155–157.

53 *RIB* 1234, 1277.

54 *RIB* 1337, 1462, 1612, 1909.

55 Turrets 33b and 34a, Bidwell 2018, 187.

56 *RIB* 1009.

57 Dio 75, 5, 4.

58 Hunter 2007, 215–217.

59 Hunter 2015b, 264.

60 Dio 76, 12.

61 Armit and Mackenzie 2013, 494–499.

62 Macinnes 1984, 244–245; Brindle 2016, 315.

63 Brindle 2016, 315.

64 Brindle 2016, 311.

65 Sue Stallibrass pers. comm.

66 Roach 2013, 110–117.

67 Richmond 1934, 99.

68 A. Birley 2019b, 173–174.

69 Jones 2011, 111–112.

70 Dio 76, 13–15.

71 McCarthy 2018, 58.

72 Hodgson 2017, 130.

73 *RIB* 1616, 1700; Allason-Jones 2013, 72.

74 Zant 2019, 135.

75 Allason-Jones 2013, 73.

76 Kent 1987, 575–577; Howgego 1995, 136–137.

77 *RIB* 1706, 1465.

78 Bidwell 2018, 145–146; Town 2019, 135; Biggins and Taylor 2004, 167–168.

79 Bidwell 2018, 92–94.

80 Taylor and Biggins 2012, 91; Biggins et al. 2014, 69; Hancke et al. 2004, 44–45.

81 Crow 2004, 78.

82 E. Birley et al. 1933, 87–90.

83 Green 2001, 36.

84 Zant and Howard-Davis 2019, 120, 148–149.

85 Buck et al. 2019, 220.

86 *RIB* 1314, 1129.

87 Allason-Jones and McKay 1985, 3–6.

88   E. Birley and Charlton 1934, 190–192; *CSIR* I 6, 152.

89   Zant 2019, 146.

90   Jackson 1988, Fig. 44.

91   *RIB* 1897, 2043.

92   Smith 1969.

93   Merrifield 1987, 44.

94   A. Birley 2013, 97–101.

95   Zant 2019, 144–147.

96   Allason-Jones 2013, 76.

97   Jobey 1979, 138–140.

98   Wilmott 2009, 272–275.

99   Roach 2013, 114–115.

100   *RIB III* 3332.

101   *RIB* 1955, 1956, 1961, 1963, 2015, 2020, 2024; Symonds 2018a, 78–81; cf.
      Bidwell 2018, 224–225.

102   See Roach 2013, Fig 7.6.

103   Bidwell and Hodgson 2009, 33–34.

104   Rushworth and Croom 2016, 469, 517–518.

105   Wilmott 2019.

106   Howard-Davis et al. 2017, 79.

107   Hodgson 2017, 151.

108   Breeze 2019b, 141.

109   D.J. Breeze pers. comm.

110   See Karst 2016, 72–80.

111   Merrifield 1987, 43.

Chapter 6

1   Elton 1996, 68; Heather 2005, 62; Collins 2012, 36–37.

2   Collins 2019b, 68.

3   Eckardt et al. 2015, 214–219.

4   Wilmott 1997, 219.

5   Tomlin 2018, 415.

6   A.R. Birley 2005, 401; Hodgson 2017, 139.

7   Hassall 1976, 113.

8   A.R. Birley 2005, 401–402.

9   Mann 1974, 38.

10   *RIB* 1613, 1912.

11 Brickstock 2010, 86.

12 Hodgson 2017, 140.

13 Tomlin 2018, 421–422.

14 A.R. Birley 2005, 411.

15 Eusebius I. 8. 2.

16 Zosimus 2. 15. 1; A.R. Birley 2005, 412.

17 *RIB* III 3218; Tomlin 2018, 425.

18 Hodgson 2017, 136–137.

19 Rushworth 2009, 299.

20 Hodgson 2017, 149.

21 Rushworth 2009, 301.

22 A. Birley 2019b, 168.

23 A. Birley 2013, 97–101.

24 Hodgson 2014, 24–25.

25 Hodgson 2017, 152.

26 Jackson 2016, 154–155; Bewley 1992, 23, 42–44.

27 Bidwell and Croom 2002, 169–170.

28 Bidwell and Croom 2010.

29 Collins 2012, 90–95.

30 Rushworth 2009, 296.

31 Collins 2012, 56; Collins 2015, 18; Gerrard 2013, 43.

32 Rushworth 2009, 305; Collins 2012, 85–88; Wilmott 1997, 229.

33 Haigh and Savage 1984, 51.

34 Gibson 1903, 15.

35 Symonds 2019a, 115.

36 Bidwell 2018, 132.

37 Ammianus Marcellinus 20, 1.

38 Ammianus Marcellinus 27, 8, 1–10; A.R. Birley 2005, 428–429.

39 Ammianus Marcellinus 28, 3, 1; 28, 3, 7–8.

40 Hodgson 1997, 65; Symonds 2017, 198–208.

41 Breeze 2019b, 114.

42 Hodgson 2017, 150.

43 Allason-Jones and McKay 1985, 12.

44 Allason-Jones and McKay 1985, 12.

45 For instance, Hodgson 2017, 150.

46 Haynes 2019.

47 Collins 2012, 105.

48 A.R. Birley 2005, 443–450.

49 Claudian 2, 252.

50 Zosimus 6, 5, 2-3. Bartholomew 1982, 263.

51 Wilmott 1997, 218–224.

Chapter 7

1 Petts 2013, 319.

2 Collins 2008, 257.

3 O'Brien 2010, 111–112.

4 Oosthuizen 2019; cf. Petts 2013, 322.

5 Bidwell 2010, 133.

6 Crow 2004, 114.

7 Roberts 2010, 131.

8 Whitworth 2000, 9–10; Collins 2019b, 75.

9 Petts 2013, 322–323.

10 Roberts 2010, 123–127.

11 Gildas 15–19.

12 Henig 2020, 6; Oosthuizen 2019, 20.

13 McKee 2006, 36.

14 Gildas 4.

15 Collingwood 1921b, 46; Hingley 2012, 37–38.

16 Ferris 2010, 555.

17 David Mason pers. comm.

18 Collins 2019b, 74–75.

19 Nolan et al. 2010, 157, 253–256.

20 Collins 2012, 130.

21 Orton and Wood 2007, 29.

22 O'Brien 2010, 118.

23 Whitworth 2000, 11; Bidwell 2010, 133.

24 Bidwell 2010, 131.

25 Bede 5, 21.

26 Oosthuizen 2019, 24–25.

27 Bede 1, 12.

28 Collingwood 1921b, 46; E. Birley 1961, 1.

29 Bidwell 2018, 159.

30 Higham 1995, 10–13.

31 Higham 1995, 13

32 D. Partlett pers. comm. See, for instance, March 2003, for a discussion of post-Soviet Uzbekistan.

33 Higham 1995, 12

34 Higham 1995, 37–38.

35 Hingley 2012, 56–57.

36 Hingley 2012, 59.

37 Cited in Crow 2004, 124.

38 Whitworth 2000, 25–26.

39 Whitworth 2000, 53–54.

40 Collingwood 1921b, 47–48.

41 Shannon 2007, 22–25.

42 Shannon 2007, 32.

43 John of Fordun 3, 10

44 Hodgson 1840, 149–152.

45 Shannon 2007, 15.

46 Cited in Shannon 2007, 10–16.

47 Leland 1769, 60.

48 Shannon 2007, 30–31.

Chapter 8

1 E. Birley 1961, 1.

2 Collingwood 1921b, 48; E. Birley 1961, 1–5; D.J. Breeze pers. comm.

3 Hingley 2012, 65–66.

4 Camden 1586, 461; *Historia Augusta, Hadrian* 12, 6.

5 Camden 1586, 461–463.

6 Camden 1610, 789.

7 Camden 1610, 800.

8 Camden 1610, 795.

9 Camden 1586, 463; E. Birley 1961, 3.

10 Cited in E. Birley 1961, 3–4. See Hingley 2012, 82 for an interesting take on this.

11 Camden 1610, 791; Hingley 2012, 107.

12 Camden 1586, 464–466.

13 Cited in Crow 2004, 120.

14 Callwell 2016, 255.

15 Camden 1610, 802.

16 Camden 1722, 1198.

17 Breeze 2014a, 1.

18 Hingley 2012, 75.

19 Crow 2004, 127–128.

20 Hingley 2012, 89, 98.

21 Bosanquet and Birley 1955: 167.

22 Camden 1722, 1055; E. Birley 1961, 14.

23 Gordon 1726, 1.

24 Gordon 1726, 136.

25 Hingley 2012, 105–107.

26 Hingley 2012, 108–113; E. Birley 1961, 17.

27 Hingley 2012, 93, 115.

28 Cited in Hingley 2012, 94.

29 Cited in Hingley 2012, 121.

30 Hingley 2012, 129–131.

31 *RIB* 1389; Hodgson 2011.

32 Bidwell 2018, 5.

33 Whitworth 2000, 21, 25.

34 *RIB* 1637, 1638.

35 Hodgson 1840, 149–322.

36 E. Birley 1961, 22.

37 Breeze 2014a, 18.

38 Breeze 2016, 1–11.

39 Breeze 2020.

40 Clayton 1855.

41 Bell 1852, 7.

42 Forster 1899, 204.

43 Breeze 2006.

44 Neilson 1912, 39.

45 Breeze 2014a, 22–23.

46 Gibson 1903.

47 Charlton 2004.

48 Leach and Whitworth 2011, 71–126.

49 Leach and Whitworth 2011, 91.

50 Witcher et al. 2010, 111–112.

51 Breeze 2019b, 165.

Chapter 9

1 Mortimer 2007, 8.

2 For instance: *CSIR* I 6, 472, 473.

3 *RIB* 944; *CSIR* I 6, 469; Alcock 1986, 121.
4 Cowen and Richmond 1935, 318.
5 Hodgson 2009b, 22.
6 Künzl 2012, 22.
7 Hingley 2012, 76–79.
8 Bruce 1863, 109–110, 156.
9 Hingley 2012, 96–97.
10 Hingley 2012, 157–169.
11 Hingley 2012, 157–169.
12 Hingley 2012, 217.
13 Kipling 1906, 173.
14 Kipling 1906, 154.
15 Kipling 1906, 169.
16 Kipling 1906, 174, 176.
17 Kipling 1906, 173.
18 Sutcliff 2004, 134.
19 Christie 1977, 21-22.
20 Higgins et al. 2017.
21 Collins and Gillis 2016, 49; Collins 2019b, 78.
22 Martin 1996, 183.
23 Collins and Gillis 2016, 51.
24 Hutton 1990, 10-11.
25 Wainwright 1968, ii, 35.
26 Mortimer 2007.
27 Nagra 2017.
28 Hingley 2012, 151.
29 Dobson 1970.
30 Catling 2019, 65.
31 *The Beano* 27 July 2019.
32 *RIB* 1952.

Chapter 10

1 Faulkner 2007, 34.
2 Mann 1990.
3 Summarised in Symonds 2019c, 49.
4 Hingley et al. 2018, 285–287.

BIBLIOGRAPHY

Abbreviations

AA   Archaeologia Aeliana

BAR   British Archaeological Reports

CBA   Council for British Archaeology

JRA   Journal of Roman Archaeology

LCL   Loeb Classical Library

TCWAAS   Transactions of the Cumberland and Westmorland Antiquarian and
           Archaeological Society

Ancient sources

Ammianus Marcellinus: J.C. Rolfe (translator) 1972 *Ammianus Marcellinus*
    (volumes 2 and 3, LCL 315 and 331) London.
Bede: B. Colgrave and R.A.B. Mynors (eds.) 1969 *Bede's Ecclesiastical History of
    the English People* Oxford.
Caesar *Gallic War*: H.J. Edwards (translator) 1917 *Caesar: The Gallic War* (LCL
    72) London.
Cicero *Letters to Atticus*: D.R. Shackleton Bailey (ed. and translator) 1999 *Cicero:
    Letters to Atticus* (volume 1, LCL 7) London.
CIL X: T. Mommsen (ed.) 1883 *Corpus Inscriptionum Latinarum: inscriptiones
    Bruttiorum, Lucaniae, Campaniae, Sardiniae Latinae* (volume 10, part 1) Berlin.
CIL XI: E. Bormann (ed.) 1901 *Corpus Inscriptionum Latinarum: inscriptiones
    Aemiliae, Etruriae, Umbriae Latinae* (volume 11, part 2) Berlin.
CIL XIV: H. Dessau (ed.) 1887 *Corpus Inscriptionum Latinarum: inscriptiones
    Latii Veteris Latinae* (volume 14) Berlin.
Claudian: A.R. Birley 2005.
CSIR I 1: E.J. Phillips 1977 *Corpus Signorum Imperii Romani: Great Britain,
    volume I, fasicule 1, Corbridge, Hadrian's Wall east of the North Tyne* Oxford.
CSIR I 6: J.C. Coulston and E.J. Philips 1988 *Corpus Signorum Imperii Romani:
    Great Britain, volume I, fasicule 6, Hadrian's Wall west of the North Tyne and
    Carlisle* Oxford.
Dio: E. Cary (translator) 1924 and 1927 *Dio's Roman history* (volumes 7 and 9,
    LCL 175 and 177) London.
Eusebius: A.R. Birley 2005.

Fronto: C.R. Haines (ed. and translator) 1920 *The correspondence of Marcus Cornelius Fronto with Marcus Aurelius Antoninus, Lucius Verus, Antoninus Pius, and various friends* (volume 2, LCL 113) London.

Gildas: M. Winterbottom (ed. and translator) 1978 *Gildas: The ruin of Britain and other works* London.

Historia Augusta: D. Magie (translator) *The Scriptores Historiae Augustae* (volume 1, LCL 139) London.

John of Fordun: W.F. Skene (ed.) 1872 *John of Fordun's chronicle of the Scottish nation* (The Historians of Scotland volume 4) Edinburgh.

Livy: B.O. Foster (translator) 1949 *Livy: History of Rome, books XXI–XXII* (volume 5, LCL 233) London.

O.Krok: H. Cuvigny 2005 *Ostraca de Krokodilô, La correspondence militaire et sa circulation* Cairo.

Pliny *Natural History*: H. Rackham (translator) 1968 *Pliny: Natural History in ten volumes* (volume 4, LCL 370) London.

P.Mich. VIII: H.C. Youtie and J.G. Winter (eds.) 1951 *Papyri and ostraca from Karanis* (Michigan Papyri volume VIII) London.

P.Ryl. II: J. De M. Johnson, V. Martin and A.S. Hunt (eds.) 1915 *Catalogue of the Greek Papyri in the John Rylands Library, Manchester, volume II: Documents of the Ptolemaic and Roman periods* Manchester.

Procopius: H.B. Dewing 1928 *Procopius: History of the wars, books VII.36–VIII* (volume 5, LCL 217) London.

RIB: R.G. Collingwood and R.P. Wright 1965 *The Roman inscriptions of Britain, volume 1: Inscriptions on stone* Oxford.

RIB III: R.S.O. Tomlin, R.P. Wright and M.W.C. Hassall 2009 *The Roman inscriptions of Britain, volume III: Inscriptions on stone found or notified between 1 January 1955 and 31 December 2006* Oxford.

Strabo: H.L. Jones (translator) 1969 *The geography of Strabo* (volume 2, LCL 50) London.

Suetonius: J.C. Rolfe 1914 *Suetonius* (volume 2, LCL 38) London.

T.Vindol. I: A.K. Bowman and J.D. Thomas 1983 *Vindolanda: The Latin writing-tablets* (Britannia Monograph Series 4) London.

T.Vindol. II: A.K. Bowman and J.D. Thomas 1994 *The Vindolanda writing-tablets (Tabulae Vindolandenses II)* London.

T.Vindol. III: A.K. Bowman and J.D. Thomas 2003 *The Vindolanda writing-tablets (Tabulae Vindolandenses III)* London.

Tacitus *Agricola*: M. Hutton (translator) 1970 *Tacitus: Agricola, Germania, Dialogus* (LCL 35) London.

Tacitus *Annals*: J. Jackson (translator) 1937 *Tactius: The Annals* (volumes 4 and 5, LCL 312 and 322) London.

Tacitus *Germania*: M. Hutton (translator) 1970 *Tacitus: Agricola, Germania, Dialogus* (LCL 35) London.

Tacitus *Histories*: C.H. Moore (translator) 1925 *Tacitus: The Histories* (LCL 111) London.

Zosimus: A.R. Birley 2005.

Modern sources

Abdy, R.A. 2019 *The Roman imperial coinage, volume II – part 3: from AD 117–138 Hadrian* London.

Alcock, J.P. 1986 'The concept of genius in Roman Britain', in M. Henig and A. King (eds.) *Pagan gods and shrines of the Roman Empire* Oxford, 113–133.

Allason-Jones, L. 1988 'Small finds from the turrets on Hadrian's Wall', in J.C. Coulston (ed.) *Military equipment and the identity of Roman soldiers: Proceedings of the Fourth Roman Military Equipment Conference* (BAR International Series 394) Oxford, 197–233.

Allason-Jones, L. 2009a 'Life and society: Introductory overview', in Symonds and Mason (eds.), 147–149.

Allason-Jones, L. 2009b 'Some problems of the Roman Iron Age in N England', in Hanson (ed.), 217–224.

Allason-Jones, L. 2013 'The *vicus* at Housesteads: A case study in material culture and Roman life', in Collins and Symonds (eds.), 71–84.

Allason-Jones, L. and Jones, D.M. 1994 'Jet and other materials in Roman artefact studies', *AA*[5] 22: 265–272.

Allason-Jones, L. and McKay, B. 1985 *Coventina's Well: A shrine on Hadrian's Wall* Chollerford.

Alston, R. 1995 *Soldier and society in Roman Egypt: A social history* London.

Armit, I. 2012 *Headhunting and the body in Iron Age Europe* Cambridge.

Armit, I. and Mackenzie, J. 2013 *An inherited place: Broxmouth hillfort and the south-east of the Scottish Iron Age* Edinburgh.

Austin, N.J.E. and Rankov, N.B. 1995 *Exploratio: Military and political intelligence in the Roman world from the second Punic War to the Battle of Adrianople* London.

Baatz, D. 2007 'Zur Funktion der Kleinkastelle am Obergermanisch-Raetischen Limes', in A. Thiel (ed.) *Forschungen zur Funktion des Limes* Bad Homberg, 9–25.

Barrett, J.C. and Boyd, M.J. 2019 *From Stonehenge to Mycenae: The challenges of archaeological interpretation* London.

Bartholomew, P. 1982 'Fifth-century facts', *Britannia* 13: 261–270.

Bell, R. 1852 *The Roman Wall: An attempt to substantiate the claims of Severus to the authorship of the Roman Wall* Newcastle.

Berger, D., Soles, J.S., Giumlia-Mair, A.R., Brügmann, G., Galili, E., Lockhoff, N. and Pernicka, E. 2019 'Isotope systematics and chemical composition of tin ingots from Mochlos (Crete) and other Late Bronze Age sites in the eastern Mediterranean Sea: An ultimate key to tin provenance?', *PLoS ONE* 14: e0218326 [https://doi.org/10.1371/journal.pone.0218326].

Bewley, R.H. 1992 'Excavations on two crop-mark sites in the Solway Plain, Cumbria. Ewanrigg settlement and Swarthy Hill 1986–1988', *TCWAAS*[2] 92: 23–47.

Bidwell, P.T. (ed.) 1999 *Hadrian's Wall 1989–1999* Carlisle.

Bidwell, P.T. 2003 'The original eastern terminus of Hadrian's Wall', *AA*[5] 32: 17–24.

Bidwell, P.T. 2005 'The system of obstacles on Hadrian's Wall: Their extent, date, and purpose', *Arbeia Journal* 8: 53–75.

Bidwell, P.T. 2008a 'Did Hadrian's Wall have a wall-walk?', in Bidwell (ed.), 129–143.

Bidwell, P.T. (ed.) 2008b *Understanding Hadrian's Wall* Kendal.

Bidwell, P.T. 2009 'Roman pottery with a brief reference to barrels', in Symonds and Mason (eds.), 121–125.

Bidwell, P.T. 2010 'A survey of the Anglo-Saxon crypt at Hexham and its reused Roman stonework', *AA*[5] 39: 53–145.

Bidwell, P.T. 2018 *Hadrian's Wall at Wallsend* South Shields.

Bidwell, P.T. 2019 'Wall miles 48 and 49 (magnetometer surveys)', in Collins and Symonds (eds.), 186.

Bidwell, P.T. and Croom, A.T. 2002 'The Roman pottery', *AA*⁵ 31: 139–172.

Bidwell, P.T. and Croom, A.T. 2010 'The supply and use of pottery on Hadrian's Wall in the 4th century', in Collins and Allason-Jones (eds.), 20–36.

Bidwell, P.T. and Hodgson, N. 2009 *The Roman army in Northern England* Newcastle upon Tyne.

Bidwell, P.T. and Snape, M. 2002 'The history and setting of the Roman fort at Newcastle upon Tyne', *AA*⁵ 31: 251–283.

Bidwell, P.T. and Speak, S. 1994 *Excavations at South Shields Roman fort* (volume 1) Newcastle.

Bidwell, P.T. and Watson, M. 1996 'Excavations on Hadrian's Wall at Denton, Newcastle upon Tyne, 1986–89', *AA*⁵ 24: 1–56.

Biggins, J.A., Charlton, D.B. and Taylor, D.J.A. 2014 'Survey of the Roman outpost fort at Risingham (Habitancum), Northumberland', *AA*⁵ 43: 47–71.

Biggins, J.A. and Taylor, D.J.A. 2004 'Geophysical survey of the *vicus* at Birdoswald Roman fort, Cumbria', *Britannia* 35: 159–178.

Birley, A. 2013 'The fort wall: A great divide?', in Collins and Symonds (eds.), 85–104.

Birley, A. 2019a 'Communities in the conflict zone: Ten years of discoveries at Vindolanda', *Current Archaeology* 353: 34–39.

Birley, A. 2019b 'Vindolanda', in Collins and Symonds (eds.), 164–177.

Birley, A.R. 1997 *Hadrian: The restless emperor* London.

Birley, A.R. 1998 'A new tombstone from Vindolanda', *Britannia* 29: 299–306.

Birley, A.R. 2002. *Garrison life at Vindolanda: A band of brothers*, Stroud.

Birley, A.R. 2005 *The Roman government of Britain* Oxford.

Birley, A.R. 2014 'Two governors of Dacia Superior and Britain', in V. Iliescu, D. Nedu and A. Barboş (eds.) *Graecia, Roma, Barbaricum. In memoriam Vasile Lica*, Galaţi, 241–259.

Birley, A.R., Birley, A. and de Bernardo Stempel, P. 2013 'A dedication by the "cohors I Tungrorum" at Vindolanda to a hitherto unknown goddess', *Zeitschrift für Papyrologie und Epigraphik* 186: 287–300.

Birley, E. 1930 'Excavations on Hadrian's Wall west of Newcastle upon Tyne in 1929', *AA*⁴ 7: 143–174.

Birley, E. 1953 *Roman Britain and the Roman army: Collected papers* Kendal.

Birley, E. 1961 *Research on Hadrian's Wall* Kendal.

Birley, E. and Charlton, J. 1934 'Third report on excavations at Housesteads', *AA*⁴ 11: 185–205.

Birley, E., Charlton, J. and Hedley, P. 1933 'Excavations at Housesteads in 1932', *AA*⁴ 10: 82–96.

Bosanquet, R.C. and Birley, E. 1955 'Robert Smith and the "Observations upon the Picts Wall" (1708–9)', *TCWAAS*² 55: 154–171.

Breeze, D.J. 1972 'Excavations at the Roman fort of Carrawburgh, 1967–1969', *AA*⁴ 50: 81–144.

Breeze, D.J. 2003 'Warfare in Britain and the building of Hadrian's Wall', *AA*⁵ 32: 13–16.

Breeze, D.J. 2006 *J. Collingwood Bruce's handbook to the Roman Wall* (14th edition) Newcastle upon Tyne.

Breeze, D.J. 2009 'Did Hadrian design Hadrian's Wall?', *AA*[5] 36: 87–103.

Breeze, D.J. 2014a *Hadrian's Wall: A history of archaeological thought* Kendal.

Breeze, D.J. 2014b 'Commemorating the Wall: Roman sculpture and inscriptions from Hadrian's Wall', in Collins and McIntosh (eds.), 59–64.

Breeze, D.J. 2015 'The Vallum of Hadrian's Wall', *AA*[5] 44: 1–29.

Breeze, D.J. 2016 *Hadrian's Wall: Paintings by the Richardson family* Edinburgh.

Breeze, D.J. 2017 'The placing of the forts on Hadrian's Wall', *AA*[5] 46: 21–39.

Breeze, D.J. 2018 *Maryport: A Roman fort and its community* Oxford.

Breeze, D.J. 2019a *The frontiers of Imperial Rome* (2nd edition) Barnsley.

Breeze, D.J. 2019b *Hadrian's Wall: A study in archaeological exploration and interpretation* Oxford.

Breeze, D.J. 2020 *The pilgrimages of Hadrian's Wall 1849–2019: A history* Kendal.

Breeze, D.J. and Dobson, B. 1976 *Hadrian's Wall* (1st edition) London.

Breeze, D.J. and Dobson, B. 2000 *Hadrian's Wall* (4th edition) London.

Breeze, D.J. and Ferris, I. 2016 'They think it's all over. The face of victory on the British frontier', *Journal of Conflict Archaeology* 11: 19–39.

Brickstock, R.J. 2010 'Coins and the frontier troops in the 4th century', in Collins and Allason-Jones (eds.), 86–91.

Brindle, T. 2016 'The north', in A. Smith, M. Allen, T. Brindle and M. Fulford (eds.) *The rural settlement of Roman Britain* (Britannia Monograph series 29) London, 308–330.

Bruce, J.C. 1863 *The wallet-book of the Roman Wall* Newcastle.

Bruce, J.C. 1867 *The Roman Wall: A description of the mural barrier of the north of England* (3rd edition) London.

Bruce, J.C. 1889 'An inscribed slab from Newburn', *AA*[2] 13: 192–196.

Buck, T., Greene, E.M., Meyer, A., Barlow, V. and Graham, E. 2019 'The body in the ditch: Alternative funerary practices on the northern frontier of the Roman empire?', *Britannia* 50: 203–224.

Callwell, C.E. 2016 *Small wars: Their principles and practice* UK.

Camden, W. 1586 *Britannia* London.

Camden, W. 1610 *Britain* London.

Camden, W. 1722 *Britannia* (volume 2) London.

Catling, C. 2019 'Sherds', *Current Archaeology* 357: 64–65.

Charlton, J. 2004 'Saving the Wall: Quarries and conservation', *AA*[5] 33: 5–8.

Christie, A. 1977 *The thirteen problems* London.

Clarke, S. and Jones, R. 1994 'The Newstead pits', *Journal of Roman Military Equipment Studies* 5: 109–124.

Clayton, J. 1855 'Account of excavations at the Mile Castle of Cawfields, on the Roman Wall', *AA*[1] 4: 54–59.

Collingwood, R.G. 1916 'The exploration of the Roman fort at Ambleside: Report on the third year's work (1915)', *TCWAAS*[2] 16: 57–90.

Collingwood, R.G. 1921a 'The purpose of the Roman Wall', *Vasculum* 8, 1: 1–5.

Collingwood, R.G. 1921b 'Hadrian's Wall: A history of the problem', *Journal of Roman Studies* 11: 37–66.

Collingwood, R.G. 1929 'Roman signal-stations on the Cumberland Coast', *TCWAAS*[2] 29: 138–165.

Collingwood, R.G. 1930 'A system of numerical references to the parts of Hadrian's Wall and the structures along its line', *TCWAAS*[2] 30: 108–115.

Collins, R. 2008 'The latest Roman coin from Hadrian's Wall: A small fifth-century purse group', *Britannia* 39: 256–261.

Collins, R. 2012 *Hadrian's Wall and the end of empire: The Roman frontier in the 4th and 5th centuries* New York.

Collins, R. 2015 'Economic reduction or military reorganization? Granary demolition and conversion in later 4th-century northern Britannia', in R. Collins, M.F.A. Symonds and M. Weber (eds.) *Roman military architecture on the frontiers: Armies and their architecture in Late Antiquity* Oxford, 18–31.

Collins, R. 2019a. 'Great Whittington', in Collins and Symonds (eds.), 145–146.

Collins, R. 2019b. 'The late and post-Roman frontier', in Collins and Symonds (eds.), 68–78.

Collins, R. 2020 'The phallus and the frontier: the form and function of phallic imagery on Hadrian's Wall', in I. Ivleva and R. Collins (eds.) *Un-Roman Sex: Gender, sexuality, and lovemaking in the Roman provinces and frontiers* London, 274–309.

Collins, R. and Allason-Jones, L. (eds.) 2010 *Finds from the frontier: Material culture in the 4th–5th centuries* (CBA Research Report 162) York.

Collins, R. and Gillis, S. 2016 'Beyond the archaeology: The cultural afterlife of Hadrian's Wall', *Current Archaeology* 321: 48–51.

Collins, R. and McIntosh, F. (eds.) 2014 *Life in the Limes: Studies of the people and objects of the Roman frontiers presented to Lindsay Allason-Jones* Oxford.

Collins, R. and Symonds, M.F.A. (eds.) 2013 *Breaking down boundaries: Hadrian's Wall in the 21st century* (JRA Supplementary Series 93) Portsmouth, RI.

Collins, R. and Symonds, M.F.A. (eds.) 2019 *Hadrian's Wall: 2009–2019* Kendal.

Collis, J. 1996 'Celts and politics', in P. Graves-Brown, S. Jones and C. Gamble (eds.) *Cultural identity and archaeology: The construction of European communities* London, 167–178.

Cool, H.E.M. 2006 *Eating and drinking in Roman Britain* Cambridge.

Cowen, J.D. and Richmond, I.A. 1935 'The Rudge Cup', *AA*[4] 12: 310–342.

Craig, C.R., Knüsel, C.J. and Carr, G.C. 2005 'Fragmentation, mutilation and dismemberment: An interpretation of human remains on Iron Age sites', in M. Parker Pearson and I.J.N. Thorpe (eds.) *Warfare, violence and slavery in prehistory: Proceedings of a Prehistoric Society conference at Sheffield University* (BAR International Series 1374) Oxford, 165-180.

Creighton, J. 2006 *Britannia: The creation of a Roman province* London.

Croom, A. 2001 'Some finds from the 1997–8 excavations at South Shields Roman fort', *Arbeia Journal* 6/7: 68–73.

Croom, A. 2018 'An Iron Age bridle bit from the River Tyne', *AA*[5] 47: 1–3.

Crow, J.G. 1991 'A review of current research on the turrets and curtain of Hadrian's Wall', *Britannia* 22: 51–63.

Crow, J.G. 1999 'Milecastle 37 (Housesteads) and the central sector of Hadrian's Wall', in Bidwell (ed.), 127–130.

Crow, J.G. 2004 *Housesteads: A fort and garrison on Hadrian's Wall* Stroud.

Cunliffe, B. 1995 *Danebury: An Iron Age hillfort in Hampshire, volume 6: A hillfort community in perspective* (CBA Research Report 102) York.

Cunliffe, B. 2005 *Iron Age communities in Britain: An account of England, Scotland and Wales from the seventh century BC until the Roman conquest* Abingdon.

Cunliffe, B. 2017 *On the ocean: The Mediterranean and the Atlantic from prehistory to AD 1500* Oxford.

Curle, J. 1911 *A Roman frontier post and its people: The fort of Newstead in the parish of Melrose* Glasgow.

Cuvigny, H. (ed.) 2006 *La route de Myos Hormos, L'armée romaine dans le désert Oriental d'Égypte* (volume 2) Cairo.

de Durand, E. 2010 'France', in T. Rid and T. Keaney (eds.) *Understanding counterinsurgency: Doctrine, operations, and challenges* London, 11–27.

Dobson, B. 1986 'The function of Hadrian's Wall', *AA*[5] 14: 1–30.

Dobson, S. 1970 *Hadrian and the Geordie Waall* Newcastle.

Donaldson, G. 1988 'Thoughts on a military appreciation of the design of Hadrian's Wall', *AA*[5] 16: 125–137.

Eckardt, H., Müldner, G. and Speed, G. 2015 'The late Roman field army in northern Britain? Mobility, material culture and multi-isotope analysis at Scorton (N Yorks)', *Britannia* 46: 191–223.

Edgeworth, M. 2011 *Fluid pasts: Archaeology of flow* London.

Elton, H. 1996 *Frontiers of the Roman Empire* London.

Faulkner, N. 2007 'Trains, trenches and tents: The archaeology of Lawrence of Arabia's war', *Current World Archaeology* 23: 26–34.

Ferris, I. 2010 *The beautiful rooms are empty: Excavations at Binchester fort, County Durham 1976–1981 and 1986–1991* (volume 1) Durham.

Ferriter, D. 2019 *The border: The legacy of a century of Anglo-Irish politics* London.

Foglia, A.B. 2014 'Turrets as watchtowers: A GIS and source-based analysis of appearance and surveillance capabilities', *AA*[5] 43: 27–46.

Forster, R.H. 1899 *The amateur antiquary: His notes, sketches, and fancies concerning the Roman Wall in the counties of Northumberland and Cumberland* London.

Fulford, M. 2006 'Corvées and *civitates*', in R.J.A. Wilson (ed.) *Romanitas: Essays on Roman archaeology in honour of Sheppard Frere on the occasion of his ninetieth birthday* Oxford, 65–71.

Garrow, D. and Gosden, C. 2012 *Technologies of enchantment: Exploring Celtic art: 400 BC to AD 100* Oxford.

Gerrard, J. 2013 *The ruin of Roman Britain: An archaeological perspective* Cambridge.

Gibson, J.P. 1903 'Mucklebank wall turret', *AA*[2] 24: 13–19.

Gibson, J.P. and Simpson, F.G. 1911 'The milecastle on the Wall of Hadrian at the Poltross Burn', *TCWAAS*[2] 11: 390–461.

Gillam, J.P. 1961 'Roman and native, AD 122–197', in I.A. Richmond (ed.) *Roman and native in north Britain* London, 60–90.

Gillam, J.P. 1975 'Possible changes in plan in the course of the construction of the Antonine Wall', *Scottish Archaeological Forum* 7: 51–56.

Gordon, A. 1726 *Itinerarium Septentrionale: Or, a journey through most of the counties of Scotland and those in the north of England* London.

Graafstal, E.P. 2012 'Hadrian's haste: A priority programme for the Wall', *AA*[5] 41: 123–184.

Graafstal, E.P., Breeze, D.J., Jones, R.H. and Symonds, M.F.A. 2015 'Sacred cows in the landscape: Rethinking the planning of the Antonine Wall', in D.J. Breeze, R.H. Jones and I.A. Oltean (eds.) *Understanding Roman frontiers: A celebration for Professor Bill Hanson* Edinburgh, 54–69.

Green, M.J. 1984 *The wheel as a cult-symbol in the Romano-Celtic world* Brussels.

Green, M.J. 1986 *The gods of the Celts* Gloucester.

Green, M.J. 1999 *Pilgrims in stone: Stone images from the Gallo-Roman sanctuary of Fontes Sequanae* (BAR International Series 754) Oxford.

Green, M.J. 2001 *Dying for the gods: Human sacrifice in Iron Age and Roman Europe* Stroud.

Haigh, D. and Savage, M. 1984 'Sewingshields', *AA*[5] 12: 33–148.

Hancke, T., Charlton, B. and Biggins, J.A. 2004 'A geophysical survey at High Rochester Roman fort', *AA*[5] 33: 35–50.

Hanson, W.S. (ed.) 2009 *The army and frontiers of Rome: Papers offered to David J. Breeze on the occasion of his sixty-fifth birthday and retirement from Historic Scotland* (JRA Supplementary Series 74) Portsmouth, RI.

Hanson, W.S. and Maxwell, G.S. 1983 *Rome's north west frontier: The Antonine Wall* Edinburgh.

Harbottle, B., Fraser, R. and Burton, F.C. 1988 'The Westgate Road milecastle, Newcastle upon Tyne', *Britannia* 19: 153–162.

Hartley, B.R. 1972 'The Roman occupations of Scotland: The evidence of the Samian ware', *Britannia* 3: 1–55.

Haselgrove, C. 2016 *Cartimandua's capital? The late Iron Age royal site at Stanwick, North Yorkshire, fieldwork and analysis 1981–2011* (CBA Research Report 175) York.

Hassall, M.W.C. 1976 'Britain in the Notitia', in R. Goodburn and P. Bartholomew (eds.) *Aspects of the Notitia Dignitatum* (BAR International Series 15) Oxford.

Haverfield, F.J. 1905 *The romanization of Roman Britain* London.

Haynes, I. 2013 *Blood of the provinces: The Roman Auxilia and the making of provincial society from Augustus to the Severans* Oxford.

Haynes, I. 2019 'Altar pits and temples', in Collins and Symonds (eds.), 205–209.

Heather, P.J. 2005 *The fall of the Roman Empire* London.

Henig, M. 2020 'Letter to the editor', *Current Archaeology* 360: 6.

Heslop, D.H. 2009 'Newcastle and Gateshead before A.D. 1080', in D. Newton and A.J. Pollard (eds.) *Newcastle and Gateshead before 1700* Chichester, 1–22.

Higgins, K., Siegel, A., Reis, R. and Peteri, T. 2017 *Hadrian's Wall* USA.

Higham, N.J. 1995 *An English empire: Bede and the early Anglo-Saxon kings* Manchester.

Hill, P.R. 2001 'Hadrian's Wall from MC0 to MC9', *AA*[5] 29: 3–18.

Hill, P.R. 2006 *The construction of Hadrian's Wall* Stroud.

Hill, P.R. 2013 'The northern gate-tower of milecastle 37', in Collins and Symonds (eds.), 68–69.

Hill, P.R. and Dobson, B. 1992 'The design of Hadrian's Wall and its implications', *AA*[5] 20: 27–52.

Hingley, R. 2009 'The indigenous population', in Symonds and Mason (eds.), 149–152.

Hingley, R. 2012 *Hadrian's Wall: A life* Oxford.

Hingley, R., Bonacchi, C. and Sharpe, K. 2018 'Are you local? Indigenous Iron Age and mobile Roman and post-Roman populations: Then, now, and in-between', *Britannia* 49: 283–302.

Hodgson, J. 1840 *History of Northumberland* (part 2, volume 3) Newcastle.

Hodgson, N. 1997 'Relationships between Roman river frontiers and artificial frontiers', in W. Groenman-van Waateringe, B. van Beek, W. Willems and S. Wynia (eds.) *Roman frontier studies 1995* Oxford, 61–66.

Hodgson, N. 2003 *The Roman fort at Wallsend (Segedunum): Excavations in 1997–8* Newcastle upon Tyne.

Hodgson, N. 2008 'After the Wall-Periods: What is our historical framework for Hadrian's Wall in the twenty-first century?', in Bidwell (ed.), 11–23.

Hodgson, N. 2009a 'Pre-Hadrianic military installations and the question of the "Stanegate frontier"', in Symonds and Mason (eds.), 13–15.

Hodgson, N. 2009b 'A review of research on Hadrian's Wall 1999–2009', in N. Hodgson (ed.) *Hadrian's Wall 1999–2009: A summary of excavation and research* Kendal, 5–51.

Hodgson, N. 2011 'The provenance of *RIB* 1389 and the rebuilding of Hadrian's Wall in AD 158', *The Antiquaries Journal* 91: 59–71.

Hodgson, N. 2012 'The Iron Age on the Northumberland coastal plain: General conclusions', in N. Hodgson, J. McKelvey and W. Muncaster (eds.) *The Iron Age on the Northumberland coastal plain* Newcastle upon Tyne, 183–222.

Hodgson, N. 2014 'The accommodation of soldiers' wives in Roman fort barracks – on Hadrian's Wall and beyond', in Collins and McIntosh (eds.), 18–28.

Hodgson, N. 2017 *Hadrian's Wall: Archaeology and history at the limit of Rome's empire* Marlborough.

Hodgson, N. 2019 'Newcastle upon Tyne – Roman bridge', in Collins and Symonds (eds.), 128.

Holder, P. 2004 'Roman place-names on the Cumbrian coast', in R.J.A. Wilson and I.D. Caruana (eds.) *Romans on the Solway: Essays in honour of Richard Bellhouse* Kendal, 52–65.

Horsley, J. 1732 *Britannia Romana: Or the Roman antiquities of Britain* London.

Howard-Davis, C., Leary, R. and Ward, M. 2017 'Evaluation of Beckfoot Roman cemetery, 2006', *TCWAAS*³ 17: 43–84.

Howgego, C. 1995 *Ancient history from coins* London.

Hunter, F. 2007 'Silver for the Barbarians: Interpreting *denarii* hoards in north Britain and beyond', in R. Hingley and S. Willis (eds.) *Roman finds: Context and theory* Oxford, 214–224.

Hunter, F. 2015a 'Powerful objects: The uses of art in the Iron Age', in J. Farley and F. Hunter (eds.) *Celts: Art and identity* London, 80–105.

Hunter, F. 2015b 'The lure of silver: *denarius* hoards and relations across the frontier', in D.J. Breeze, R.H. Jones and I.A. Oltean (eds.) *Understanding Roman frontiers: A celebration for Professor Bill Hanson* Edinburgh, 251–269.

Huntley, J.P. 2013 'The world is a bundle of hay: Investigating land management for animal fodder around Vindolanda, based on plant remains', in Collins and Symonds (eds.), 33–51.

Huntley, J. and Stallibrass, S. 2019 'Landscape and environmental evidence', in Collins and Symonds (eds.), 78–98.

Hutton, W. 1990 *The history of the Roman Wall* Newcastle upon Tyne.

Inall, Y. 2020 'New light on Iron Age warfare in Britain', in P. Halkon (ed.) *The Arras culture of eastern Yorkshire: Celebrating the Iron Age* Oxford, 67–84.

Iron, R. 2008 'Britain's longest war: Northern Ireland 1967–2007', in D. Marston and C. Malkasian (eds.) *Counterinsurgency in modern warfare* Oxford, 167–184.

Isserlin, R.M.J. 1997 'Thinking the unthinkable: Human sacrifice in Roman Britain', in K. Meadows, C. Lemke and J. Heron (eds.) *TRAC 96: Proceedings of the sixth annual Theoretical Roman Archaeology Conference* Oxford, 91–100.

Jackson, D. 2016 'Neolithic to Romano-British occupation at Durranhill, Carlisle: Archaeological investigations 1997–8 and 2011', *TCWAAS*³ 16: 145–176.

Jackson, R. 1988 *Doctors and diseases in the Roman Empire* London.

James, S. 1999 *The Atlantic Celts: Ancient people or modern invention?* London.

James, S. 2002 'Writing the legions: The development and future of Roman military studies in Britain', *Archaeological Journal* 159: 1–58.

Jobey, G. 1978 'Burnswark Hill, Dumfriesshire', *Transactions of the Dumfriesshire and Galloway Natural History and Antiquarian Society* 53: 57–99.

Jobey, G. 1982 'The settlement at Doubstead and Romano-British settlement on the coastal plain between Tyne and Forth', *AA*⁵ 10: 1–23.

Jobey, I. 1979 'Housesteads Ware – a Frisian tradition on Hadrian's Wall', *AA*⁵ 7: 127–143.

Jobey, I. and Jobey, G. 1987 'Prehistoric, Romano-British and later remains on Murton High Crags, Northumberland', *AA*⁵ 15: 151–198.

Jones, C.P. 2005 'Ten dedications "to the gods and goddesses" and the Antonine plague', *JRA* 18: 293–301.

Jones, G.D.B. 1976 'The western extension of Hadrian's Wall', *Britannia* 7: 236–243.

Jones, G.D.B and Woolliscroft, D.J. 2001 *Hadrian's Wall from the air* Stroud.

Jones, R.H. 2011 *Roman camps in Scotland* Edinburgh.

Karst, C. 2016 *Puteus altissimus: Brunnen und Schächte im römischen Britannien, Gallien und Germanien als religiös markierte Orte* (Pharos 37) Leidorf.

Kent, J. 1987 'The monetary system', in J. Wacher (ed.) *The Roman world* (volume 2) London, 568–585.

Kipling, R. 1906 *Puck of Pook's Hill* London.

Koch, J.T. 2007 *An atlas for Celtic studies: Archaeology and names in ancient Europe and early medieval Ireland, Britain, and Brittany* Oxford.

Kristiansen, K. 1996 'European origins – "civilisation" and "barbarism"', in P. Graves-Brown, S. Jones and C. Gamble (eds.) *Cultural identity and archaeology: The construction of European communities* London, 138–144.

Künzl, E. 2012 'Enamelled vessels of Roman Britain', in D.J. Breeze (ed.) *The first souvenirs: Enamelled vessels from Hadrian's Wall* Kendal, 9–22.

Leach, S. and Whitworth, A.M. 2011 *Saving the Wall: The conservation of Hadrian's Wall 1746–1987* Stroud.

Leary, J. (ed.) 2014 *Past mobilities: Archaeological approaches to movement and mobility* London.

Leland, J. 1769 *The itinerary of John Leland the antiquary* (volume 7, part 1) Oxford.

Macinnes, L. 1984 'Brochs and the Roman occupation of lowland Scotland', *Proceedings of the Society of Antiquaries of Scotland* 114: 235–249.

Mann, J.C. 1974 'The northern frontier after AD 369', *Glasgow Archaeological Journal* 3: 34–42.

Mann, J.C. 1990 'The function of Hadrian's Wall', *AA*⁵ 18: 51–54.

Manning, W.H. 1972 'Ironwork hoards in Iron Age and Roman Britain', *Britannia* 3: 224–250.

March, A.F. 2003 'State ideology and the legitimation of authoritarianism: The case of post-Soviet Uzbekistan', *Journal of Political Ideologies* 8.2: 209–232.

Mattern, S.P. 2010 'Counterinsurgency and the enemies of Rome', in V.D. Hanson (ed.) *Makers of ancient strategy: from the Persian wars to the fall of Rome* Princeton, 163–184.

Martin, G.R.R. 1996 *A game of thrones* New York.

Mattingly, D.J. 1995 *Tripolitania* London.

Mattingly, D.J. 2006 *An imperial possession: Britain in the Roman Empire, 54 BC–AD 409* London.

McAtackney, L. 2014 *An archaeology of the Troubles: The dark heritage of Long Kesh/Maze prison* Oxford.

McCarthy, M.R. 2002 *Roman Carlisle and the lands of the Solway* Stroud.

McCarthy, M.R. 2018 *Carlisle: A frontier and border city* London.

McCarthy, M.R., Padley, T.G. and Henig, M. 1982 'Excavations and finds from The Lanes, Carlisle', *Britannia* 13: 79–89.

McCluskey, A. 2018 'The "functions" of Hadrian's Wall: A view from the trenches', in C.S. Sommer and S. Matešić (eds.), 159–163.

McKee, I. 2006 'Gildas: Lessons from history', *Cambrian Medieval Celtic Studies* 51: 1–36.

Megaw, J.V.S. 1970 *Art of the European Iron Age: A study of the elusive image* Bath.

Merrifield, R. 1987 *The archaeology of ritual and magic* London.

Meyer, A. 2019 'The Vindolanda calendrical clepsydra: time keeping and healing waters', *Britannia* 50: 185–202.

Miket, R. and Maxfield, V. 1972 'The excavation of turret 33b (Coesike)', AA^4 50: 145–178.

Mortimer, P. 2007 *Off the Wall: The journey of a play* Nottingham.

Mullen, A. 2019 'Sociolinguistics', in Collins and Symonds (eds.), 102–105.

Nagra, D. 2017 *British Museum* London.

Neilson, G. 1912 'Obituary notice of J.P. Gibson F.S.A., A vice-president of the Society', AA^3 8: 37–45.

Nesbitt, C. 2016 'Multiculturalism on Hadrian's Wall', in M. Millett, L. Revell and A. Moore (eds.) *The Oxford handbook of Roman Britain* Oxford, 224–244.

Nolan, J., Harbottle, B. and Vaughan, J. 2010 'The Early Medieval cemetery at the Castle, Newcastle upon Tyne', AA^5 34: 147–287.

O'Brien, C. 2010 'The emergence of Northumbria: Artefacts, archaeology, and models', in R. Collins and L. Allason-Jones (eds.), 110–119.

Oosthuizen, S. 2019 *The emergence of the English* Leeds.

Orton, F. and Wood, I. 2007 *Fragments of time: Rethinking the Ruthwell and Bewcastle monuments* Manchester.

Parker, A. 2017 'Protecting the troops? Phallic carvings in the north of Roman Britain', in A. Parker (ed.) *Ad Vallum: Papers on the Roman army and frontiers in celebration of Dr Brian Dobson* (BAR British Series 631) Oxford, 117–130.

Petts, D. 2013 'Military and civilian: Reconfiguring the end of Roman Britain in the North', *European Journal of Archaeology* 16.2: 314–335.

Porch, D. 2013 *Counterinsurgency: Exposing the myths of the new way of war* Cambridge.

Potter, T.W. 1979 *The changing landscape of South Etruria* London.

Poulter, J. 2009 *Surveying Roman military landscapes across Northern Britain* (BAR British Series 492) Oxford.

Proctor, J. 2009 *Pegswood Moor, Morpeth: A later Iron Age and Romano-British farmstead settlement* (Pre-Construct Archaeology Monograph 11) Durham.

Proctor, J. 2012 Faverdale, Darlington: Excavations at a major settlement in the northern frontier zone of Roman Britain (Pre-Construct Archaeology 5) London.

Reid, J.H. and Nicholson, A. 2019 'Burnswark Hill: The opening shot of the Antonine reconquest of Scotland?', *JRA* 32: 459–477.

Richmond, I.A. 1934 'The Roman fort at South Shields', *AA*⁴ 11: 83–102.

Richmond, I.A. and Gillam, J.P. 1952 'Milecastle 79 (Solway)', *TCWAAS*² 52: 17–40.

Roach, L. 2013 'From the Severans to Constantius: The lost century', in Collins and Symonds (eds.), 105–121.

Roberts, B.K. 2010 'Northumbrian origins and post-Roman continuity: an exploration', in R. Collins and L. Allason-Jones (eds.), 120–132.

Roberts, P. 2019 'Kitchens and toilets', in P. Roberts (ed.) *Last supper in Pompeii* Oxford, 163–180.

Ross, A. 1968 'Shafts, pits, wells – sanctuaries of the Belgic Britons?', in J.M. Coles and D.D.A. Simpson (eds.) *Studies in ancient Europe: Essays presented to Stuart Piggott* Leicester, 255–285.

Ross, A. 1974 *Pagan Celtic Britain* London.

Ross, A. and Feachem, R. 1976 'Ritual rubbish? The Newstead pits', in J.V.S. Megaw (ed.) *To illustrate the monuments: Essays on archaeology presented to Stuart Piggott* London, 229–237.

Rushworth, A. 2009 *The grandest station: Excavation and survey at Housesteads Roman fort by C.M. Daniels, J.P. Gillam, J.G. Crow, D.J. Smith and the RCHME 1954–95* (volume 1) Newcastle.

Rushworth, A. and Croom, A. 2016 *Segedunum: Excavations by Charles Daniels in the Roman fort at Wallsend (1975–1984)* (volume 1) Oxford.

Shannon, W.D. 2007 *Murus illes famosus (that famous wall): Depictions and descriptions of Hadrian's Wall before Camden* Kendal.

Simpson, F.G. 1976 *Watermills and military works on Hadrian's Wall: Excavations in Northumberland 1907–1913* Kendal.

Simpson, F.G. and Richmond, I.A. 1937 'The fort on Hadrian's Wall at Halton', *AA*⁴ 14: 151–171.

Smith, A. and Fulford, M. 2016 'Conclusions: The rural settlement of Roman Britain', in A. Smith, M. Allen, T. Brindle and M. Fulford (eds.) *The rural settlement of Roman Britain* (Britannia Monograph Series 29) London, 385–420.

Smith, D.J. 1969 'The forgotten Whitfield Hoard of bronze vessels', *AA*⁴ 47: 172–181.

Smith, D.J. 1984 'A Romano-Celtic head from Lemington, Tyne and Wear', in R. Miket and C. Burgess (eds.) *Between and beyond the Walls: Essays on the prehistory and history of north Britain in honour of George Jobey* Edinburgh, 221–223.

Sommer, C.S. and Matešić, S. (eds.) 2018 *Limes XXIII. Proceedings of the 23rd International Congress of Roman Frontier Studies, Ingolstadt 2015* (Beiträge zum Welterbed Limes Sonderband 4) Mainz.

Stallibrass, S. 2009 'The way to a Roman soldier's heart: Did cattle droving supply the Hadrian's Wall area?', in J. Hendriks (ed.) *TRAC 2008: Proceedings of the Eighteenth Annual Theoretical Roman Archaeology Conference, Amsterdam 2008* Oxford, 101–112.

Stevens, C.E. 1941 'Gildas Sapiens', *English Historical Review* 56: 353–373.

Stevens, C.E. 1966 *The building of Hadrian's Wall* Kendal.

Sutcliff, R. 2004 *The eagle of the Ninth* Oxford.

Swinbank, B. and Spaul, J.E.H. 1951 'The spacing of the forts on Hadrian's Wall', *AA*⁴ 29: 221–238.

Symonds, M.F.A. 2005 'The construction order of the milecastles on Hadrian's Wall', *AA*⁵ 34: 67–81.

Symonds, M.F.A. 2013 'Gateways or garrisons? Designing, building and manning the milecastles', in Collins and Symonds (eds.), 53–70.

Symonds, M.F.A. 2015 'Review of David J. Breeze, Hadrian's Wall: A history of archaeological thought', *AA*⁵ 44: 303–306.

Symonds, M.F.A. 2017 *Protecting the Roman Empire: Fortlets, frontiers, and the quest for post-conquest security* Cambridge.

Symonds, M.F.A. 2018a 'Terminating milecastle 50: Ritual activity in the Hadrian's Wall milecastles', *TCWAAS*³ 18: 67–85.

Symonds, M.F.A. 2018b 'Who goes there? The evolution of access through Hadrian's Wall and the Antonine Wall', in Sommer and Matešić (eds.), 153–158.

Symonds, M.F.A. 2019a 'The purpose of Hadrian's Wall: The Dorothy Charlesworth Lecture delivered at the Shakespeare Centre, Kendal on 6th November 2017', *TCWAAS*³ 19: 97–122.

Symonds, M.F.A. 2019b 'Design and construction of the Wall', in Collins and Symonds (eds.), 29–43.

Symonds, M.F.A. 2019c 'The Wall and its constituent parts', in Collins and Symonds (eds.), 43–56.

Symonds, M.F.A. 2020a 'Fords and the frontier: Waging counter-mobility on Hadrian's Wall', *Antiquity* 94.373: 92–109.

Symonds, M.F.A. 2020b 'Hadrian's Wall: A Roman frontier revisited', *Minerva* 31.2: 32–40.

Symonds, M.F.A. 2020c 'Thinking small: Fortlet evolution on the Upper German *Limes*, Hadrian's Wall, Antonine Wall and Raetian *Limes*', in D.J. Breeze and W.S. Hanson (eds.) *The Antonine Wall: Papers in honour of Professor Lawrence Keppie* Oxford, 201–217.

Symonds, M.F.A. and Breeze, D.J. 2016 'The building of Hadrian's Wall: A reconsideration. Part 2: The central sector', *AA*⁵ 45: 1–16.

Symonds, M.F.A. and Mason, D.J.P. (eds.) 2009 *Frontiers of knowledge: A research framework for Hadrian's Wall, part of the frontiers of the Roman Empire World Heritage Site* (volume 1) Durham.

Taylor, A. 2008 'Aspects of deviant burial in Roman Britain', in E.M. Murphy (ed.) *Deviant burial in the archaeological record* Oxford, 91–114.

Taylor, D.B. 1982 'Excavation of a promontory fort, broch and souterrain at Hurly Hawkin, Angus', *Proceedings of the Society of Antiquaries of Scotland* 112: 215–253.

Taylor, D.J.A. and Biggins, J.A. 2012 'A geophysical survey at the Roman fort at Bewcastle, Cumbria', *TCWAAS*³ 12: 85–96.

Tomlin, R.S.O. 2018 *Britannia Romana: Roman inscriptions and Roman Britain* Oxford.

Tomlin, R.S.O. 2019 'Inscriptions', *Britannia* 50: 495–524.

Tomlin, R.S.O. and Hassall, M.W.C. 1999 'Inscriptions', *Britannia* 30: 375–386.

Town, M. 2019 'Rutherford Lower School', in Collins and Symonds (eds.), 134–136.

Vyner, B.E. 2007 'A Great North route in Neolithic and Bronze Age Yorkshire: The evidence of landscape and monuments', *Landscapes* 8.1: 69–84.

Wainwright, A. 1968 *Pennine Way companion: A pictorial guide* Kendal.

Webster, P. 2003 'An early fort at Caerwent? A review of the evidence', in P. Wilson
    (ed.) *The archaeology of Roman towns: Studies in honour of John S. Wacher*
    Oxford, 214–220.
Welfare, H. 2000 'Causeways, at milecastles, across the ditch of Hadrian's Wall',
    AA[5] 28: 13–25.
Welfare, H. 2004 'Variation in the form of the ditch, and of its equivalents, on
    Hadrian's Wall', *AA*[5] 33: 9–23.
Welsby, D.A. 1985 'The pottery from two turrets at Garthside on Hadrian's Wall',
    TCWAAS[2] 85: 71–76.
Whittaker, C.R. 1997 *Frontiers of the Roman Empire: A social and economic study*
    London.
Whitworth, A.M. 2000 *Hadrian's Wall: Some aspects of its post-Roman influence
    on the landscape* (BAR British Series 296) Oxford.
Willis, S. 1999 'Without and within: Aspects of culture and community in the Iron
    Age of north-eastern England', in B. Bevan (ed.) *Northern exposure:
    Interpretative devolution and the Iron Ages in Britain* (Leicester Archaeology
    Monographs 4) Leicester, 81–110.
Wilmott, T. 1997 *Birdoswald: Excavations of a Roman fort on Hadrian's Wall and
    its successor settlements: 1987–92* London.
Wilmott, T. (ed.) 2009 *Hadrian's Wall: English Heritage research 1976–2000*
    London.
Wilmott, T. 2019 'Birdoswald cemetery', in Collins and Symonds (eds.), 186–191.
Witcher, R., Tolia-Kelly, D.P. and Hingley, R. 2010 'Archaeologies of landscape:
    Excavating the materialities of Hadrian's Wall', *Journal of Material Culture*
    15.1: 105–128.
Woodfield, C.C. 1965 'Six turrets on Hadrian's Wall', *AA*[4] 43: 87–200.
Woolliscroft, D.J. 1989 'Signalling and the design of Hadrian's Wall', *AA*[5] 17: 5–19.
Woolliscroft, D.J. 1999 'More thoughts on the Vallum', *TCWAAS*[2] 99: 53–65.
Woolliscroft, D.J. and Hoffmann, B. 2006 *Rome's first frontier: The Flavian
    occupation of northern Scotland* Stroud.
Zant, J. 2009 *The Carlisle Millennium Project: Excavations in Carlisle 1998–2001*
    (volume 1) Oxford.
Zant, J. 2019 *The Maryport Roman settlement project: Excavations in the Roman
    extramural settlement, 2013–14* (Lancaster Imprints 27) Lancaster.
Zant, J. and Howard-Davis, C. 2019 *Roman and medieval Carlisle: The Northern
    Lanes, excavations 1978–82, volume one: The Roman period* (Lancaster
    Imprints 25) Lancaster.
Zartman, I.W. 1995 'Introduction: Posing the problem of state collapse', in
    I.W. Zartman (ed.) *Collapsed states: The disintegration and restoration of
    legitimate authority* London, 1–11.

INDEX

Personal names are usually listed by surname or last name, but Roman emperors are entered under the names they are commonly known by today. So, Publius Aelius Hadrianus appears as 'Hadrian', while Titus Aurelius Fulvus Antoninus is entered as 'Antoninus Pius', and so forth.

Page numbers in italics refer to illustrations.